OUR APPALACHIA

Our Appalachia

An oral history edited by
**Laurel Shackelford
and Bill Weinberg**

Photographs by DONALD R. ANDERSON

ⓦ HILL *and* WANG　*New York*
A DIVISION OF FARRAR, STRAUS AND GIROUX

Printed in the United States of America

Published simultaneously in Canada by McGraw-Hill Ryerson, Ltd.

Designed by Karen Watt

Photographs, except where otherwise credited, by Donald R. Anderson

Library of Congress Cataloging in Publication Data
Main entry under title:
Our Appalachia.
    Includes bibliographical references and index.
    1. Appalachian region, Southern—Social life and customs.
2. Appalachian region, Southern—Biography.   I. Shackelford, Laurel.
II. Weinberg, Bill.   III. Anderson, Donald R.
F217.A65097 1977   975 [B]   76-48625
ISBN 0-8090-7462-1

FRONTISPIECE: The Cheek pushboat which was owned by the Cheek family of Beaver Creek in Floyd County, Kentucky. The Cheeks used the boat to transport merchandise—barrels of salt and flour and slabs of bacon—from Allen up the Big Sandy River to Whitehouse, Kentucky. c. 1900

To those who refuse to leave the land they love

ACKNOWLEDGMENTS

Sharing is a way of life in the mountains and, appropriately, the essence of *Our Appalachia*. From Mayking, Kentucky, to Winnipeg, Canada, neighbors and outlanders gave time, counsel, and financial assistance. We are grateful. Warm thanks must first go to all the mountain people—and there are thousands—who have welcomed, and continue welcoming, Appalachian Oral History Project interviewers into their homes and graciously allowed us to ply them with questions. Along with them we salute the scores of student interviewers and wish there were space to name each one. Unfortunately, we must limit our written recognition to students who contributed to the few interviews that appear here. They have our gratitude and are: Darrell Bentley, Jenkins, Ky.; Archie Bowling, Saldee, Ky.; Tom Burnett, Chagrin Falls, O.; Medda Campbell, Terre Haute, Ind.; J. B. Combs, Jackson, Ky.; Harriet Connor, Nashville, Tenn.; Phillip Craft, Mayking, Ky.; Josia Dye, Pine Top, Ky.; Karen Easterling, West Liberty, Ky.; Joey Elswick, Wayland, Ky.; Luther Frazier, Price, Ky.; Loretta Gullett, Busy, Ky.; Diane Hall, Galveston, Ky.; Mary Lou Jackson, Booneville, Ky.; Connie Cottle Kimyabayki, West Liberty, Ky.; Darrell Lewis, Crewe, Va.; Regina Maciaq, Campton, Ky.; Darrell Madden, Pippa Passes, Ky.; Sandra Miller,

Jackson, Ky.; Tim Morris, Busy, Ky.; Frieda Mullins, Pippa Passes, Ky.; Hester Mullins, Kite, Ky.; Lorraine Napier, Wooton, Ky.; Jeff Noble, Jackson, Ky.; Larry Rayburn, Pippa Passes, Ky.; Annette Reems, Berea, Ky.; Ken Slone, Garner, Ky.; Darrell Sparkman, Pippa Passes, Ky.; Rex Wilson, Weeksbury, Ky.; Sue Wooton, Wooton, Ky., and Mary Yates, Mystic, Conn.

Many other people helped by supervising specific projects, interviewing and suggesting persons to interview, reading manuscript, typing, comparing transcripts with original tapes for accuracy, and by funding the Appalachian Oral History Project. Again, we are able to recognize and publicly acknowledge only those persons and organizations which made the greatest contributions to *Our Appalachia*. They are: Fran Ansley, Knoxville, Tenn.; Brenda Bell, Maryville, Tenn.; Edward A. Bennett, Louisville, Ky.; Kate Black, Pyramid, Ky.; Carole Currie, Asheville, N.C.; Charles Dahlenburg, Vest, Ky.; Carole Ganim, Pippa Passes, Ky.; Bill Hughes, Wheelwright, Ky.; The Johnson Foundation, Racine, Wis.; Marc Landy, Cambridge, Mass.; Helen Lewis, Wise, Va.; J. Patrick Morgan, Boone, N.C.; McKinley Little, Minnie, Ky.; The National Endowment for the Humanities, Washington, D.C.; The Rockefeller Foundation, New York, N.Y.; Della Smallwood, Dorton, Ky.; Brenda Slone, Pippa Passes, Ky.; Steele-Reese Foundation, New York, N.Y.; Dan Stein, Chewelah, Wash.; George Stevenson, Emory, Va.; Sari Tudiver, Winnipeg, Canada; Jack Williams, Jackson, Ky.; and Brenda Wright, Pippa Passes, Ky.

The historical photographs that add much to *Our Appalachia* came to the Appalachian Photographic Archives at Alice Lloyd College from a number of sources. We wish to specially recognize the following for their generosity: Mrs. Dorthula Childress, Wheelwright, Ky.; Astor Dobson, Hindman, Ky.; Lionel Duff, Hindman Settlement School, Hindman, Ky.; The Filson Club, Louisville, Ky., for access to the R. C. Ballard Thurston Collection; Frank Harmon, Prestonsburg, Ky.; Henry P. Scalf, Stanville, Ky.; Mrs. Geneva Smith, Mallie, Ky.; the Smithsonian Institution, Washington, D.C.; the Southwest Virginia Museum, Big Stone Gap, Va.; and Albert F. Stewart, editor, *Appalachian Heritage* magazine, Alice Lloyd College, Pippa Passes, Ky.

Other thanks date back to 1971 when William S. Hayes, president of Alice Lloyd College, and Troy Eslinger, president of Lees Junior College, acknowledged that education transcends the classroom and, with the initiative of Marc Landy, began the Appalachian Oral History Project. Their continued support was later augmented by the help of Herbert W. Wey, chancellor of Appalachian State University, and Thomas F. Chilcote, president of Emory & Henry College. *Our Appalachia* is a small tribute to the foresight of these mountain educators.

Special thanks are due to Arthur Wang, who showed both sensitivity and interest in working with us on this book.

Finally . . . Thank you, Ron Daley and Mike Mullins of Pippa Passes. You never stopped helping.

CONTENTS

OUR APPALACHIA

INTRODUCTION

Our Appalachia portrays the people, the life, the history, and the culture of a region of America that is both little known and little understood. We call the region Central Appalachia but its name and its boundaries are suggestive only. *Our Appalachia* is about people—mountain people—the hills of eastern Kentucky and southwestern Virginia and the ranges and valleys of western North Carolina. The mountain people talk about a way of life not walled in by state or county lines. Their thoughts, struggles, feelings, and recollections will be familiar to many people in southern Ohio or northern Georgia, rural Pennsylvania or eastern Tennessee, areas beyond our immediate scope but within Appalachia.

The impetus for this book grew out of the need for a social history of Central Appalachia.* It has provided the opportunity to let residents of the region tell their own story—an opportunity they have seldom had. It presents the struggles and the joys, the high points and the low, the strengths and the weaknesses of

---

* Harry M. Caudill's *Night Comes to the Cumberlands,* published in 1962, remains the classic history of the coal industry's involvement in eastern Kentucky.

being part of America's largest geographically contiguous sub-culture.*

Members of the Cherokee Nation had the region largely to themselves until the early 1700's when they were joined by pioneers, most of whom were Scotch-Irish and Palatine Germans. They had come to America in search of the religious freedom and democratic institutions it offered and settled in Pennsylvania. During the first half of the eighteenth century Pennsylvania's coast became thickly populated and descendants of the earlier settlers moved south and west to the Central Appalachian region where people were few and land was cheap. Between 1720 and 1770 approximately 600,000 Scotch-Irish and 110,000 Germans, as well as many English, Irish, and French Huguenots, migrated to the southern Appalachians. Horace Kephart, a writer and naturalist who traveled extensively in Central Appalachia during the early 1900's, studied the history of these early settlers. In *Our Southern Highlanders* he characterized them as people who "had little or nothing to do with slavery, detested the state church, loathed tithes, and distrusted all authority save that of conspicuous merit and natural justice."

The early pioneers made their living by farming and hunting and of course they clashed with the Indians on whose lands they encroached. As the migration of white settlers continued, the Cherokees were outnumbered and moved farther south and west. Major waves of migration followed the Revolution, when many soldiers received land in the wilderness for their wartime services in lieu of cash, and in the 1820's as people rushed south in search of Georgia's gold. By 1830 nearly one million permanent settlers occupied Central Appalachia. Between 1830 and 1850 the last sustained migration occurred. This time the impetus

---

* Appalachia is usually considered to consist of West Virginia and portions of eleven other states: New York, Pennsylvania, Ohio, Maryland, Kentucky, Virginia, Tennessee, North Carolina, South Carolina, Alabama, and Georgia. Central Appalachia is most often defined as including sixty counties in eastern Kentucky, northern Tennessee, southwestern Virginia, and southern West Virginia.

was escape, not discovery, as descendants of the earliest settlers fled economic depression and exhausted farm lands in the South.

Our Appalachia presents a substantial piece of twentieth-century life in Central Appalachia. It is not a definitive history of the region. Instead, it tells the highly personal story of men and women whose lives quietly shaped the region's history. We do not claim their spoken history will tell the whole story, but we believe there will be people deep in the valleys and hollows who will read and muse, "Yes, that is the way it was." Or, "I did it a little differently, but still that is just about the way it was."

The first section, "A Simpler Time," deals with life in the mountains before extensive railways were built or the coal industry and tourism became important. It was a hard life, and the quality of a man's existence depended upon his independence, energy, and self-sufficiency. Cash was scarce and barter was the usual way of acquiring needed goods and materials. Central Appalachia during this period was an agrarian society in which people lived off the land.

Some of the men and women who speak of a simpler time are talking about life as they recall it in the 1930's or 40's, long after the simpler mode of living had passed for most mountain people. They nonetheless speak from their own life experiences—experiences which can be viewed as a mirror into the past. For this first section, we sought people whose childhoods reflected as much as possible life in the early twentieth century, or people who had a strong oral tradition in their family that made them intimately familiar with the lives their parents led as children.

The second section, "A Culture under Attack," deals with the social transition that occurred as the early struggle of men against nature was replaced by a more devastating one: the struggle of man against man, and man against society. Mountain people, accustomed to the struggle of man against the elements, adjusted slowly to the very different demands of an industrial age.

Twentieth-century America has been preoccupied with growth through industrialization. Any person or group that questioned the values of industrialization was left behind. Central Appalachia was rich in natural resources; these were needed to fuel the country's growth and if the men and women who resided in the area were slow to climb aboard the industrial bandwagon, or were not aggressive enough in demanding their fair share, then who was to blame? The industrial captains of the nation were, if nothing else, singleminded, and it should not be surprising that in their determination they paid small heed to the devastation of a culture.

The imposition of outside influences on the agricultural economy of Central Appalachia did not go unchallenged. Part Two tells of the struggles—the battle for land ownership and natural resources, the impact of the Depression, union wars, the pinch of automation, and finally, the most desperate struggle of all, the fight to remain in the region, on land the people love.

In the years following World War II, thousands of the children of Appalachia left for the industrial North. Many who remained were forced to accept welfare to survive. Today mountain people face still greater pressure as they attempt to balance the nation's energy needs with the preservation of their ecology; to mesh modern life with traditional ways; and to reconcile a rich culture with an unhealthy economy. In the short final section, "Digging In," those who are involved in the making of the region's future discuss the issues mountain residents are facing and must continue to face.

Our Appalachia emerged from the work of the Appalachian Oral History Project, a five-year-old, four-school consortium based at Alice Lloyd College. The four schools—public and private, two-year and four-year, large and small—are Alice Lloyd College in Pippa Passes, Kentucky; Lees Junior College in Jackson, Kentucky; Appalachian State University in Boone, North Carolina; and Emory & Henry College in Emory, Virginia. Using student as well as staff interviewers, the project began in 1971 to tape the recollections of mountain residents throughout Central Appalachia. To make this reservoir of information available to the general public, work on *Our Appalachia* began in 1973.

This book would not have been possible twenty-five years ago; it required the technological, educational, and philosophical changes that have occurred in the country during that time. It is based on oral history, a technique that involves the use of tape recorders. As might be expected, there was a significant lag between the new technology and our understanding of the ways in which it might be used. One use is recording the history and culture of people who rely upon oral traditions. In Central Appalachia, as in many parts of the world, most information is not written down but is passed on by word of mouth from generation to generation. Tape recorders help preserve this rich reservoir. Occasionally people exaggerate and sometimes their statements may be factually incorrect. We chose not to footnote the few inaccuracies—and there are very few in light of the scope of material covered and the number of people who cover it—because oral history has room for human error.

Just as the oral-history technique was obtaining wide popularity, the country's outlook changed dramatically. From the latter half of the nineteenth century to the 1960's most Americans applauded the concept of the United States as a melting pot. Cultural differences were muted by the desire of immigrants to be assimilated into the mainstream of American life and by a similar attitude on the part of our racial minorities. In the 1960's the melting-pot idea came under attack.

This was perhaps one of the major side effects of the Civil Rights Movement. As black Americans struggled to recapture their identity as a part of the battle for equal rights and opportunities, other minorities began to look more closely at their heritage and to emphasize differences rather than similarities. The rush for assimilation had been so prevalent in American history that many initially viewed this trend toward ethnicity and racial pride as downright un-American. It was reinforced, however, by the youth movement of the late 1960's in which many of the sons and daughters of American elites searched in vain for roots which had long since disappeared, and by the 1970's the "myth of the melting pot" has given way to the "importance of a pluralistic society."

Ironically, as the country began to appreciate racial, ethnic, and regional differences, the pressure to obliterate these differences became even more intense. Nowhere is this more true than in Central Appalachia. It is no longer a question of whether it is desirable to maintain the qualities that have made mountain life unique, but rather a question of whether it is possible.

Finally, it is significant that many of the contacts which led to the interviews that are included in *Our Appalachia* were made by the students who live in and attend school in the mountains. The staff of the Appalachian Oral History Project did the bulk of the interviewing for *Our Appalachia,* but nearly one third of the interviewees were contacted initially by student interviewers. In addition, the Appalachian Oral History Project has in its collection thousands of interviews done by students. By virtue of their Appalachian heritage, the students brought to each interview a knowledge and sensitivity that few people from outside the mountains could achieve. They do not have to spend hours establishing a rapport with the resident historians, or narrators, because most already have it. Like the people they interview, the students, as well as their parents, have lived in the hills and hollows of Appalachia all their lives. They speak the same language and do not have to be told what expressions such as "roasting ears," "red dog," and "hunting for sang" mean.

Even though a student and resident historian may not know each other personally, they often begin the interview by tracing their family trees until they meet. Often students are able to interview their own neighbors and kin and these conversations have resulted in some of our finest tapes.

Hester Mullins, from Kite, Kentucky, was one of our student

Hester Mullins

interviewers. Hester, who saw her first town (population 786) at the age of fifteen, is now a student at the University of Kentucky in Lexington. She talked about her experiences working with oral history.

I've been isolated here in Knott County most of my life and at first I didn't appreciate the people; I was wary, distrustful [of them]. When [I started] working for oral history I began to appreciate the qualities the people did have, their fellowship, [their] rapport. I couldn't believe so many people could open their hearts to me—never lay eyes on you before and when you walk in [they] hug you, say, "Welcome in, child. Sit down and make yourself at home." [They] tell you so many personal things about their life, things they might not have even told their own children.

I don't think any of my friends, unless they have worked [with oral history] have even the vaguest idea of the kind of life their daddy and grandparents lived. If they did they would have appreciated them more. We are brought up as selfish little brats, our wants and needs are all that concern us. After you begin to mature you realize who your people were, what they were, and what they stood for.

The person I most enjoyed talking to was my own grandmother, Melvinia Thornsberry. The spirit she had in her, the mischief, I loved that. Through her I understood my own parents a lot better; what they had to live through, how hard things were for them. [When we were] kids she'd gather us around and tell us big scary stories. I remember [her] telling us how hard it was living through the Depression. She was talking about how you had to make moonshine to live, and how people would buy that when there wasn't anything else. She was saying you had to make it to live. I made the remark [that] if I had to do that I would just starve.

[I was] ashamed of the fact that Grandpa had made moonshine [but] when I started [interviewing] Grandma I found out he once had been a magistrate, he ran a store, he had been a schoolteacher, he could repair all kinds of tools, he built barns for people, and cleared ground. I realized he was the type of man who did what he had to do to make a living. In his boots I would have done the same thing. I felt ashamed of myself because I didn't try to understand what she was trying to tell me, which is exactly what people outside of [our] culture do; they don't understand. I really felt ashamed of myself. Then I [began] to feel glad because I felt I can be proud of my heritage because they fought to survive.

I love to interview the older people because they tell you what you want to know, they're relaxed, and they're tickled to death when you go in to talk to them. You can't leave unless you eat *and stay a couple of hours. [After the interview] older people, especially, [like] you to play the whole tape back for them to find out what they said. They all want copies. My great-uncle went out and bought a tape recorder to hear his tape. His children and his grandchildren were tickled to death to hear "Pa" talk.*

I've interviewed more women than men and I don't get to talk much to them about [politics]. The women here in Knott County have worked the same as men, you know. The man is recognized as the head of the household, but she keeps it together. Women like to talk about their life, the culture of women, the danger with the midwife, the children, the games they played, and how they put up food. They're much more descriptive about conditions back then. A man, he's concerned with politics, and mining, and logging.

Since I've gone to Lexington I've been thrown out of this little culture of mine and it scares me. It shook my world up finding people down there really don't care anything about you; all they perceive [is] what you look like, how you act, and how you treat them. Sometimes when you try to [know] people down there you can't get any further than the stone wall that they present. You feel like they don't even have a heart or a heritage. I live off campus, I'm not thrown in situations where I meet a lot of people. I'm alone a lot and I'm looking at four walls most of the time. I feel like I'm going to go crazy because I have a great need to be with people, to understand and relate to them, and there I'm isolated from that. I feel so lost.

[I went to the university] because I wanted to prove to myself that I could make it outside this area. Once I get what I want from U.K., which is a law degree, I can come back here and be just as hillbilly as I want to be. I can't wait to come back: it is my home and it is my culture. We do need progress, we need to raise our living standards and goals for our peace of mind, and for the well-being of the county and eastern Kentucky. I don't think that in any way we should ever get into mainstream America—that's the worst thing we can do—but there are certain

things that we can draw from it and still retain the beauty of the mountains and the closeness of the people.

There is no "typical mountaineer." The region has been plagued by overnight experts, who, in the words of one mountain person, "pop in, pop off, and pop out." Such writers have most often concentrated on "sociological" pieces about the Appalachian people. Over the years, bad sociology becomes bad history. There is a crying need for a history of the Central Appalachian region that will, without romanticizing, counteract some of the misconceptions and stereotypes which bombard us daily through television and comic strips.

One cannot go out into the hollows of eastern Kentucky or along the ridges of western North Carolina without realizing that there are thousands of people throughout the mountains with a great deal to say. Seldom before has anyone stopped to listen to them. One of the first things that many of our resident historians exclaim upon being asked for an interview is "I don't know anything." *Our Appalachia* is a testament to their humility.

Each excerpt is drawn from one to six hours of interviews that took place over a period of days or years. Each resident historian has reviewed his particular excerpt in the book. In order to bridge the gap between oral and written language with clarity some words have been deleted and some sentences rearranged, but only those words that appear in brackets were not actually spoken by the narrators.

Although oral history furnishes the basis for this book, there is visual history as well. Donald R. Anderson, an Associate Professor of Fine Arts at the University of Louisville and former Director of the Photographic Archives there, spent two years with the Appalachian Oral History project collecting old photographs and taking new ones. His work provides the visual images which are an integral part of *Our Appalachia*.

It is an American cultural characteristic to forget about our elderly. In many cultures age is respected as a sign of wisdom; in the United States our aged are frequently cast off or forgotten. In the mountains there remains a greater respect for elders than in the country at large. But even here out-migration and death have left many a mountain man or woman alone in his later years. We hope that in the process of completing *Our Appalachia* we have not only taken, but also given, and through our interest, have bolstered a sense of meaning in those whose book this really is.

Exploitation in the mountains has occurred through publication as well as through the more common means of controlling natural resources from afar. When the work on *Our Appalachia* began, it was decided that all royalties would go to the Appalachian Oral History Project to assist it in continuing its work. This was our way of saying thanks to the mountain residents who shared their innermost thoughts and their lives with us.

A Simpler Time

1

GOD, BADMEN, AND SCHOOLMARMS

Coal had not been discovered by outsiders yet. In the 1890's people who had coal on their land often used it for heating. The coal on the hearth was no more important than the quilts on the bed and few dreamed it would ever be otherwise. Mountain people had a history of adapting their surroundings into means for living. Creek beds were roadways. Felled trees became log cabins, barns, churches, schools, farm tools, brooms, and bedsteads. Seeds of fruits and vegetables were harvested in autumn, dried during winter, and replanted in the spring. These labors required a strength beyond brawn and mountain people accepted the challenge.

In many ways it was the kind of back-to-nature living that people who feel trampled and smothered by metropolitan life seek today, or think they seek. On the surface there is something romantic about making a house from poplar logs held together with a mixture of yellow mud, water, and horsehair, or creating a Drunkard's Path quilt from scraps of handwoven fabric. However, when a person's day-to-day existence depends upon his ability to transform nature's bounty into life's necessities, the challenge loses its romance and becomes hard, sometimes desperate.

So it was with the people of Central Appalachia as the nine-

teenth century drew to a close. Wounds caused by the Civil War faded in the region but lingered privately in homes and communities. Tourists had discovered, and forgotten, North Carolina's hills and spas and the Virginia and Kentucky coalfields had only recently been visited by outside industrialists. There was no industry except logging, a brutal, seasonal occupation confined to land near waterways. Mountains, wider than they are tall, staved off travel, communication, and outside influences. Cash was scarce and the notion that quality of life was somehow linked to dollars was foreign to most people. The way a man lived depended upon his energy, self-sufficiency, and ability to join together with others like himself.

Life revolved around the home. Families relied upon one another to provide schools, churches, and law enforcement, to clear land, build barns, pull teeth, and rear orphan children. When someone living deep in a hollow became seriously ill, family members would convert the dining-room table into a stretcher, cover it with a corn-shuck mattress and carry the patient through forests and creeks to the mouth of the hollow. There kinfolks or neighbors who had been alerted to the trouble would carry the stretcher five or ten more miles, where they were relieved by another ambulance team. This continued until the patient reached a hospital, which might be thirty miles or more from his home. One member of the family would have made the entire journey with him; scores of other people would have helped.

Jim Byrd, who was born in 1899, remembers this spirit of fellowship and determination in mountain communities and says: "People had to take care of their neighbors. There was nobody else to do it. No funeral homes, no doctors . . ." Like the other people who will talk about a simpler time, Jim is remembering a way of life that belonged primarily to his parents and grandparents, a way of life that had already begun to fade in the early 1900's when he was a youngster in Valle Crucis, North Carolina.

Jim is a builder by trade—of houses, lakes, railroads, gun forts, banjos, and office buildings—and when his family began to grow he would leave the mountains for weeks and months at a time to

Jim Byrd

work in distant states while his wife, Celia, and the boys tended the farm. If there was no construction work available, Jim traveled to the orchards of Washington to prune trees and pick apples. "A lot of people back at that time [would] tell me when they got in debt they couldn't sleep good at night. I told them that was a bad mistake. I said I found out when I got in debt that I'd better sleep good of the night and get up early of the morning."

His sons are grown now and debts are no longer a problem, but Jim Byrd is still rising early in Valle Crucis to tend his garden and do cabinetwork for neighbors.

Back when I was growing up, about February you'd go clearing land, clearing it off for a crop. They'd send one of us old boys out and invite everybody in the whole community to come to the working. They'd come, too. I've seen forty and forty-five and they'd just clean off acres a day, pile it ready to burn. They was grubbing, sawing logs, cutting logs, spreading them, piling them in big grips, and getting them ready to burn. When it got dry they burned it off clean. There was no overseer. They all knowed how to work.

The womenfolks would come to the house and have a quilting.

They'd have two or three quilt tops and you'd pad them with sheep's wool. Man, it was a sight in the world what was going on! There'd be a lot of girls there, seventeen- and eighteen-year-old, helping them quilt. We all would come in of an evening and we'd want to shake the cat. Four girls—one at each corner—would get a hold of that quilt and another one would throw the cat in, and they got to shaking it as hard as they could shake and whichever one that cat jumped toward was going to get married first. That's a fact, there's no joke to that. It happened all over this country at all the workings.

[At corn shuckings] they'd have a big heap of corn as big as this room. They'd gather the corn all in and pile it up and they'd all gather plum around and shuck. Back then when they'd grow corn they'd have speckled ears [red and white ones] and they'd have solid red ears. Then they'd have a "stewball"; if it had fifteen red grains in it, it was a stewball. It was a habit, an old saying, that the first one that got a red ear got to kiss the prettiest girl around the corn ring. And if you got a stewball you got to kiss her and hug her neck, too.

I was just an old mischief boy in my teens and my daddy he'd shuck his corn maybe two days before every corn shucking and put it in the crib and I'd pick me out some red ears and when I got ready to go to a corn shucking I'd stick me a red ear or two in my pocket and a stewball. Whenever they got to shucking and one would holler, "I've got a red ear," he'd kiss the girl and in a few minutes I'd slip one out of my pocket, holler, "Yes, and I've got a red ear!" They'd shuck on trying to find a stewball and directly I'd slip my stewball out of my pocket. I'd holler, "Stewball!"

Had a lot of fun at them old corn shuckings. My daddy used to go to them, he had an old homemade banjer, he made it himself. A "hump banjer" is what they call them. He'd kill a cat, tan the hide and make the [banjo] head. He'd take that banjer and whenever the corn shucking was over they'd have what they called a dance. There was no dances like they have in dance halls now. [They did a dance called] "snatch partners." Everyone would get their partner, have one [boy] in the middle, and they'd start going around. That one in the middle, he'd make a run, go and grab a girl, and call, "Snatch partner!" [Then] everyone would grab a girl, call "Snatch partner!" and on around the ring you'd go.

Many a time me and my dad went to hoe out a crop when [people] were sick, typhoid or something like that. And then in '18 the flu struck, that was during the World War, it struck everything in this country and it killed them just like killing flies. Me and my daddy and my brother-in-law, Andrew Townsend, we was having to wait on this whole country. We got [ourselves] a big bottle of horse temperature medicine, it was right yellow-looking stuff, and of a morning before we'd start out we'd take that old temperature medicine and rub it right across our lips. My dad had a heavy mustache and him and my brother-in-law would take that temperature medicine and be yeller across their [whiskers]. We'd go wait on [people] day and night: washed them, dressed them, lay them out when they was dead, put them in the casket, dig graves. [We] worked ourselves to death and we never did take the flu. We didn't use a thing in the world but that old horse medicine.

Most people made caskets. Caskets [in a store] run from twenty-five to thirty-five dollars, but there wasn't one in fifty in this country that had twenty-five, thirty-five dollars. We *had* to make them.

Old Aunt Fanny Townsend, my wife's aunt, she'd been up in Virginia and come back home and took a cold and pneumonia and died on the head of Clarks Creek. [Her] daughter, Zettie, had a young baby at home and she wanted to see her mother. I took a team and wagon and went to the head of Clarks Creek and got [Aunt Fanny] on the wagon and come down to Zettie. I stopped my horses and wagon—right smart little snow on the ground— and we got the casket out of the wagon and carried it in the house. I opened the casket up and let Zettie see her mother.

Closed the casket back, loaded it back on the wagon, took it to the head of Dutch Creek to an old cemetery way up on the hill.

[People] was happy to carry in all the food and everything, take care of the widder, right on and on. Had no welfare, they didn't know what welfare was. [The men] would go out and put [her] crops out, hoe corn out and tend it. We didn't have what you call this old plain lazy stuff much back then. They all had to work and they knowed it. They grow what they eat and eat what they grow.

(Appalachian Photographic Archives)

Gathering around the open coffin of a loved one for a final family portrait is an old mountain custom. Clell Back, of Quicksand, Kentucky, died in 1923 and lies surrounded by members of his family. The young people touching the coffin are Clell's children. His mother, Lena Back, is the sixth person from the right

What did people do on Sundays?

Had to go to church before twelve, wasn't no way of getting out of that unless you was sick. After twelve we'd go and wrestle till time to go to work Sunday evening. We had wrestling rings and my dad knowed a place up on the mountain—pretty, grassy, and soft. We'd get twenty-five or thirty of us over.

Used to have rooster fights. My Grandpaw Byrd was pretty big on that and my daddy was, too. He kept them game roosters, trained them to fight. Grandpaw, he had two champion roosters and he thought a lot of them. My grandpaw and grandmaw went off [one] Sunday visiting and [Dad and his brother, Uncle Harrison Byrd] decided they'd take their young roosters and put them in the lot with my grandpaw's champion roosters and see them fight. They turned their roosters in there and my grandpaw's roosters just eat them up right quick.

That made them mad. They went and got them a couple of thorns and they caught my grandpaw's roosters and jabbed them thorns right through the head and killed them both.

My grandpaw come back that evening and went to feed his roosters. He found them both laying there dead and he just raised Cain. He said, "Now, George and Harrison, what happened to my roosters?" "Oh," [one] said, "Pap, we took our young roosters down there in the lot and put them in there to fight your roosters and do you know our roosters spurred yours right square through the head? We couldn't help it." Just told a lie, you know.

In much of Central Appalachia, counties were required to convene their courts of law semiannually on dates specified by the state legislature. These occasions were known as "court day," but as Jim Byrd explains, horses often took preeminence over justice at court day.

Dad would buy up old poor horses in the wintertime, or in the fall, and feed them till spring. He'd feed a couple of old horses and get them looking pretty good and he'd make me go with him and ride one and he would lead the other. He never would ride a horse. And they had what you call a jockey lot out in the courthouse [yard]. Everybody had horses there and they'd get on them horses and ride and say, "Who'll give me so much?" Ride them around in rich suits, they'd price them and trade.

Daddy'd have his tied up and if one was heaving or a stumpsucker* . . . If he was a stumpsucker he wouldn't tie him to a post because he'd grab that post and just rare back and say, "Rooooooop!" and everybody'd know he was a stumpsucker and just didn't have no wind. Wind-broken. Fed moldy hay or something like that make him heavey, like a person with asthma. If he was heavey they'd take that old axle grease like you grease them old wagons with back then, put a clevis in their mouth so as to hold their mouth open, and pull the tongue way out. Put a paddle of that axle grease right on the root of the tongue. Then they wouldn't choke for a good long while. I've helped do it a many a time.

Me and Dad, neither one, never would swap horses till we put the harness on them and tried them out and see what they'd do. If they rode to suit us then we'd swap horses. If they didn't we wouldn't.

What actually happened in the courtroom on court day?

I never did know much about that court and what went on. Back at that time it give me the cold chills to go in there and set down and let them try someone because they got what was coming to them back then. They'd try the women and the girls, just give them the same as they give the men. It ain't like it is now.

Back when I was growing up if you done a pretty dirty crime, a dirty deed, you went to jail and stayed in there from fall to spring, or spring to fall, till your trial. You stayed in there six

---

* A "stumpsucker" is a horse that sets its teeth against a solid object, pulls back, arches its neck, and swallows air. Horsemen consider the vice a serious one because it is usually incurable and causes the animal to be a poor worker.

months because they just had court every six months. Back then nobody would go your bond. People didn't have the money to put up cash bond and they sure wouldn't sign over their farm for a bond. Had their home and had to keep it. If I had got into a little trouble back when I was growing up my daddy wouldn't go my bond because he told me from the time I was little if I got in jail to stay in jail and that's the reason I took the chills every time I went into the courthouse.

If you stole a horse or something like that [you] stayed in jail till court and then you went to the road for so many years. If you carried a pistol you stayed in jail until court come for carrying a pistol. Have your trial and you could pay off $300 and the cost of going to the road. And if you stole something or another you'd go to the road by day. No way out of it. Of course, the jails wasn't crowded back then because boys obeyed the rules.

Who usually took care of the roads?

Well, it was done by free labor. They set up so many days a year. They worked about ten days a year to the man. There wasn't no such thing back then as to refuse. They come around a couple or three days before you had to work and summoned you to go out on these roads. They summoned you to put in two days, if they wanted you for two days, or four days, or five. And if you'd tell them you couldn't go, then you'd pay them seventy-five cents a day and they hired somebody else. You paid the boss man, whoever the boss man was, appointed by the county.

If you were sick they'd excuse you, but when you got well you made that time up. That was the only way there was of keeping the roads up. And they worked, you had to work, there wasn't no such thing as standing around like kids these days.

Leisure time was scarce. Most social gatherings were tied to working, and the long farm work days kept the entire family busy from dawn to dusk. But mountain people always found time for their first love—politics.

It is hard to describe the feeling that existed in an eastern Kentucky hollow or a southern Virginia town when the subject of politics arose. Ruby Watts, of Pine Top, Kentucky, explains it in part by saying, "People. I like people. I eat, drink and sleep politics, honestly I do. And when an election comes around, I'm just interested." Politics was serious business because it could affect a man's social standing as well as his pocketbook. It was a means to a job and a way of paying off debts. But it also was a game to be enjoyed, a lesson in life to be studied, and an avocation to be indulged.

Mountain people seldom talked for long without mentioning a political gathering of some kind. Politics touched nearly every aspect of life in Central Appalachia from the election of local officials to the selection of schoolteachers. One of the most knowledgeable sources for information about political gatherings in the mountains is Ruby Watts. Ruby has a warm, effervescent personality, the kind image makers sometimes spend years cultivating in their political protégés. His success in local politics is rooted in personal qualities, not formal education. He is proud of his position in the county but does not flaunt his status. Indeed, there is not even a sign on his office door saying Ruby Watts is Judge Pro Tem of Knott County, Kentucky.

Ruby begins by talking about his schooling and about his first campaign for Knott County tax commissioner in 1929 when he was twenty-four years old. He described the elections, campaign rallies, and county fairs that were the heart of mountain politics.

I went to Nealy; that's the only school I ever went to. It was just a one-room, never but one teacher there. I went through the fifth grade. Of course, that was a high grade at that time.

[From 1961 to 1969] I was working for the U.S. government, the Department of Agriculture, and the qualifications of the job required you to have a college education and I didn't have it. But [Congressman] Carl Perkins and others sat on [President] Kennedy's doorstep and pleaded my cause and he finally waived my

Ruby Watts

education, Kennedy did. All the state committee and my supervisors knew that my education was limited and they didn't take advantage of me at no time. When they met down at Atlanta, Georgia—thirteen states met—we were supposed to introduce ourselves, tell where we lived, what we were doing, and where we graduated from. Treva Howell, she was my immediate boss, and she knew my qualifications were limited. She was sitting over among them and she was wondering, "Now, what's he going to say?" All of them were saying they were graduated from the University of Kentucky, University of Morehead, or Eastern, or Western, Murray, or Pikeville, and Harvard and Oxford. Best colleges in the world.

When it come to me I got up, I told them who I was, where I lived, who I worked for, and that I graduated from the University of Nealy. [Later, Treva Howell] told me, "I knew you'd come up with something, but I never thought of that."

I've wondered how I got along with what little education I had, what would have happened to me if I'd been a graduate from some college. I might have been the biggest fool in the county. I've seen fellows that's got college degrees that didn't get by as well as I have. I never was afraid of my job, whatever I've done I tried my best to do it as good as I could and most of the time it was satisfactory.

I remember the first election I ever was in. It was the primary. I didn't work my home precinct [on election day], I worked the precinct that was one of the farthest points from home. I knew less people there than I knew anywhere else. I went in the evening before, got acquainted with some of the people and some of the election officers. They were voting down at a dwelling house and I learned the boys liked a dram and I got them one. There was a store nearby—there weren't any restaurants close—and at lunchtime I asked the boys what they liked to eat. They told me what they'd like and I went and got it for them. Everybody I talked to, nearly, thought that it would be a pretty even vote between just the two of us running.

The boys wouldn't talk to me as much as they went in to vote as they would after they came out, so I could tell I was getting along fairly good and I was right well pleased with what was happening to them. I stayed around till late in the evening, till the voting was pretty well over with. They counted the vote and came to the door and cried the vote off and I carried the precinct pretty good. So, there was always something that would encourage people to be for you.

My hard race was in November. I ran against one of the best men in the county and I never would mention his name. I just campaigned for myself. Ever now and then someone would ask me, "Who's running against you?" I'd say, "The best man in the county and if I wasn't a candidate I'd be for him myself." I still wouldn't mention any names.

Did you make a lot of speeches?

I never did get into that speaking because I always felt that most of the time you'd say something that you'd rather you hadn't said afterwards. While the other fellow was speaking I was always walking down on the ground shaking hands and hugging necks. They had [rallies] all over, but while they were speaking I was doing it another way.

We would have county fairs a month or less from election day and there was always a crowd here in Hindman. One of the things that's followed me through life was in October 1929 we had a county fair here and I'd made arrangements with a bread truck in Hazard to bring a truckload of pies and cakes and other goodies into Hindman and I'd treat them out. They got in here about one o'clock and everybody was hungry and everybody started giving these pies out and, of course, everybody was my friend because I was really doing something for them. Finally, they got around to giving me one of these pies and the pie was in a paper plate. I was still handing out pies and shaking hands and hugging necks and before I knew it I had that pie two thirds eat up and someone called my attention that I was eating the paper plate.

I'd say the first race I ever ran [was for tax commissioner and it] cost me about a thousand dollars. I didn't have that much and it cost me all I had. My friends gave me my board and spending money.

Back in those days the [primary] election was the first Saturday in August. It was always the hottest part of the year. I was trying to shake hands and get hold of everybody I could and I came across one woman that I knew well. She said to me, "How are you doing?"

I said, "I'm hot and bothered."

She said, "Well, you're in much better shape than I am because I'm hot and not being bothered." Wherever I'd go then they'd ask me had I run across anybody that was hot and not being bothered.

I never would run from one precinct to another on election day and I noticed a lot of people did that. I'd work everywhere else except home, then on the last two days I'd always be right there on the ground. I would always have someone standing at the door giving them a card asking them to vote for me. Most of your races that people were interested in were sheriff, and the clerk, and the judge. Tax commissioner was way down the line and that last word as people went in that door helped a lot. I paid three dollars so I always had someone to help me out.

The election officers counted the vote at the polls. Most of the time it would be ten or eleven o'clock at night before they would get through and they would cry off the vote at the door and show how many each candidate got. [Then] they'd bring it to Hindman. None of them hardly would get here till Monday except the ones that was here in town.

Did you ever consider running for state office?

No, I never was interested in that. I was always interested in county politics. I like the people here and the closer you stay with them the more contact you have with your people. I worked for the government for nearly nine years and I lost a lot of my contact. After I got back here in the judge's office I really took advantage of it again. I never let nobody come in here and go out without talking to them. If I can't do nothing for them at least I make them think I tried.

My advice to a person if he has to get into politics is to contact as many people as he can. Run your own race, meet the people, talk with them, [don't] depend on certain people in certain precincts to take care of you, just go and see everybody. I think the only type of politics to play is personal contact. I took advantage of every opportunity to get acquainted with people in the county. I talked to them about nearly everything. I knew what creek everybody lived on and I knew who they married. That was my way of getting friendly with people and learning their background, where they were born, and where different families had married into. When I'd go in and call them by name they wondered how I knew who lived there.

In 1924 when you started working as Lee Hall's deputy tax commissioner did you have any idea of making politics your career?

No, I didn't. Times were real rough and I needed a job. I got married August 22, 1924, and Lee Hall offered me a job and I took it. I worked for him for five years. I did some of [his] book work so I learned from that what people owned and who their neighbor was.

In 1929 me, Bruce Martin, and others got together. Bruce was an old schoolteacher and a politician. He wanted to be tax commissioner and we got together and we agreed that we'd take the examination to qualify to be a candidate for tax commissioner and we wouldn't run against each other. We had an agreement: for me to run in '29 and he'd run in '33.

I wrote some people down at Frankfort and a member of the state tax commission furnished me with all the material that I needed to pass this examination. I knew Adam Campbell right well, he was the county attorney, and his wife and my wife were first cousins, and Adam helped me quite a bit. He put us in a room to ourselves. I had all my literature hid in that room, I had the statutes hid in there also—which I wasn't supposed to have—but Adam didn't know it. He just turned us loose in there and when a question come up on revenue and taxation, why, I had the statute in there and I had all this other literature in there. We all passed, but we worked hard. Honestly, I worked I'd say three months or longer on it.

What was the main difference between the way you won an election then and now?

In those days there were certain fellows in the precincts that people looked up to. If they got in trouble, they were the ones they'd go to and get them to help them out of trouble. If they needed accommodations, they would accommodate them and then when elections would come along they would feel it necessary to go along with them because of past accommodations, and the accommodations they expected in the future. They don't do that anymore. You've got to talk to everybody in person, nearly everybody likes to be talked to.

It's always been my thinking that the best time to see a person is around three o'clock in the morning. You get more out of a person at that time and they think more of it, too. I said, "I laid down and couldn't sleep. Got to thinking about [you] and just had to get up and come and see [you]." They think, "Doggone, he thinks I'm important or he wouldn't be out here to see me that time of morning." A lot of people would think maybe you're bothering them, but you're not. They always greeted me and they liked it.

Of course, I used my letter-writing system in all the campaigns that I ever made. I would write three, four hundred letters each time I was a candidate and I would put a stamped addressed envelope in it and ask for an answer back [saying] whether they would support me or wouldn't. [In 1949 when I was running for Knott County sheriff] I wrote a fellow in Quicksand,* he was a merchant and a leader in that section, and asked him about his support for me. He wrote back right quick and told me he would support me.

[Later] I sat down with my contender—he was a right strong contender—[and] I asked him about several people, who they'd be for. He didn't know or he'd say they'd be for him. Finally, I asked him about this merchant and he said, "He's for me."

I said, "How sure [are] you that he's for you?"

"I'm sure."

I said, "Have you seen him?"

"No."

"I'll tell you what I'll do. I'll leave it up with him which one should run and I haven't been to see him either."

* A section of Knott County.

He took off just like Snider's pup and we went to see [the merchant]. I said, "We're both candidates for sheriff and I know you're a good friend of this fellow, and I know you're a good friend of mine. It might put you in a hard place but we won't feel bad at you. We're going to leave it up to you which one of us should make the race. That's our agreement."

He took me. Said, "Well, I have to be for Ruby."

That settled it, [my contender] quit. I never did tell him [about the letter]. I never did tell nobody about those letters I was writing all over the county, but it worked wonders. I'd say a hundred of them or more would answer. I never did get a letter back saying they wouldn't support me.

Four years I was tax commissioner. [In 1933] I worked for Bruce Martin as deputy tax commissioner. I made his books for him and I went out and done some assessing.

Have you ever been defeated in a race?

Yes, I was defeated for sheriff in 1937, I was hoping you wouldn't ask me about that. That's the only race I ever lost. These factions were still there when I was trying to run in the middle. I never was mixed up in factions. I would plead with them to get along, especially on certain races. I never would get interested in all the races at the same time which they would. We had two factions—the Combs and Hayes—and they would try to run a candidate for every office on both sides. But I'd never do that. I'd always try to leave them room to either single me out or single some other candidate out. I've always thought that my plea with both factions had something to do with my success in politics. I'm still pleading with them to not go into it because let an election that's [passed] be gone. That type of politics won't last. It might last for a while but it won't last forever.

In 1937 me and General Fugate, John Sturgill, and Farris Hayes all run for sheriff. I defeated John Sturgill bad, and Farris Hayes real bad, and then General defeated me by a small vote. When they saw that General was really going to get the nomination they had a brother of mine back in the room upstairs here wanting to run him on the Hog Back ticket.* When the vote was counted and I had lost, I got the General up on a table. I knew they had brother Lawrence back in the room then trying to get him to run Hog Back ticket. I got up on the table and laid my arm around his neck and I said, "Now, General, in the past when candidates got defeated [in the primary] they [ran on the Hog Back ticket in the general election]. I'm for you and if they undertake to Hog-Back you this fall you can just bet that I'm on your side." Of course, Lawrence came out after a while and told me they were trying to get him to run. I said, "Now, Lawrence, I done told General that I was against Hog Back ticket and I certainly don't want to be against you. Don't run." So, he told me that he wouldn't run. Prior to my time they had run on that independent, or Hog Back ticket. That was the first time in years [no one did]. [For years] our sheriff and jailers were elected on the Hog Back ticket. The legislature passed a law against it around '40 [and] to get on the ballot you have to run through the primary.

I was on the highway patrol [from] 1938 until March of '41. When Happy Chandler was elected [governor] in '35 he changed the name of state police to highway patrol. Jobs were scarce and I was offered a job, paid a hundred dollars a month. I was one of the first highway patrol that was stationed in Hazard.† I still lived in the county and I kept my contacts pretty well. Of course, in

---

* Candidates who were affiliated with neither the Republicans nor the Democrats were said to be running on the Hog Back ticket. Hog Back candidates either entered the campaign after the primary, or had competed in the primary under the rooster (Democratic) or log cabin (Republican) symbol and lost. In the November election they chose their own symbol—often a hen, plow, or mattock—for the ballot. The Hog Back practice was outlawed in the 1930's when the Kentucky legislature passed a statute requiring all candidates for public office to declare their party affiliation and participate in their party's primary in all races except nonpartisan judicial positions.

† Hazard is the seat of Perry County, which is adjacent to Knott County, and is considerably larger than Hindman. In 1930 Hazard had a population of 7,021, and Hindman had 508 residents. Many Knott Countians went to Hazard to do business, which enabled Ruby to maintain ties with his constituents.

Hazard you see more people from Knott County than you would see in Hindman. There was a road going into Hazard and they'd go to Hazard and trade. It was a good place to talk to people on the street and I took advantage of that because they wouldn't be afraid someone would hear them talk to you and they'd tell you whether they were for or against you. Back in those days people's words were [their] promise much more than they are now. Now they rattle off to you so to get rid of you.

In 1941 sixteen of us started out running for sheriff, and it finally got down to three of us in the primary: myself, and Alonzo Howard, and Mark Amburgey. I got some of them off and the other fellows got some of them off. They [were] on there to hurt somebody, not to be elected, because they knew they couldn't be elected. Some fellow that didn't want me to be elected would put on somebody they knew that could take some votes.* We just went out and talked to them, and got other people to talk to them, and showed them that they couldn't win and I could.

The primary was the only election I had that year, didn't have any [opposition] in November. Of course, being tax commissioner, people hadn't forgotten that. I'd been on the highway patrol and I was able to help a lot of people get their driver's license. [When] I'd come into Hindman I'd let people ride in the police car. While I was highway foreman [from 1946 to 1948, if] I would have excess dirt I'd always put it in front of their homes if they needed some dirt. I tried to do everything good for people and nothing bad against them.

I tried to convince them that my experience as a highway patrolman would be a lot of help to the people of the county. [In] my experience on the highway patrol I'd learned quite a bit how to handle prisoners and I didn't have any trouble. It was a hot race, buy my majority was large, it was nine hundred and some.

One of my elections was contested. They accused me of buy-

* Such candidates are called "cutters" in mountain political circles.

ing gingerbread* and using other ways of influence on voters. Giving them money. They figured what they done, I done the same thing. You never know what people will swear in a contest. [I got my] case settled before it came to court. It's rough to be contested.

Did you ever have trouble collecting taxes from people who had been against you in the election?

No, everybody was real nice. When I was real nice with them, then they was real nice with me. Actually, [my opponents] were about the easiest people there was to work with. In a lot of cases your friends would expect more out of you. I made the point of trying to make friends out of [my opponents]. I remember [one time] I went out front here and there was a fellow standing there. I casually knew him and I asked him what he was doing. He said he had a son down in jail and he couldn't get nobody to go his bond. I knew he was against me in the election [for tax commissioner] but I said, "What's he charged with?"

He told me it didn't mean much, just an appearance bond is all he needed signed. I said, "Well, if it'll help any I'll sign his bond."

He said, "It sure will and I'll appreciate it. I'll let you know now that I was against you in the election."

"Yes, I knew it. I know of no reason that I should want your son to be down here in jail. If we can get him out, let's get him out."

He said, "If I ever have a chance to help you again I'll do it." And he was always for me after that. I'd always take advantage of things like that.

When the people got in trouble on making moonshine and selling and either myself or some of my deputies caught somebody, I would always go with them to court and try my best to

* In the past, mountain politicians often bought gingerbread cakes from elderly women and distributed them to people in the hope of gaining a few extra votes. By doing this, candidates earned the goodwill of the gingerbread bakers and of the people who received a free piece of cake. The practice has almost died now and today "buying gingerbread" is usually a euphemism for vote buying.

get them out if they promised to quit, and I had right good success out of it. I always thought it was better if we could get them to promise to quit [and] get them on probation than it was to prosecute them and send them to jail for four to six months; then they'd go right back into it.

I remember in one section of the country they'd been reporting a still for a couple of years. We'd hunted for it and weren't able to find it. And one day a woman came in and told me where a still was. Of course, she mentioned a few names—her and her hubby had had a falling out—and she told me that I could find this still if I'd go where she told me to go.

I went and we didn't see anybody. They had evidently learned that she had come to town, maybe would cause them some trouble, and they had quit and got away. It was the granddaddy still that I ever heard of in Knott County—we figured it would hold about 210 gallons—and it was hot. Nobody never would own up to it. [World War II] was on, I gave it to somebody that was handling copper.

When I was tax commissioner I got paid by the percentage of the amount of real estate and personal property [I taxed]. If it came to a million dollars, I got so much on the million. We got ten cents for each list that we taxed and I believe five cents for every dog.

Prior to Lee Hall being elected [in 1923] we had people [who], before they would start asking questions, would make them hold up their hands [and] swear that they would give true answers to all questions they would ask them. Then they would go down this list. They would ask them about boats and automobiles and there wasn't nothing like that in this country, wasn't no roads here and there wasn't an automobile in the county or a boat.* This [list of questions] was put out for the whole state and they did have automobiles in Louisville and Lexington and places like that, and they had boats on the rivers and lakes. When they got through

* As unlikely as this statement may seem, according to an article in the *Louisville Post* on April 8, 1924, there was only one registered passenger car in Knott County at that time.

they'd make them hold up their hands and swear that they had told the truth.

I just did it a little different than anyone else had ever done before. I'd go on horseback, I'd ride up to their home, get down and go in. If it was lunchtime and these people asked me to eat, I'd always go right in and flop down and eat with them and they appreciated it. If they didn't have much to eat I bragged on it just as good as if it was one of the best dinners anybody ever sat down to. And I would talk with them. I'd find out who their kinfolks was, who they married, who their children married, and people liked it.

I knew the real estate, how many acres of land you've got and what your timber would be worth, what your improvements on the land would be worth and I'd add it up and I'd tell them how much it all came to. Then I'd ask them how many head of cattle [and hogs] they had. I never would ask them how many chickens they had, they would have to [voluntarily] tell how many chickens they had. I never would mention their dogs, either. Sometimes they'd tell me they had a dog and then I'd put down a dog, or if I saw a dog around there I'd put it down.

When I got through with them I'd say, "You're upon your honor if you told me the truth." It was just something different and they liked it, and they would always invite me to come back again.

Actually, it comes to a point where most people have to have some encouragement to be interested in elections and they get encouragement in different ways. You did whatever you thought would make them be for you in the elections. If it was hoeing corn, pulling fodder, digging potatoes, gathering corn, milk the cows, hugging the women, or diapering babies—whatever it took.

Like Ruby Watts, Moss Noble of Jackson, Kentucky, has had an almost lifelong interest in local politics. Ruby is a Democrat and Moss is a Republican. The practices Moss discusses have long

been common ones in most mountain counties and are favored by
Democrats and Republicans alike.

Moss was born in 1900 in the Breathitt County, Kentucky,
town of Noble, which was undoubtedly named after his forebears.
After he graduated from George Washington University's law
school in 1931 he returned to Jackson, the county seat of Breathitt
County, to begin a law practice. His interest in politics coincided
with the hanging of his lawyer's shingle. He ran for office only
twice, and the results were discouraging. "There were too many
disadvantages. The Republican party was too much [of] a minority to overcome" the Democrats.

Moss has held three appointive public posts, however, the most
recent one as assistant United States attorney for the eastern Kentucky district. He served from 1958 to 1973, when he retired and
resumed law practice in Jackson.

I was appointed tax collector in 1943 [and] the town was in dire
need of money. The budget had got in such bad shape they
couldn't pay the light bills and they didn't have any street lights.
The city waterworks was privately owned and the water companies were about to turn off the city water unless the bills were
paid. They elected a reform ticket here with a very aggressive
man for mayor who [tried] to go about collecting some of the
taxes and restoring the solvency of the town. I was appointed tax
collector and given a list of delinquent taxes. I went out and
talked to the people; told them I came for their taxes, period. I
told them that meant they could pay voluntarily and get it over
with, or they could pay [through] the nose later on. I made people pay taxes that didn't like to pay taxes. One of them was the
county judge. He never paid any taxes until I went in office. The
gimmick I used on him was catching him with a bunch of people.
I'd go up before a big crowd of people and ask him to pay his
taxes.

I served one term as city tax collector [and] was not reap-
pointed.

I've had some connection with the Republican politics of Breathitt County since 1936. At that time the Republican party was very much in the minority and the problem was twofold: first, to get as many people as we could interested and willing to vote the Republican ticket; and second, to see that the elections were conducted strictly according to law and to keep down any irregular practices.

[In] a number of precincts in the county there were not enough Republicans to provide election officers. [At] that time each party was allowed two election officers per precinct and in those precincts where there were no Republican election officers the opposition party had pretty free hand. They did just about what they wanted to, which included, in some instances, voting out the entire registration and doing things to disenfranchise the Republican voters that came by, [such as] failing to sign their ballots. I recall one precinct in the county where there were some thirteen, fourteen, Republican votes cast and all of them were invalidated because the clerk intentionally failed to sign his own name on each ballot.

Under Kentucky law it was against the law for any person to vote in public; all the votes had to be secret. Even a blind person was required to select a person to cast his vote for him and that person was sworn to cast the vote in the manner in which the blind person directed. It was common practice for blind people and ignorant people who asked to be given instructions on how to vote, not [to be] voted the way they asked but the way the worker wanted to vote. In other words, the voter was defrauded.

[There was also] the chain ballot [that] operates in this fashion: a precinct worker for a given party will go himself, or send somebody, in to vote, and instead of putting his legal ballot in the ballot box he'll bring it out unfolded and deposit a piece of paper in the ballot box to indicate that he'd voted. He'll take [the official ballot] outside and contact some person that arranged to buy his vote. [That person would] vote this ballot in the manner he wanted it voted and furnish it to [a] floater with instructions that the floater [is to] go in the voting booth as if to mark his ballot. Actually, what he'll do [is] take the voted ballot that has been furnished him by the worker out of his pocket and place that in the ballot box and carry the unvoted ballot out and deliver that to the precinct worker. Then the precinct worker will take that ballot and repeat the process with as many voters as he can buy. The advantage of the chain ballot is that the precinct worker knows that he's getting ballots marked the way he wants them voted put in the ballot box.

What too often happened was that if the voters didn't come out [party leaders] just voted them anyway. I remember the gubernatorial election in 1943 in which I was somewhat active in behalf of the Republican party. The election day was a very bad day; it was cold and [there was] some snow and a great deal of rain. I recall one precinct where there was some 350 registered voters and when the returns were brought into the courthouse to be counted, the entire registration was voted out almost alphabetically. I took down names of people who appeared as having voted and I found people that hadn't lived in the county for a number of years. I found some people that I knew were living in Illinois and Ohio and yet they voted as if they'd been there. I learned afterwards that the number of illegal votes cast in that precinct changed the result of the office of secretary of state, which the Republican nominee lost by only forty-five votes. I presented that [information] to the grand jury and brought in witnesses to establish that these people were out of the state at the time, but for some reason the grand jury saw fit to return no indictments. I later heard from the grapevine that the grand jury thought everybody violated the election law, so nobody ought to be indicted.

The most noted incident is the Clayhole precinct [in] 1921. There were some very hot races that year, particularly the state senator's race, and all indications were that the race would be very close. The late M. F. Crain of Lexington lived in Breathitt County at that time and he was the Republican nominee for state senator. Doctor J. D. Whitaker from Cannel City was the Democratic nominee and word got out that the Democratic party was going to take Clayhole precinct and the opposite party took steps to keep that from happening and they sent guards there. An altercation came up [in] the afternoon, four men were killed and about nineteen others wounded, and of course the ballot box was destroyed.

One gimmick used in this county quite extensively was the campaign slate. This was utilized largely in those years when county officers were elected. The dominant politician in the county would establish a "slate." In other words, he'd pick some man to run for each county office, like one man for county judge, another man for sheriff, another man for jailer, and so on. The man that was organizing this slate would fix a price the candidate would [have to] pay to be put on the slate. The going price was mighty small sums in minor offices to as much as $5,000 [for] major offices. It was a form of vote buying, of bribing. When the slate was established word would go out and all the people that belonged to that faction of the party would vote the slate and generally the man on the slate would be nominated.

It's generally understood that there's a great deal of vote buying. People would be seen consulting with the precinct workers, going into the voting place and then coming back and meeting with the election workers after they voted, which indicated that there was possibly a payoff. Normal price [was] five dollars, but there are cases where the race appeared to be very close [and] votes were being sold for as much as six dollars.

[The power of the Democratic party in Breathitt] goes back to the Civil War days. A large part of Breathitt County was allied with the Confederacy and nearly all the old Confederate soldiers were Democrats. Nearly all of the Union soldiers were Republicans. It just happened that in the history of Breathitt County there emerged some very strong individuals who more or less manipulated the Democratic party. For a great many years here during the days of the New Deal the Democratic machine controlled everything. The Democrats campaigned all the time. It was twenty-four hours a day, three hundred and sixty-five days a year. [They dispensed] patronage [and] everybody that was given a job was given to understand how they had to vote. If they didn't register right and didn't vote right, they were fired from whatever job they might have had. Every job from the state, to the schools, to the courts, to the federal government was controlled by the party and they naturally had economic power of life and death over the citizens of the county. [If an employee didn't vote the way party leaders wanted him to vote] he was thrown out on his ears. Promptly. Disloyalty was strictly not tolerated.

Nearly every individual had some contact with some governmental agency and when all those agencies were dominated by one political party there was the opportunity for political pressure, and that was used to the hilt. The independent individual, the person not connected with any of these machines, was afraid to say anything, afraid reprisals [would] be taken against him. I had this problem. It got so hot in the courts here that I found it to my advantage to give up my practice and take a job with the United States government [in] 1958.

When any political machine is operating smoothly there are a great many victims, people that machine has to run over to get somewhere, and it fell my lot to represent the victims. I was generally the attorney for the victims and plenty of obstacles were thrown in my path. I wasn't afraid. I had too many relatives here and I had the reputation of being a law-abiding citizen.

If community life in the mountains were likened to handwoven fabric, politics would be the warp and religion the woof. In many parts of the region one county encompasses several hundred square miles of land, which made for unwieldy governance before the days of paved roads and automobiles. For this reason county officials, especially those concerned with law enforcement, often had little clout beyond the county seat and matters of local dis-

cipline that could not be handled within the family were often dealt with through the church. Just as socializing was a part of every election and county fair, fellowship was an integral part of church services and Association* meetings. The duties of fellowship included caring for one's neighbor and, if necessary, censoring or punishing him if he strayed from beliefs and standards of behavior set by the church.

Like Ruby Watts, Luther Addington, of Wise, Virginia, has had a many-faceted career. He was born in 1899 and before graduating in 1922 from Emory & Henry College in Emory, Virginia, Luther had hunted ginseng, tracked minks, possums, and skunks, managed a railroad store, written scrip for a coal company, "slung hash" in a college dining room, sold books door-to-door ("A thing like that is where you get a lot of experience in how people live"), stacked lumber, and built roads. Since then, he has sold Fuller brushes, written detective stories and children's books, and been the Wise County school superintendent for thirty-five years. One of Luther's avocations has been delving into the history of the Baptist Church in southwestern Virginia. He talked about the role of the church in community life and how church members sometimes acted as both jury and judge.

[During the 1800's] the Regular Primitive Baptist was the predominating religion in Scott County, Virginia, the area I grew up in. † It was a way of life of people in my vicinity. Most of the people belonged to the church in order to be considered an upstand-

---

* In the mountains an "Association" is the governing body of a group of Baptist churches in one locale or county that share common beliefs. For many years Association meetings were the largest and most important annual public gatherings.
† The Regular Primitive Baptist Church in southwestern Virginia is a fundamentalist sect which uses lay ministers and follows a strict interpretation of the Bible. Many such sects exist in Central Appalachia; as theological disputes have developed new churches have been formed by the dissident believers. The most prevalent fundamentalist sects in eastern Kentucky are the Old Regular Baptists and the Primitive Baptists.

Luther Addington

ing equal in the community. To be excluded from the only group
that was really meeting and had any influence in the community
was right much of a jolt to anyone.

The Baptists came down from the old Calvinistic crowd and
seemed to be the people who were coming out into the mountains [in the 1790's]. Of course, a little later the Methodists and
Presbyterians [came too]. Daniel Boone and Squire were Baptists. They were among the first. Squire Boone preached over
here on Clinch River and had a little church.

The Primitive Baptist Church served as a welding focus for the
people in those communities. It was a place to come together.
The services were set once a month as a rule. Usually they met of
a morning: they'd have their service about ten o'clock, and it

would start with singing. Some one person would "line" the song. That is, he would read one line. Everybody would sing that. Then after the singing there would usually be a prayer, most often by the pastor, and then after that he preached. If there was one preacher [it would end] about twelve-thirty or one. Sometimes an extra preacher would come in and it'd be longer. They were long-winded. After the preaching there would come the business part, "Assemblying in love and fellowship." After the business meeting was over people would linger and visit with each other for a long time. One fellow would maybe tell the other how his corn crops were coming along and what was going on in the community. They pretty well found out what others were doing that way.

Once a year they'd have what they called an Association, or the annual meeting, and they'd have dinner on the grounds. The Associations were held first [at] one church, then another. There were five, six, or seven churches, and a whole bevy of [preachers].

Now the Associations were considered big affairs. People from a distance would come and stay through it all and visit somebody in the community. The preachers liked to [congregate at] the same place because they could sit around the fire and talk, and they certainly liked to talk. It is told that a group of these preachers at the Association went to one house and the host built up a big roaring fire. They formed a semicircle around it. One of the grandsons had been out in the cold playing. He came in cold, wanted to warm, but he couldn't get to the fire. So he kept walking behind this semicircle of preachers rubbing his hands together and said, "Cold." Nobody would listen to him. Finally he said, "Hell fire!"

One preacher looked around and says, "Young man, I don't know what to think of you using such language as that. I'll bet you don't know what kind of place that is anyhow."

"Well, I really don't, unless it's just like it is here: You can't get to the fire for the preachers."

I can remember if somebody died in the community they'd always go to the church and tap that bell as many times as there were years in the person's life. About a year after the death they'd always have the Memorial Service. Of course, they'd have a service when the person died and it was usually a sermon. The preacher would use the occasion as a time to admonish the people by [the dead person's example and say] they ought to live the right kind of life, even though they had to live it through grace. Something would be said about the person who had died, maybe a short biography.

I found a minute book, the first entry in it was 18 and 8, and in it one gets something of the life of that community because it seemed to revolve around the church. When you pick up the minute book and read it you can see how the church was really the court. You hear little about any justice of the peace, but in the minute book you find that after the regular service was over, the moderator—every church had a moderator: he could be a preacher, or he could be just a regular member—would "open the doors," as they called it. There were two reasons to open the doors of the church: to find out whether there were any people being charged for misconduct in the community; or whether there was anybody who wanted to join the church. The parlance of the church was a "reference": "Are there any references?"

They would say when they opened it, "Are all in love and fellowship?" And if there were no voices to the contrary, that meant those who were there were all in love and fellowship with each other. However, there might be members on the outside who couldn't have answered that question positively and sometimes they would bring up the case of somebody who wasn't there. Somebody would say they had a complaint to bring up against somebody not there a'tall. And then they'd appoint a committee to bring that person to the next meeting, "in course" they always said, in order to give an account of himself and to see what was going to happen.

Now one fellow, Sam Salyers, lived over there [during the

early 1800's] and his name runs all through the book because he was in and out of the business meeting for one little misdemeanor or another. One time it was for "walking in an un-Christian-like manner," they said. He had been drinking too much of the spirits. Then another time he was brought in for making spirits. Now, if he apologized and said he'd done wrong, they would forgive him and let him go ahead.

The Primitive Baptists were rather strict in their beliefs about the mode of dress. A woman's dress had to be long enough to cover her ankles. It was sort of a sin, you know, for her to expose her ankles. It didn't matter how beautiful they might be. Of course, didn't any of them wear breeches back then, but they would have frowned on it.

To show how strict they were, they tried a woman who had come to church while pregnant. That was an offense. She was excluded from their fellowship for not knowing any better than to come to church in that particular situation.

I found that my own ancestors—although they were considered good enough to become deacons of that church—one of them, my great-grandfather, was brought in for walking in an un-Christian way in his community [in 1810]. He'd been drinking some. One time he denied it and that case lingered on. Time after time they would "notice" him to come back to the next [meeting]. Finally, he withdrew his membership, said he was going to leave that church, but after he thought it over he decided he'd come back and let his name go back on the books. That very often happened to people who would come in and repent.

Now occasionally somebody was brought in for stealing and they said, "Well, now you have to pay for the value of whatever [you] took." If he did that and he admitted he done wrong, they would take him back into the congregation. Now in one case a man was brought in for being a little tipsy and he would say he knew he'd done wrong and they'd let him go on. This particular individual went on committing one little offense after another and he was always forgiven by the moderator. Eventually, however, he was brought in for stealing some goods out of the moderator's store and then it was, "Good-bye, you're gone!" Some called it "de-churched," or "You're excluded," and that was just terrible for anybody who belonged to the church to be excluded, unless he was just so mean that he didn't care anyhow.

They would get into arguments as to what was right and what was wrong. Of course, one of the main questions that they discussed time and again was predestination. The Regular Primitive Baptists believed that people were destined for heaven or hell before the world began, and so there would be arguments over that question. After a while in that particular community people began to say, "Well, there's some other way to live and we don't believe that there is such a thing as predestination." Also, there came up the question of sending missionaries to places. Most of the Regular Primitive Baptists didn't believe in sending missionaries anywhere, but some of them did. Well, they argued that question and, of course, it was argued not only in that one community but in others. Then the question of "Anti's" arose. Those who didn't want missions were called Anti's, and the Anti's said, "Let's build a church of [our] own."

That's been the history of churches in the mountains over the years. Some disagreement came up and then they would split. Regular Primitive Baptists split into two factions. The Anti's continued as the Primitive Baptists and did not believe in missions. Those who did believe, they called them "Missionaries."

Were preachers paid?

No, that was another rule of the church. If somebody wanted to slip them a buck and stick it in his pocket that was all right, he wouldn't throw it away, but no salaries. They earned their living farming.

To become a preacher [a man] had to declare himself "interested in becoming a preacher." Then a committee of examiners was appointed, and on a certain day this committee would gather in the presence of the congregation and would ask him various questions about his belief. If they were satisfied that his belief was what they thought it ought to be, then he was given the right to become a pastor.*

[During the late 1800's] the early Methodist [preachers] had a circuit, maybe four or five churches, and they would go one place one Sunday and another church the next Sunday. Because they went on a circuit they became known as circuit riders. They were supported by their membership and some of them earned their own living, too. Now, one custom they had—about dead now— once a year when a new preacher would come into a Methodist community they would give him a "pounding." It started out with the idea that the members, or anybody else in the community that wanted to do so, would take a pound of groceries to his house at a certain time. That eventually spread into taking various things, whatever people might want. The more wealthy maybe gave the preacher money outside of the regular salary.†

Another hub of community activities was the school. Cora Reynolds Frazier, of Whitesburg, who has taught in eastern Ken-

---

* The *History of Scott County,* by Robert M. Addington, a distant relative of Luther's, includes a transcript of the theological examination Robert Kilgore underwent before becoming a preacher in 1808. Some of the questions and answers were: "What view have you of God?" "I view Him as a spirit almighty, eternal, immortal, invisible, without body, parts, or passion." "What think you of man in his first erectitude?" "I believe he was created in God's image in innocence and happiness." "What think you of man in his present state?" "I believe man fallen and depraved through every power of body and soul."

† The first official circuit in Wise County, Virginia, was formed in 1839. It was called the North Estilville Circuit and the Reverend Reuben Steele was the preacher. In his book, *Kentucky's Last Frontier,* historian Henry P. Scalf says: "These early Methodist ministers owned little in the way of worldly goods. A small farm, usually far from the scene of his ministry and attended by his family while he carried on, a horse, and the necessary needs for considerable time spent on the trails, were usually the sum total of his worldly physical possessions. In his saddle-bags he carried a Bible, hymnal, shoemaker's tools, a small hammer used to nail on a horseshoe, an extra shirt, and a few tracts issued by his church. Thus equipped he 'rode the circuit.' Since there were no church houses for a long time . . . he preached at any place available to him—in taverns, public buildings at the county seats, at cabin homes, and in the open air. With the exception of Monday, he preached every day of the week."

Cora Frazier

tucky schools for more than fifty years, explains how parents had a hand in both the recreation and discipline of schoolchildren.

I'd try to talk correctly around the children, [but] when the parents would come I would talk just the way they talked so they would be comfortable and I'd make them like me. That was the most important thing—to get them to like you and be sure that I stayed in the schoolhouse and worked with the children and put in my time. I didn't let them have two hours at noon or longer recesses than they were supposed to have, or I didn't turn out and take off and go where I wanted to go in the afternoon.

I organized a PTA [in 1924] and we had meetings every

Wednesday night. We gathered at the schoolhouse and had a good time. The children would entertain one week and the parents would entertain the next. We didn't do it just once a month, we had it every week. The goal of the PTA was for the betterment of the school and the community and the children, and to work out the problems between teachers and the children, if they had any problems. We had projects where we made money and we bought books and things for our schools, equipment of all kinds.

In the fall we'd have pie suppers. The mothers would bake beautiful pies, and they would take them to the schoolhouse and have auctions and bid on the prettiest girls. They'd have beautiful boxes made out of silk paper all decorated up. The boys in the community would bid on the pies. If your pie was put up and everybody knew that [a certain boy] wanted your pie, well, they'd run it just as high as they could run it. Sometimes they'd tell [who brought the] pie, and sometimes they wouldn't because some girls wouldn't want certain boys to bid on their pie. They'd put the girls up on the stage—all the girls that would go up there—and every which one they put the most money on would be the prettiest girl in the community. I won in spelling bees, but I never took the cake in beauty.

When I went to school* they had switches, but I never had a switch because they're too easy to break the skin off a child and a paddle won't. I can't see why they wanted to take the reading of the Scripture for two or three minutes out of the school when there's Scripture that will discipline the child. A good teacher generally knows what to read to children to discipline them, and I've got a little key that will tame any wild boy. I know it does. In Proverbs, the Ephesians, and Psalms there's not any better counsel in the world that you can give to young people. In Proverbs it tells you that foolishness is bound in the heart of a child, but the

* Cora Frazier entered the first grade in 1912 and graduated from Whitesburg High School in 1923.

rod of correction will drive it far from [him]. All of it is wonderful. Psalms, Proverbs, and Ecclesiastes, those are my favorites, and I used them while teaching in a hard school and I didn't have any trouble.

I never touched a child with my hands in my teaching, except boys. Sometimes I'd grab them by the shoulders and shake them a little bit. Sometimes, if they used bad language or had fights on the school grounds, I whipped them. It might have been wrong, but I did. Turn them across a desk, paddle them good, and they'll learn. The parents generally made me [a paddle], bored holes in it, and sent it to school to me. [They sometimes] came right to the schoolhouse [to complain about the paddlings]. Some came with sticks in their hands. I'd ring the bell and call the children in, and I'd ask the children to tell the parents just what happened. I wasn't afraid. I knew the law was on my side. We generally had a county judge that just really backed you up.

The influence of politics on local schools went far beyond judicial support of Scripture reading and paddlings. Cora taught at a time when voters and politicians determined who the local schoolteacher would be. Every other year people voted for a "trustee." Whoever won had the privilege of recommending the next schoolteacher to the county superintendent. Often a person ran for trustee because he had a son or daughter, niece or nephew, who wanted the job. The position was a coveted one.

Cora Frazier, like many mountain schoolteachers, is as correct and proper as she is gracious. High on the walls of her parlor in Whitesburg there are two old photographs. One is of her mother, Mahala Hall; the other shows her husband, Troy Frazier. Both are dead now but whenever Cora mentions either in conversation she pauses, then nods toward the picture. Does she seek their approval? Are they listening? It is a private pause that momentarily unmasks this mountain woman.

A childhood accident prevented Cora from going to school until she was eight years old. She fell in the fire when she was small and recalls: "My right leg was drawn up under my body. A faith doctor blew on my leg, and with the help of Daddy and Mother and with home remedies that Mother made out of the white of an egg and alum this drew the fire out. They straightened my leg."

Cora described the influence of politics on the schools and how she dealt with the politically sensitive problem of discovering a moonshine still behind her school.

The first school I ever taught was on Bottom Fork at Mayking, [Kentucky, and] a trustee recommended me to the county superintendent, and whoever he recommended that superintendent had to hire. Every little school in the county had one trustee. We used to have primaries in May for the county elections and state, but this school election was a special time of the year. It was in August. Those elections were hotter than the President's because there were so many teachers that didn't have any jobs. The ones that had the largest number of votes and relatives that could vote in their behalf [would] get the school.

What made the elections so hot?

It was about the only paying job there was in this country, and they praised the teacher highly. They wouldn't hire anybody with a bad reputation. You had to be a good moral person and have good character. You were the most respected person in the whole community, and if you didn't behave that way it was a disgrace to the profession.

When I came back from college* there were only two schools in Letcher County that hadn't been recommended. I visited both of these trustees and said I would teach them a good school if they would recommend me to be hired. I made up my mind that whichever came first I would teach that school. I hoped [it would

* Cora Frazier graduated from Eastern Kentucky State Teachers College in Richmond, Kentucky. In 1966 the name of the school was changed to Eastern Kentucky University.

be] the one closest to home, and sure enough [it was]. The first trustee I had weighed coal at Elk Horn Coal Company at Millstone [Kentucky]. Most all the others I ever had were wealthy people, wealthy compared to what the people had in this country. They were in business, and doctors, and [had] big coal interests. The school that he recommended was a rather large school. I remember getting eighty dollars a month. Your salary was based on the number of students that were in school.

The county superintendent was Professor George Clark from Knott County, and he was a fine person. He would tell you exactly what he could do and what he couldn't, and I liked that very much. When I went to him he said, "Now, Miss Cora, you're just too small, too young, you just can't teach that big school." I lacked two weeks of being eighteen.

The trustee came down and had it out with Professor Clark. He told [Clark] he was going to have me; didn't matter whether he'd recommend me or not, and he had more power than he did. Of course, I appreciated that. The superintendent finally agreed, and they let me have the school, and we had a wonderful school on Bottom Fork.

Then, I was principal of the school at Colson [from 1941 to 1942]. That year I had the ball team. These boys didn't think I could coach a team, but I coached it and they won the county championship. I have a trophy for that. I was real small, I didn't weigh over a hundred pounds, and the ball court was so dusty I tied a red bandanna handkerchief on my head. The whole team was big—tall boys, fine young men—but they had never gone to school regular and they were really poor in seventh and eighth grade. They wouldn't be able to add seven and eight sometimes. I got to worrying something was wrong with them. They kept excusing themselves [to go to] the willow bed above the ball court. I wouldn't even tell my husband, but I kind of got suspicious and afraid.

[One day] I threw the ball to one of the boys and said, "You all just go ahead and play and I'll be back just in a minute." And I went up to the willow bed. There was the finest still running in there that you ever looked at. It had all that copper worm laid out and they were just making liquor left and right up in that willow bed. They were doing it at night, of course, and these boys were going up there and drinking that still beer. I brought two big jugs of still beer down to the schoolhouse.

It was about time for the bell to ring at noon, and the boys began looking at each other, and winking, and laughing. We went on inside, and I never said a word. The teachers all were suspicious and whispering to each other. I had three or four teachers under me. I went to each door and said, "Open up the doors. We're going to have a fifteen-minute conference before we turn out school this evening."

Fifteen minutes before school was to turn out I got up on a little stage and said, "Now, boys and girls, the families that are connected with anything up here in the willow bed, you tell your daddies that I said to get it away from my school and I'll never go to any officers or anybody. All I want is that away from the school and there'll never be another word said on my part." I knew how desperate they were—all of them—and they were making a living out of it. I was against it, but I didn't want to have any trouble.

That night they moved everything out from there.

When I came to the county office with my report—I brought all the teachers' reports in at the end of the month—the superintendent said, "Well, I've got another job for you."

I said, "I'm sorry, but I'm not too well. I don't need another job. If I live to get this one out, I'll be a-flying."

He laughed, "Oh, but I've got a better job for you. The revenue men were here and they want to hire you for a revenue man."

"Well, I don't want any revenue job."

He laughed, and he said, "Why didn't you tell me about that?"

"Well, I didn't know it needed telling."

In pioneer communities throughout the nation, disputes easily got out of hand because there was often no recognized law en-

*forcement structure. If one man committed a crime against an-
other it was usually left to the injured person's family to take action in the absence of any outside law enforcer. It is not
surprising, then, that the job of righting local wrongs, or at least
of temporarily quieting them, sometimes fell to a small group of
people who came to be known as "badmen." These men were acknowledged to be good with guns, good at looking out for themselves, and good at protecting their kinfolks and friends. They
generally answered to no one. By prosecuting wrongdoers with
gunfire or threats, they acted as law enforcers; by stirring up un-
necessary trouble they were breaking the law themselves. This
paradox of law enforcer versus law breaker, which becomes so apparent when W. T. (Chid) Wright talks of his father, has led to
controversy in the mountains about badmen. Kinfolks of a particular badman tend to minimize the number of persons he killed,
and to feel his deeds were done in the course of enforcing the law.
People not related, or who were in opposition to certain badmen,
tend to exaggerate the number of persons killed and to talk about
the lawless nature of the man's activities. Both have some basis
for their view.*

*Chid is the son of Alice Harmon and "Devil" John Wright, one
of the most respected—and feared—men who roamed a small
part of Central Appalachia in the late nineteenth century. "Devil"
John had the reputation of having killed scores of men; whether
he ever killed more than a handful of people has yet to be proven.
John was an enigmatic man: he protected the law by running the
Ku Klux Klan out of the area; he flirted with it by taking more
than one wife, and he scorned it by offering revenuers a drink of
his splendid homemade whiskey.*

*Chid, who was born in McRoberts, Kentucky, in 1897, is a re-
tired coal miner, schoolteacher and long-time member of the
Pound Town Council in Pound, Virginia, where he lives. He is
also the author of a book about his father called* Devil John
Wright of the Cumberlands. *He described his father as both a law
man and a family man.*

This Ku Klux business started out* with the purpose of cleaning up the country and making people behave themselves and do things like they should do. If somebody was violating the law and the legal authorities weren't doing anything about it, [the Ku Klux wanted] to clean it up. I've also heard that they didn't want [people] to let their corn get too weedy. If they found too many different men going to a woman's house after night they would lay for them and whip the woman, and the man too if they weren't afraid that he might be a little too formidable for them.

[First] somebody would warn them† in some way about what they were expected to do. Then, they would set a bunch of switches that had blood on them down beside the door and those people would be looking for a good licking if they didn't get the thing done. And then if the happenings still continued—they

* State histories are unclear about when Ku Klux Klan groups emerged in Central Appalachia, but it is certain they were in operation by the 1850's.
† The errant citizen.

W. T. (Chid) Wright

would have some way of finding out—they'd go back and whip her and she wouldn't know who whipped her. And they wouldn't talk anything about it. They would ride and have their faces concealed and they used sheets over them, too. No doubt they carried arms.

Looked like they started with pretty good things in mind and then [in about 1905] they got into a little trouble when they killed Mime Hall, that's a widow woman, and after that happened some of the citizens got together to put the thing down. This night there was some men there at Mime Hall's and they started shooting. They killed her by accident and after that happened the citizens banded together—Pap was the leader—and [the Klansmen] had to leave.

I've heard [Pap] tell about having to shoot one man, and we knew about a Jonathan Wells that he went to get in West Virginia. I believe he was wanted for some crime, possibly a murder, and they had a reward for him. Wells was working in a shoe factory. When Dad went to get him, Dad had his pistol in his coat pocket and he had hold of it because he thought he'd better try to play safe, didn't know what Wells might do, and when Wells started shooting [Pap] shot from his coat pocket and he didn't take his gun out of his coat. The bunch of people who saw the thing thought that Wells had shot himself.

What about the feuding between Claib Jones* and John Wright?

Claib Jones was a man that lived out of the section of Letcher County where John lived. He seemed to be a kind of man that had a bunch of followers and did about whatever he pleased; had things going just about the way he wanted them to. It looked like Claib Jones might have been pretty brave and maybe a little bit jealous of John Wright. I don't know what their difference was.

* James Claybourn Jones, 1826–1914, was another so-called Kentucky "badman."

Just seemed to me like it was two fellows, one wanted to be more powerful than the other. And Claib was coming into John's county there. Looked like he was possibly carrying the offensive a little bit in that connection.

They were at a mill about the mouth of Millstone, Claib Jones and some of his men. And John Wright passed by there and they knew John was coming along. I think he was riding Old George. That was his racehorse. Some of them concealed themselves and they shot at John as he was passing by. They were ambushing him. One bullet hit him in the arm, I'm not sure which. Cut the triceps of the arm that it hit. A bullet went through the hat band—the hat was on his head—and he was blind in his left eye the latter part of his life and he attributed that to the bullet going so close to his eye that it injured the sight. They used to call Pap "Leather Eye" behind his back.

[Pap] was the Lord and king to me. He knew everybody and everything. He was more important than anybody else as far as I was concerned. He was the most important man on earth and I believe that he was about the smartest man that I ever did hear tell of, and I've had several college teachers in my time. But as for knowing the people and everything generally he kind of had a world education that a fellow doesn't get out of school books.

What was it about John Wright that made his word law among the children?

Our mother always told us the neighborhood regarded John Wright as a dangerous man. He was supposed to have killed about ninety men—which was an exaggeration—and we didn't know what he was going to do to us. Maw could pound around on us all she wanted to, and that was [true] through all his families. The [children] didn't pay too much attention to what their mother said, but if Dad was in the radius of several miles we knew that we'd better do exactly what was supposed to be done.

You know, if a fella kills some one man or two and the news starts traveling, by the time it's crossed a few state lines it's multiplied considerably. Some of them called him "Old Bad John," and some called him "Old John," and some of them called him "Devil John." And, of course, all his children called him "Pap."

I respected him a lot and I was afraid of him, too. He never did whip me but a little bit, but he didn't have to because I knew that whatever he said had to go. He did everything that was lawful and maybe was like Thomas Jefferson, he might have stretched the thing just a little bit in a place or two. He was just a character that all the men as well as his own children respected for about the same reason.

John Wright looked much like me. He was about six feet and a half inch in his sock feet. At his best he weighed 165 pounds. He had just ordinary dark hair and his mustache and beard was red. He let his beard grow a time or two but it didn't grow much, and ordinarily, until he got kind of old, he wore a mustache. He wore, ordinarily, a broad-brimmed hat. Most of the time he wore a black velvet shirt. He wore a vest, summer or winter, and buttoned the two bottom buttons of it up most of the time, and he wore a coat if it was cold weather. He wore what you call "Congress shoes," shoes you pull on, don't have string in them. A fine make of shoe. He hardly ever wore boots and if he did he let somebody else lace them up for him.

Pap carried, when he traveled most of the time, two pistols. Called one "Old Remodel" and the other was a Mulvan Hubbard. The Mulvan Hubbard was a .45 and the Remodel was a .44. And he generally had whiskey in one side of his saddle pockets. Most of the time he had it in the right side; generally a quart-sized bottle. I was always very quick to go and get his horse and put him up especially if he hadn't taken the saddlebags off, because when I'd go to the barn I'd look in the saddlebags. I didn't bother his pistol, but if his bottle was in there I'd nip a little of whatever he had. He brought back some gin one time that I thought tasted awful good and I didn't know it was kind of sneaking, but I took a little too much of it. Next morning Dad said it looked like that bottle must have leaked quite a bit the night before.

Most of the time he was pretty pleasant. About the best thing he could do for company was to give them a drink of whiskey. And generally it was moonshine, and moonshine meant corn whiskey that they made without a license to make it.

How did John Wright change as he got older?

As he got older once in a while he'd drink enough whiskey so you could tell he'd had a drink. And he'd talk a little bit more when that happened. He finally did join the church and was baptized. I don't reckon he swore any after that but otherwise he didn't act different that I could tell.

A good old Baptist preacher used to come and pass the weekends with him, stay around for a considerable length of time. He was a pretty good preacher, a very persuasive talker, and I figured that him and Ellen* talked Pap into joining the Baptist church and being baptized. It was the most people that I'd seen at one gathering in this country at that time. I suppose there was possibly two thousand people there at Fairview, Virginia. He was a very outstanding character in Letcher and Wise counties and all around here and he was called "Devil John." Maybe a bunch of them were kind of anxious to see them beat the devil out of him there in the water pond.

[His funeral] wasn't as heavily attended as the baptizing by any means.† They had the funeral at the house and couldn't many people get inside the house. There was a lot of people from Jenkins and all around here and of course all his children that could get there.

* Ellen Saunders was John Wright's second wife.
† John Wright was eighty-seven at the time of his conversion. He died two years later on January 30, 1931.

2

HEARTHSTONES AND HOMELIFE

Ever since settlers wended their way through the mountains in the eighteenth and nineteenth centuries to clear a bit of new ground far from the intrusion of a neighbor's halloo, home held a special place in the mind of mountain people. For them, the homeplace itself was important and regional literature is filled with references to the wrench of watching an old house crumble. However, home was far more than puncheons and hearthstones. It included every inch of land and every tree owned by the family, the air they breathed, the water they drank, the hills and valleys surrounding them, the county they lived in.

From the time white people settled the region in the late 1700's until the discovery of coal more than a century later, home was where men and women worked, socialized, read the Bible, educated the children, and raised the family's food. When churches served as the local court and there was no formal meeting place, members met in private dwellings. In the absence of a local jail, the home of the sheriff became a prison for runaways and convicted ne'er-do-wells.

Underlining the activities of the home were the unspoken joys that sprang from a good harvest, the discovery of wildflowers and whippoorwills, the passing of winter into spring, and the birth of a newborn. There were also sorrows.

When people join together in sorrow, as rural families have done a million times over, they find strength and unity. Over the years this unity broadens into a deep personal feeling that tells mountain people they belong. People elsewhere had this sense of belonging too, but the feeling was heightened by the isolation and repose of life deep in a mountain hollow. Once mountain people attained a harmony with self and home (for many it was their birthright) it became indelible, yielding to neither distance nor time. Author Elizabeth Madox Roberts said it well: "The places you knowed when you was a little shirt-tail boy won't go outen your head or outen your recollections."

Alice Slone, Verna Mae Slone, and Henry Scalf talk about homelife. Each still lives near the old homeplace and only Alice has ever left home for more than two years. They belong. In discussing homelife each touches on some of the same themes: the working contribution that every family member was expected to make; the passing on of values from generation to generation, and the role of birth, marriage and, most important, death in a family cycle.

Alice Slone was born in 1904 and reared on Caney Creek, near Pippa Passes, Kentucky, at a time when people met the chill of winter by papering their walls with old newspapers, magazines, and Sears, Roebuck catalogues. Children learned to read by studying their wall coverings. When Alice was in the eighth grade, Mrs. Alice Spencer Geddes Lloyd, a Boston Brahmin who started a school on Caney Creek, realized the young woman had potential for leadership and sent her to high school in Cleveland, Ohio. Sixteen years later, in 1932, Alice Slone had graduated from Ohio State University and returned to the mountains at Mrs. Lloyd's request. The following year she began the Lotts Creek Settlement School near Cordia, Kentucky, where she has lived ever since.

Alice Slone

In recent years Alice has publicly and privately bemoaned the ruining of God's land by man's strip-mining machines. Her philosophy about the future of the land reflects the strength and perseverance that are her heritage: "There is that inborn thing in every human being which will triumph over the situation because it isn't of the human being himself. It came here with him, lived here with him, and it doesn't die when he goes out. If you have this feeling about life then nothing is really hopeless. It is a terrible thing to think of destroying your environment, the beauty, the basic things that God did create, but I have faith—and it's almost a conviction—that we will come through."

Alice discussed her childhood, a simpler time, when man and the land seemed to her to work together.

You asked what was life like? Well, in some ways it was very ideal, of course, because we did have the beautiful woods, we had everything that nature gives, but we had none of the things that civilization gives. The woods themselves offered food. There were roots, berries, the sap of trees. We lived well.

Now, anything could hit you for a lean year. If your father stayed well and your mother stayed well, you had a pretty good life. The weaving went on, the carding, the spinning. But if something happened to your family and your father died, then things got very hard for you. You traded off your pork to get work done to raise the corn, to bring in more funds to help buy shoes for the children. When the spring came you could be very hungry. If your meal corn that you raised was gone, then you were in trouble because you had no breadstuff.

My father died when I was six years old. This left my mother with six of us children and my brother Commodore still at the institute and not yet teaching. Those were the lean years for us. Now many people had them because of sickness, or sometimes—most often, I think—the problem was alcohol. If a father drank then the family suffered very greatly because he was not providing for them, or he made moonshine which was worse. He'd be in trouble with the law and then he'd have to avoid the law, and then the families would have a very terrible time. Then we had some who were just not such good providers. In fact, a saying is, "There's always one runt in the family," one not as intellectually provided for as the others. There were people, as I think back over it, we [called] "sorry" if they didn't work. For the man that doesn't provide for his family the term "sorry" was the lowest term you would label [him] with.

Our people were from Virginia and from North Carolina. Our family that came from North Carolina leaned toward the Union, and my mother's family that came out of Virginia stayed with the South and they were called "Rebs" or "Rebels." My mother was thirteen when the Civil War took her father. Very shortly after the Civil War [she] married into a family on the Union side, which is unusual because they held bitterness for a long time.

Quite often according to my family oral history one member of the family would come in one door while the other one left by the other door. They didn't want to meet because as opposing soldiers they just didn't want to have to face each other in battle. This was during the Civil War. Afterwards, I guess, they all came home and laid down their arms and all that kind of thing and everybody went back to trying to rebuild. In the mountains I think you were more divided than in any other place because here is where you really had your father and son division. That division is still, in a sense, strong. If a person says, "I am a Republican, a dyed-in-the-wool Republican," then he was apt to be Union.

I was told that the feuding here on Lotts Creek originally grew out of the Civil War. One of the early lessons I learned was that there was one time when you could tell a lie, and that was when your father was home and the opposing side asked if he were home, you would lie and say, "No," he was not home. We were that close to it, the Civil War, in that this was still training in our family. Mother was thirteen when they were coming into the homes and asking, "Where's your father? Where is your brother?" so that would have been deeply ingrained in my mother at thirteen.

But do you ever remember her setting you down and saying you should never lie except in this one situation?

You lived *with* your children, you didn't sit down and talk *to*. Wherever the parent was the child was, participating in all the activities that were going on. The individual attention that the children received was the fact that they were participating in the family needs. The times when you might be instructed in that way would be in the evenings after you came in from work and you would be sitting in the shade of the house resting and reminiscing, or on Sundays after church, after you'd gone to the family church or graveyard. You could come home and you'd not work. You would sit around wherever the shade of the house was.

What would you talk about?

Relatives and relatives' history. The kind of things I'm talking about now. Mostly it would be family history. How we are from

"Old Virginia," never [just] "Virginia." (*Here Alice lapses into the speech patterns her family used during those talks.*) "We're from Old Virginia and our family come in with Dan Boone. They lived at Mayking and we took care of his house when he was gone, and one time your Aunt Lou went up to see about the house and the Indians come. And they'd killed her except she got in between the wall of the house and the chimney and she stayed in there and they come in and they looked all around and went everywhere all through the house and then they went back out and went away. And she got out and come home."

This is the kind of thing told around the fire in the evenings. Mother would be spinning, or the men might be tanning hides, or maybe taking care of some tobacco which they grew, or mending shoes, or peeling pumpkins, or peeling apples or other foods to be stored. This would all be going on as the talk was going on.

If you were in a group, men and women together, the men did most of the talking. They had the bigger tales to tell. The storytelling for the most part in our family was men telling about their hunts. They hunted here as long as there were bear in Pine Mountain and then after that they went to the Smokies. Most of my memory of what the men talked about was going to the Smokies or going to some more remote place and bear hunting. Or their trips when they would build their rafts or logs and take their coonskins and their mink and their otters, the small animal skins, and their moonshine [and] go down to Catlettsburg and sell them. And by the way, one of the early lessons my mother taught me [was] if we were going any place, especially any distance in the woods, to whittle a stick and if a bear came toward you, you rammed the stick down the bear's throat. What better way could you have for fighting a bear?

Values were instructed all the time. There was no time when you weren't instructed, in the talk and in situations. We had three months of formal school and, of course, we had the McGuffey Readers, so values were taught there, too. All your McGuffey Readers had a moral point. One I remember in particular dealt with the Brownies. The Brownies of McGuffey's text were the little people dressed in brown suits with pointed caps and laced-up boots with pointed toes. They also had pointed ears and big grins. They were the little helpful people. All our fairy stories were apt to be nicely laced with Brownies. In the McGuffey stories the children were being taught to be helpful to their families, joyfully performing the necessary tasks. Another [story] I recall very well dealt with the ants. A leaf fell from the tree and floated across [the water] and it looked as if the ant were going to not survive. Its life was going to be lost in the current. So one of the good little boys reached out and took the leaf out and put it on the land and the ant lived. This taught you respect for life. That was the way your values were taught: making a poignant story which would touch on your emotional response.

My job at four—no, six, I don't remember having a job before six because that was when my father died and things changed so for us—was to take care of the children while Mother and the older children, like Rilda, would thin the corn. Rilda was seven. If there were more than two good stalks in a hill, you pulled out the weaker ones. I wasn't big enough to thin corn in my earliest years, but I was big enough to watch for Jim Courtney who was two years younger than I, and Bob, who was four years younger, and Bertha, who was two weeks old. They were put under the cliff and I was to keep snakes away.

Just to show you that there is responsibility there [one day] I looked up this hollow log and here was a rattlesnake coiled. Well, this is a thing I shall always remember because you do have folklore that a rattlesnake can charm you. Now birds, when a snake is around, they'll fly round and round and round the snake. I had seen a bird do that and eventually the bird simply flew into the mouth of the snake. I don't know what happened there, I was too young to analyze it. I'm not that afraid of snakes, I'd pick them up and stroke them down and back, you know. To this day I don't mind picking up a snake, but I will choose what snake I'm going to pick up and *how* I'm going to pick it up. But this one, somehow it was different. It was huge and I called to my mother and said, "Mama, here's a copperhead! No, it's a rattlesnake! No, it's a garter! No, it's a viper!" All the time I was running and I didn't veer that way, I didn't veer this way. And I never had my eyes off that snake's eyes, a little six-year-old. I didn't look around to call Mother, I didn't look around for anything. My eyes and that snake's eyes were together all this time. I could get back just so far, then I stopped. Why did I stop? I don't know, but back I was pulled right up to the face of that snake. Back and forth and back and forth just like the bird. Mother would say, "Go away!" I had no will to go away and I wasn't afraid, and so back and forth, back and forth I went. Then, of course, Mother got really worried, came over with a hoe and hauled the snake out. It was too big for Mother to kill. She had to hold it down with a hoe and my brother and I together killed the snake. Where would you get more education than you got right there for living? Not in Cleveland, goodness no. [People] had to learn to live all over again when they went to Cleveland.

When the sun said four o'clock on the mountain—and to this day I know where four o'clock is on Caney Creek—it was my job to go out and start the fire for the bread for the supper. I can remember that many times, and I dreaded this, the fire was not going. I had to find a mouse's nest and I'd have to strike and strike until that fire caught unless my brother happened to come in from school on a Friday or Saturday. If he happened to ride in he'd take the flintlock rifle and shoot into that mouse's nest and, BOOM! The cotton just went flying. It had cotton in it and bark off of trees shredded so that it would catch. Mother taught me how to stand the stove lid up edgewise by that mouse's nest and strike until some spark would hit the [nest] in a way that it would catch. If for any reason the fire [went] out I would have to go a mile or so to get fire, what we call "borrowing fire." Now a lovely [saying] came out of that: "Well, what'd you come for, a chunk of fire?" If you'd come for a chunk of fire you'd dash right off to get that fire back home and preserve it so that you could start your fire for cooking. That was my job, to get the fire going, so that Rilda could make the bread and put it in the oven and Mother could take over when she came out with the rest of the meal. Then Mother'd have to go milk and Rilda'd watch the meal and I'd watch the little children.

We had to help because Mother was responsible now, and the only way that you could go on living would be to raise your garden and store your food. That's the only way you could go on. I've often thought what that must have been to Mother to worry about a seventeen-year-old son and five under the age of seven. But she managed. She managed beautifully.

When my father died he left sufficient wealth [if] you have a man to head the family and handle it. He left oxen, lots of pigs, cows, and a field newly cleared, a log house newly built, a very good sturdy log house. We had cane, corn, pumpkins, cushaws, the meat of the woods.

My father died in May when he was only forty and by June my brother was home from school. The first summer we got along fine because we had a storehouse of hams and things like that. Mother would exchange those hams for manual labor. When I was ten Mother married [again] and we had things easier because [there] was a man in the home.

The one time that I remember being thoroughly insecure and upset was one afternoon Mother closed all the doors and laid down on the bed. She had a terrible headache, she said, and she was just going to have to lie down and rest. And I was frantic. She never stopped, never stopped. She was up at four o'clock in the morning, all day long [doing] something for the care of the children and in the evening she didn't stop, she was spinning or carding. I was stricken. I thought Mother was going to die and you lived with death. You lived with the threat of death all the time. You just don't know death outside in the cities except when it hits your own family and then you don't really live with it like you do here.

I learned the threat of death from my father's going. He was struck by a cant hook [while] rolling logs, clearing our new-ground. And it struck him [on the cheekbone near his left eye]. And of course, it crushed his cheekbone. Well that set up blood poisoning and infection and it was a terrible, horrifying death. And he suffered terribly. My father, he laid ill I guess for maybe a week at least before infection set in. We had to be so quiet and children don't know how to be quiet. I was probably one of the healthiest of the children and the rowdiest because somewhere I must have been told to be quiet and I wasn't as quiet as I ought to be. And then when Father died I got the idea that I was responsible for his death. Then when [I was working with Lotts Creek School] I'd go to these homes to visit the people where there's death in the family I would realize, "I'm responsible for this. I must do something. I've got to prevent this person's death." It took me all this time to trace that back and find out where I had gotten the idea that I was certainly at least partially responsible for [anyone's death].

How was death explained to you?

You went to heaven and if you weren't good you went some other place and that was no fooling.

Whenever Mother said, "Go!" we went, although I can remember a good many little keen switches. She didn't paddle us, but she got a tiny little switch: "zizz" you went and did whatever she wanted you to do. I really was the obstreperous one. They called me "Hell-Fired Nance." I would ramble the woods. Mother didn't know where I was. No fear—climb the rocks, look in every crevice, investigate every place there was to be investigated. Try out every herb, or every root. And Mother must have been frantic with me. That's when I got my little switchings is when I'd come in. Poor Mother, I don't know how she ever lived through my existence.

If a mother was left, the father dead, the homeplace would usually go to the youngest daughter. The mother would stay with her. But all throughout the year she would go to visit her other children and stay for a certain period of time. I remember when Claib Jones's* wife, Aunt Chrissie, used to come and visit us. Mother wasn't very happy about Aunt Chrissie because she felt Aunt Chrissie wasn't a nice woman. You see, she followed Uncle Claib and fought in his battles with him. And she wore pants. Mother was more fussy at that than she was [about the battles]. Mother wasn't too happy about Aunt Chrissie coming because she didn't approve of Aunt Chrissie.

Then why did she invite Aunt Chrissie?

You don't invite. Your house is open to everyone. Never is your house closed. To anyone. Ever. Then and now, if it's inbred in you, which it is. I can't imagine how we'd feel about somebody that [said] "No, you can't come in." No matter who it was. I think we'd be horrified if you don't invite them in.

[When relatives came] all the children stayed in the big room. You just piled up, three at the head and three at the foot on feather beds. That way you could go off to sleep hearing all the stories being told around the open fire. But a girl managed to be modest. Till this day I could undress and change my clothes with a quilt in front of me. Didn't always wear night clothes, I'll have to be honest.

And don't think mountain people don't like their privacy. They do. In fact, they don't want anybody to build close to them. They haven't all down the years.

Alice Slone described the tenor and tone of family life in the mountains. Now a distant cousin of hers, Verna Mae Slone, filled in with observations on marbles, tooth pullers, badcolds, sunsets and rainbows, and the religious beliefs of one Appalachian family.

Verna Mae was born on the Onion Blade Branch of Caney Creek in Knott County, Kentucky, in 1914. She never tires of

---

* This is the same Claib Jones that Chid Wright mentioned on pages 59–60.

talking ("That's what I feed my tongue for") and her passion is correcting the misconceptions about "hillbillies" and "hillbetsies" spread by outsiders who have written books and produced television programs about eastern Kentuckians. One book, Stay On, Stranger, *a history of Caney Creek where Verna Mae lives, and of the Caney Creek Community Center, angers her more than all the other slurs and slights combined. She says it is "one big pack of lies from beginning to end and I've spent years a-trying to get people to not believe it."*

She is not always so polemical. While piecing a quilt (she has made more than seven hundred), Verna Mae enjoys nothing better than entertaining grandchildren or outsiders who are visiting with tales of illicit "wahooing"* during her school days or of her false arrest for making moonshine. "Slone" is the surname of hundreds of people along Caney Creek and as luck would have it there once was a moonshine-making Verna Mae Slone. A deputy sheriff heard of her activities and came with a warrant to the home of the wrong Verna Mae Slone. It so happened Verna Mae needed a ride into town that day, so she said nothing and accompanied the sheriff to the county seat, realizing, of course, the magistrate was a cousin of hers who would know better. At the courthouse the sheriff was told in no uncertain terms that he had the wrong Verna Mae Slone, and she went on about her business. The experience taught her the importance of having a distinctive first name if you are a Caney Creek Slone. As a result, she later named her five sons: Milburn, Orbin, Losses, Lyn, and Willie Vernon, Junior.

In remembering her homelife, Verna Mae said:

---

* Alice Lloyd began the Caney Creek Community Center in 1923. After her death in 1962 it was renamed Alice Lloyd College. While she was alive, verbal or physical contact between boys and girls was forbidden at the school, so the practice of wahooing—courting from a tree limb—arose. The boys climbed "wahoo" (magnolia) trees outside the girls' dormitory until they were parallel to the windows and could whisper or pass notes to the girls.

It would take two years to tell about my daddy. He was a wonderful man. He was brilliant. That's why I hate all these stories
and things that's told about us hillbillies that degrades him. I'd
hate to have him labeled as a hillbilly because he was such a wonderful feller. He didn't have very much education, but he was
brilliant in common sense, and he was the kindest, most gener-
ous person I ever knew. He had so many philosophies and so
many sayings that were so wise. He said what made people fight
was either that they were hungry or cold. If the kids got to
yelling he'd build a big fire and go get us something to eat. He
used it in some ways as a joke, but it was really true.

He taught me to love nature, to love thunder and lightning.
And he'd teach me to [appreciate] the sunset and rainbow. I
know when [Alice Lloyd] first [started her school] this teacher
tried to tell him about the great paintings, the masterpieces and
all that, and he said, "Listen, I look at pictures that was painted
by the most wonderful master of all. Jesus. Did you ever see a
sunset? Did you ever see a rainbow? Did you ever get up of the
morning and see the whole world covered with snow? Nothing's
more beautiful than that."

He lived by the Bible. He used it as a basic of life. But he got
drunk. Not much, now, he wasn't a drunk. And he fathered two
children out of wedlock. My two half brothers; he wasn't married
to either one of their mothers. But he was the kindest, gentlest
person that I ever saw. The night before he died he prayed to die
and for Jesus to take him out of his misery. I don't believe he
would have prayed to die if he thought he was a sinner, do you?
He was eighty-four years old. So you'd have to say he was a
religious person. He went to church, he took care of the dead, he
took care of the sick, and gave land for the graveyard. He had a
religion but you couldn't say he was a Roman Catholic, or a Prot-
estant, or a Methodist, or anything like that. And like I say, he
used the Bible as a basic for all things; very seldom you talked to
him what he wouldn't bring [up] something that he'd read in the
"Good Book." He wasn't ashamed of nothing God put on him or

that God asked him to do. He was ashamed of some of the things the Devil got him into.

My father probably had about what would be the equivalent of the fifth or sixth grade. Mostly he taught hisself. He would kid and say he only went to school three days in his life and two of them he went in place of his brother.

My mother knew one letter, "O," and that was all of the education that she had, I mean book education. She knew how to do a lot of things like sew and how to keep a family together. She'd card, and spun, and wove. They dyed by hand. Onion hulls made

Verna Mae Slone

yeller dye. Walnut hulls made a brown. They used things they could go out in the hills and get. They didn't use, as they say, "fotched-on" dyes. They made their own. And she was a Christian. She joined the church.

My mother died [when I was five weeks old] and it was pretty hard for us girls because the older one was just fourteen and then I had one sister that was older than me that was mentally retarded. She wasn't born that way, she had rheumatic fever, "brain fever" 's what they called it then. And she finally just walked in the fire and got burned up.

From the time I could walk I was taught to be good to Sissie. The only candy that we had was big long red sticks of peppermint candy. My dad would bring me and her and my next older sister candy but she wouldn't eat it. So he would say, "Now you watch Sissie and when she lays hers down you have hers. [Do] not take it away from her." And I'd watch her, maybe follow her round for an hour or two and she'd lay it down. I'd grab it and run. She wouldn't eat it. It's probably because she had bad teeth. No matter what she wanted she got it first. And, you know, I didn't resent it. I knew that she was special, that [she wasn't] responsible for what she did.

[Sissie had a dress] she loved because it was red. And she was up close to the fire and it caught fire. That's the way she got burned up. I know my dad had gone to Wheelwright.* It was at Easter and all the girls was outside watching the boys play ball. Heard her scream and run in and my older sister picked her up and carried her to the well and drawed water and poured it on her. She was burned so bad she died. I was scared to death. I can remember thinking, Now when Father comes back it'll all be okay. Of course, [the others] just forgot me and didn't pay any attention to me and I thought, now when he comes back . . . The next thing I remember was him coming in and he hugged

* Wheelwright, Kentucky, is an old coal town about twenty miles from Pippa Passes.

me so tight it hurt. After that I found out they had told him that I was the one that got burned up.

The most fun [was] when all of the family got together around the fire [to] tell jokes, pop corn, roast potatoes and boil eggs, and things like that. And then they'd set around of the night and tell riddles. That was something they loved to do. They was tickled to death if they learned a new riddle that nobody else didn't know. My father wouldn't let us believe in ghosts, course there was a lot that did. He'd let us listen at them, but then he'd say not to believe in it because he didn't believe in ghosts.

And then they had a lot of "off-colored" riddles and jokes that I wouldn't want to tell. There were a lot of them that would sound like they was going to be something bad and really they're not. The [men] had what they'd call "toasts," little rhymes they'd say as they drank their whiskey. They said:

> Hold this whiskey
> Between fingers and thumb.
> If I leave any,
> You can have some.

And this kind of sounds against the religion but it was all for a joke:

> Father, Son, and Holy Ghost,
> The one that drinks the fastest
> Can have the most.

[My father] was what we could call an undertaker; they called it "laying folks out" then. You took the feather bed off and laid [the body] on the slats on a door [that was laying across] two chairs. Their feet was tied together, and their hands was usually crossed. Then they would take a cloth and tie [it] under their chin and up over their head, and then they'd place nickels or quarters, or if there wasn't any money in the house they would use little smooth rocks on their eyes to keep them together. This had to be done before they begin to stiffen. They were placed to look as comfortable-looking as they could. Someone always stayed with them because—I don't know if it really happened—but they was afraid that cats would get in and eat on the dead bodies. They always tried to bury them the second day.

My father wanted to be dressed in a shroud and he died [in 1946] during the wartime, when you couldn't get cloth. We had money enough to [buy] it, but we just couldn't get it, so we used two real expensive sheets. He'd asked not to have his shoes put on. He said he had dressed so many people and scrouged shoes on their feet and said he would hear their bones crackle; just the horror of it he didn't want for himself.

[My father] made the worm of the fence and he built chimneys. He made chairs. He was a horse doctor, cow doctor, and he was just a person that the community couldn't have got along without. Off and on he carried the mail all of his life. He started carrying when he was about sixteen years old.

He took care of folks and he knew all the different medicines that they used and it wasn't silly. I mean, there was a lot of silliness, like carrying a buckeye in your pocket to cure rheumatism, but he didn't believe in that. They just really believe in honest prayer, in connecting with the higher power to help them. They learned a lot of this from the Indians, I imagine, and [from] grandfathers. Like they used this pussy-willow bark, they called it "possum bush," to cure the headache. And there's the same thing in it that's in aspirin. The catnip is really a plant tranquilizer. I made some the other day, it makes a good tea, and it really helps colds and it makes you sleep. We used slippery elm to cure fever. You take it, put it in water, and it makes a kind of jelly. And they used peach bark for tonsillitis and they'd use it also if you vomited. If something didn't have a rational reason to it he wouldn't believe, nor would he let us.

They called tuberculosis "consumption." We talked about having a "badcold." Now, it wasn't "bad" opposite from "nice," it was all one word: badcold. Tonsillitis, they thought the palate of your mouth fell down and you'd tie your sock around your neck to cure it. And then they had "sun pains." That was the headache; I imagine it was a migraine headache by the way they described it. It was over one eye and you was supposed to go to a spring and pick up a gravel and throw it over your shoulder for nine mornings straight. And the little babies got "liver-grown," and to keep them from it you laid them on their stomach and you took their left foot and tipped* it with their right hand, took their right foot and tipped it with their left hand over their backs. I don't know what it meant, but I know they always told us to do our babies that way so they wouldn't get "liver-grown." I remember doing mine that way. Didn't believe in it, but it was fun.

Different families would have different expressions, different ways of saying the same thing. When folks married from different families lots of times there would be friction between them because of these different words and they would have little spats over it. There was the word "foggy." My husband would say "foggy" and I would say "fawggy" and we got into it one day and kept on until we really got angry over it. And he said he was going to leave. And I said, "Well, if you leave," I said, "I'll destroy everything you've got." And he said, "Even my records?" And I said, "Even Old Fawggy Mountain Top." And the laugh got us back. We forgot all about the trouble over the word.

When they didn't have any clocks they would get somebody that did have a watch to make a notch in the floor. And when the sun got to that they would know it was a certain time. I would have a certain tree that I'd watch that shadow and I could tell you within fifteen minutes what time of day it was. Of course, that didn't work on cloudy days. Dinner and supper would probably be late when it was cloudy.

The typical farmer he could usually tell what kind of weather they was going to have. They had a lot of foolish signs, and then a lot of them was based on more fact than they thought. Like when

---

* Touched.

the smoke from the chimney didn't rise straight up, it was going to rain. Of course, that was the heaviness from the air that kept it from rising up. They didn't know why. They just had noticed that and remembered it.

[Children] made their own marbles. They would get a old rock that was laying close to the brook or the creek and then by channeling just a little bit of water they'd have it run over this rock and that water would turn [a small stone] around and around till it would get perfectly round. When it got down to the size they wanted they would take it out and put another one in. They'd probably be all summer making a set of marbles. Then they played for "keeps" where they put them all in a ring and everybody shot at them. I never would let my kids play keeps because it was a form of gambling, unless they all agreed to give them back.

After [children] got up where they wanted to date boys, they'd have a lot of games. "Picking Cherries" was a kissing game. They'd set a chair—their homemade chair with the rounds—and a boy on one side and a girl on the other one. They would catch hands and step up on each one of the rungs a-holding their weight up by their hands, and they would kiss each time they went up and the thing was to keep from falling. It's hard to hold hands and kiss and [stay] balanced on the chair rounds.

[Now] I'm a misunderstood mother. [My children] can't understand why I want to live in this house, why I don't build me a new home. Why I don't get me a new couch? Or why I don't do that? They can't understand I've got everything I want. I know I'm poor and I know this is not much but it's all I want. I've got more than President Nixon because I'm satisfied with what I've got and he h'ain't. It's a peace of mind I've got. Now, I'll tell you, if I could get some girl, or some woman, to come in and to help me houseclean about once every week, or two weeks, I'd love that. But outside of that, that's all in the moneywise that I could want.

How do you think you came by that philosophy?

Jesus gave it to me. He says our wants are few, I mean our *needs* are few. We desire a lot, but He'll give us what we need. God made us all and He didn't ask me, nor you, nor him, where to be born, and if He'd asked us we couldn't have told Him at that time. But I'm thankful that He did let me be Verna Mae Slone and let me be born in eastern Kentucky right on Caney Creek. He doesn't do anything without planning. We're the ones that upset His plans.

Henry P. (Buck) Scalf has spent a lifetime studying the people of eastern Kentucky, their idiosyncrasies, genealogy, and social history. His knowledge ranges from historical investigations of hundreds of family trees to philosophical thoughts about what may set mountain men and women apart from people elsewhere. Pondering the distinctive nature of life in eastern Kentucky has been Henry's preoccupation during a lifetime of farming, politicking, teaching, and writing. He has written and edited several books including Kentucky's Last Frontier, *a history of the eastern Kentucky region, and produced thousands of newspaper articles and columns.*

Henry says the mountaineer is a proud and stubborn individual who will go to almost any lengths to protect his home and family. Mountain men may act in ways curious to outsiders, but their behavior is usually understood, or at least accepted, by friends and neighbors. A story illustrates the point: An elderly neighbor of Henry's was one of the last survivors of an old Kentucky family. He owned several hundred acres of land that included an old family graveyard, and when he was ready to die he gave the land to a friend with one terse request: "Keep the cemetery mowed and the gate closed."

"That's an Appalachian man for you," says Henry Scalf with pride. He lives on a branch of Mare Creek near Stanville, Kentucky.

Henry P. (Buck) Scalf

I was born in 19 and 2, that was a year before the railroad came up through this section, and naturally we were living in a post-pioneer period. Life was much different and, I believe, much better. We had a sense of value of things we don't any-more. For instance, people wouldn't steal like they do now. Right down the road a little there's a path and a big poplar tree. When anybody wanted to send a letter or some article back into the Buffalo [Creek] country they would place it by that big poplar tree and put the name of the recipient on it. I remember one time Aunt Lou came over here on a visit and she left a pair of her shoes, so I took them down at Mother's direction and put them at the big poplar tree. The first person that came along and saw those shoes got down off his horse and carried them through the mountains to Aunt Lou's house and gave them to her. [There was an] obligation of every horseman that came along [to] pick it up and transport it off. It would of been a tragic thing for somebody to come along and pick up and throw that article away. You couldn't do that now; first boy that came along now would give it a good lick and throw it over in the creek.

What made people so honest then?

It stemmed from the family. A family was more of a unit than it is now. There weren't any divisive influences. We seemed to have an obligation to each other. We are kinfolks. If we were cousins we were all same as brothers and sisters. I know Mother and all the old folks used to talk about "own-born cousins."*

I've always advocated that we ought to preserve all of these things of value in our Appalachian culture that we can. One is the unity, cohesiveness, of the family. It's carried over into my family a great deal. One of my sons is here now eating lunch; he's helping me paint a house because I couldn't get somebody. He feels an obligation to help Dad get that doggone house painted. Those are the things that are worth preserving. Maybe the next generation won't produce children that will be that loyal to their family group. Oh, we have families that have their scraps, but let somebody else intrude in it [and] they'll *all* be on your back.

Thievering was something just about not heard of in these mountains. A man was so socially ostracized after being caught stealing, such a great burden upon him, that they just wouldn't hardly steal anything. In fact, I never heard of anybody stealing anything until I was a grown man. That was [about] the time our sense of values [was] beginning to disappear. About 1920. Industry is what did it. I believe they had a higher moral standard. I know Mother was very much opposed to divorce and we never had many divorced people in this country. Mother called them "grass widows." A grass widow seemed to be some kind of a mild stigma. Why, I don't know. I reckon it went back to that old religious attitude: that you're married to death do you part.

My mother-in-law was a member of the Robinson family in Martin County, Kentucky. They come out of the Meathouse Fork

* In the mountains brothers and sisters often thought of each other's offspring not as nieces and nephews, but as their "own-born children." As a result, ties between first cousins were as strong as those between siblings and they referred to each other as "my own-born cousin."

of Wolf Creek which had been an isolated section and they were reared in the most religious sort of a family. They made their word their bond. You didn't have to reduce something to writing, you reduced it to an oral agreement. When my mother-in-law died in the 19 and 50's she heired a small tract of mountain land back in that country. Her brother Sam rode a mule through the mountains and came to the funeral. When the funeral was all over he called me out and said, "Henry, I guess you're kind of spokesman for the rest of them and I want to ask you if you want to sell my son Tom Aunt Angeline's land over there?" I said, "Well, I'll talk it over with them and see what they want for the land." I went out and talked to them. The price was pretty steep. I told them, "I don't believe your Uncle Sam will pay that but I'm going to see." So I go out on the front porch and I tell Uncle Sam they want a certain sum of money for that land and he said, "Henry, that's too much. My son Tom won't pay it, so we'll just forget it." He got on his mule and he started home, and he got nearly down to [the] ford and he came back and said, "Henry, I'm going to bind Tom to take that land." That evening my wife and I were driving home, I said, "Your cousin Tom won't take that land. It's too high." My wife said, "You don't know the Robinsons. Their word is their bond and Uncle Sam has bound his Tom to take it and they'll take it."

It went on for about a year and they never had come to pick up their deed. My wife said, "Just give them time because their word is their bond." One day I was sitting in my office at Prestonsburg and a taxi came up from Inez and out jumped Tom Robinson. Tom said, "Buck, let's run up and get Norah* to sign that deed. That was too doggone much to pay for that land but Pap bound me to take it and he said I couldn't go back on it. The reason I haven't been back [is] I had to work some and gather up more money to pay for that land."

You don't find any people like that now. I knew but one dis-

* Henry's wife.

honest man until I was nearly grown. We always went on the assumption that a man was honest till we found out he wasn't.

Old-time people sixty or seventy years ago wanted their families to marry into good families. Now, give you an instance: Mother always said certain families were "fine people"; then she'd say certain other families, and she would name them, "They're no good." Now, there was an inclination among the sturdy mountain families, the better ones, to have their children marry into the better families of the region. What was considered a better family was hard-working people who went to church regularly, who went to school regularly, and who owned a little property, and those who didn't were considered beneath them.

I've heard my wife talk about a family being a bunch of "seben sleepers" and they were considered trash-sorry people. A seben sleeper was somebody that laid in bed when they ought to be up and out working. Seben was a mispronunciation of "seven." You didn't want your boy or girl to marry into a family of seben sleepers. I've heard my mother say that we never had no "bad blood"—and that's the word she used—in this country until the railroads came along. She didn't approve of marriages between people outside the region and here. She thought they were not as good people as the native stock here.

A man [that] didn't take care of his family [back then] could be sold. My grandfather told me that he saw one case of it where a man wouldn't work to support his family and the court grabbed him up and sold him for fifty cents a day for a year. Whoever bid him in would pay his family fifty cents a day. Those laws, of course, would be plainly unconstitutional now.

[When parents got older] it was just assumed that the girls were going to take care of the mothers and some of the sons were going to take care of the fathers when they got widowed. There was never any questions about it. In the mountains we thought that anybody who would put their folks in an old folks' home were sorry people. I know when Mother got up in her eighties,

Father had been dead so many years, she went to stay with my sister. My sister kept her for untold number of years as if it was her own child that she was obligated to.

I'd like to describe how my father made money, it's so damned unusual from things now. [He] owned a considerable amount of mountain land and he made a living—a good living—by several things: farming, logging, raising cattle, sheep. If you were an aggressive man you could make it pretty well in these mountains back in those days. I doubt that my father ever worked a day for somebody else. He would sow hay crops up and down this creek for about a mile and a half and each bottom would have hay in it. I dreaded to see hay raking come because it never did get over with. It lasted about three or four weeks.

He usually kept about six yoke of oxens; by yoke of oxens I mean a pair that were hooked together. One peculiar thing, mountain farmers always named their work oxens Buck and Berry. It was just a tradition and if they had another yoke to work they called them Baldy and something else, I don't remember. They had big long whips that were about ten or twelve feet long and these old "ox skinners"; two or three cracks with that and old Buck and Berry would start pulling. They were pretty cruel to those oxens.

Father never did put me in the cornfield because I was too small, but he'd make me carry water and if I didn't come back pretty soon he'd come around with a whip. He had an ox whip and, of course, he'd just hit me with the cracker end of it. Three or four licks and boy! if he told me to do anything I did it. I wouldn't dare refuse to do it because he was the autocrat of the family. He was good to us but when he passed the word that you had to do something it better be done. I know that all Mother had to do [was] tell me if I didn't do something that she'd tell my father and I'd get it done right away. It wasn't that they were cruel, they were just bred in a different school to rear their families with strict discipline.

My father made a lot of money [logging]. He usually invested it in land. He wanted land. A lot of loggers stayed at our home and Mother and my sisters, mostly my mother, did the cooking. She would get up way before daylight and by daylight all the loggers would gather up and take to the mountains. It didn't matter how bad the weather got, they didn't stay at the house. They'd all line up of a night around the fireplace in what we called the "big room" and set around in a semicircle and crack jokes and tell stories and play practical jokes on each other. I remember one time somebody sending after my brother John to get a plug of tobacco and John poured Japanese oil in it. He sent it in there to a man by the name of Grover Adams and Grover went to chewing on it and it liked to burn him up.

I remember when I was [young],* my father would ride around to see his neighbors and friends and get them to vote. The most important people in the community would usually round up the votes. My father didn't have much trouble rounding up votes. He didn't have to buy them, even the low-class people that he talked to, they didn't require money, they just required a little talking to from my father. Of course, as industry came in and times changed a little bit these low-class people would sell votes much more than they would fifty years ago. I remember one typical election: I helped organize the whole precinct. There was plenty money available. There was a high percentage of vote sellers [in that] precinct and [there was] a man with a list of the registered voters at the poll. He checked them off as they voted.

Now [from about 1930 to 1950] we had what we called "haulers."† Haulers were men who would haul folks from a mile or two miles away to bring them to the polls, but they had been rousted out from their homes to go vote by what we call "rous-

* He is referring to the 1910's and 1920's.
† This practice is still prevalent today, as any mountain politician knows.

ters." You'd go around and say, "Get ready and let's go vote. Bill Jones [will] be here with a car or a truck in a few minutes to get you and take you to the polls." But when they got to the polls we had "strikers" who would grab them and tell how much money they could get by voting a certain way. When somebody went in and voted he was entitled to about five or ten dollars for voting; when he came back out of the door this "striker" would grab him and take him around behind the house to see that he got his money. That's how we organized the precinct. It worked. Now, if there'd been a lot of furious competition there, there might have been a little shooting going on, might have been trouble.

A lot of voters will betray you. The sorriest man in the world is a vote seller. He'll swear that he's going to vote for your man to get your money, then he'll go to the other man and say, "I'll vote for your man," and he'll get money from both sides. A man said to me one day, "So-and-so is a high-class vote seller," and I said, "What the hell's a *high-class* vote seller?" He said, "That's a man that takes your money and votes the way he tells you."

I remember the illness of my father. He and his brother John went to work [logging] one day in December and it was a terribly bad cold day and their pants and clothing froze on them and they had to come to the house. I remember Uncle John said, "Bill, this will kill us," and my father hardly ever saw a well day after that. He came down with tuberculosis. They called it the Great White Plague then, and he lingered along about eighteen months. He went to hospitals and got turned out. Doctors would tell you there was nothing they could do, not for TB. He died in 1912. Mother got on a mule and she rode miles and miles through the woods over to Buffalo Creek to church. She wanted to see her cousin Isaac Stratton and ask him to come over and preach a memorial service on the cemetery where my father was buried. He came the fourth Sunday in August. The news went out all over this section. I remember the first two or three meetings Mother couldn't bed [all the people who came], and she'd lay down quilts on the floor and let people sleep on the floor.

Preacher Stratton preached that memorial service for fifty-four years and that meeting is still going on. Preachers come and go. Die. The first song they sing usually is "A twelve month more hath rolled around / Since we last met to worship on this ground." It's one of the old hymns that come out of the *Sweet Songster*. The last song they sing has got to be a tradition: "God be with you till we meet again." When that's done we children walk up to Father's and Mother's tombstones and we stand there and have our pictures made. *The Courier-Journal* was up here one time and they took pictures of it.

Not as many people come as used to. You never see a mule no more. Everybody comes in cars, trucks, and they have dinner on the ground.

We had a lot of folklore in the last sixty years to build up around this meeting. One was that if any of the children didn't go, if they strayed off and went somewhere else, they'd have a death in the family before the year was out. And you know, it happened two or three times and I almost believed it.

I could tell you of [another] old custom that has practically died out. Preacher Collins down the road here a mile or two, his wife died a few years ago and she had seven sisters. I set up that night and I was there until about daylight and I heard one of the sisters say to the other, "Are you going to stand up with me?" And the sister said, "Why, yes, we're all going to stand." I thought that was kind of unusual, so a little after six o'clock those sisters of hers came in and stood around the casket from that time up until ten o'clock when the services to preach the funeral started. They stood there nearly four hours at the casket. I often thought that that was the greatest tribute they could pay their sister.

3

WORKING

During the nineteenth century everyone in Central Appalachia worked. Farming was the main occupation, but the hills and forests provided an abundance of game and some form of hunting was practiced during each season of the year. In summer it was deer, bear, and turkey; in winter beaver and otter were trapped for pelts. To survive on the frontier, however, the pioneer had to be a horseman, miller, toolmaker, and carpenter. For decades whittling knives and axes were in constant motion, outworked only by the pioneer's ingenuity. Many of the first settlers brought chisels and saws with them. Blacksmiths fashioned other tools for a price or fair trade. Still there were gaps in the builder's tool box, gaps that were often filled by inventing a substitute.

As the area became more settled, mountain men and women confronted scarcity by trading with neighbors and kinfolks. At first most of the trading was informal: midwives delivered babies and farmers transported corn to the mill; in return they received similar favors or garden stuff. As communication increased, opportunities for trading expanded. Trappers sent furs and hides to department stores in the East and Midwest and received clothing, tools, and kitchen utensils in return. Whole families scoured the hills for ginseng, sent the dried herbs to export firms, and were rewarded—often for the first time in their lives—with cash money.

The ginseng that was so prized by mountaineers a century ago still grows in Appalachia, but its exact whereabouts usually remains a secret guarded by hunters such as Leonard Eversole. Leonard lives in Buckhorn, Kentucky, and used to hunt everything that grew or ran wild in the hills–everything from ginseng and yellowroot to muskrat and mink. He said, "In those days a man worked for a quarter a day if he was lucky. Anything that brung more than a quarter a day, why he just run after it." Health problems prevent Leonard from hunting the fox and coon that remain, but the lure of the forest lingers: "When hunting season comes and someone catches a squirrel or two, I just squirm and twitch."

Hunting ginseng was a good hobby for anybody. My daddy learned it to me. When I was a little boy he took me senging with him and when he would find a bunch he would show it to me. In the spring of the year when it first started coming up everything was so green it was hard to find. I've found the best time to find it was from about the middle of September to the fifteenth of October when it turns a pretty yellow color and there ain't another weed in the hills that favors it. You can see a bunch of it from here to that truck yonder, a small patch yellow and the rest of the stuff green.

An old man kept a store over here on Middle Fork and he would buy seng. When it would be too wet weather [and people] couldn't work they would hit the hills and seng. They would get a great big bunch of seng, half a pound, dry it out, take it up there and [trade for] a pretty good wagonload of meal and flour, salt bacon. I'll tell you another thing: I'd seng all day and not find over eight or ten little old roots. That night I would say, "I'm heading right back there. I've been running over it in too big a hurry."

I know where a bunch is now and I would love to go and get it. It's [growing] right out between two roots of a beech tree. The only way to get it would be take a chopping ax. Many a time I would pass by it in the fall of the year and I would cut that top off to keep somebody else from finding it.

One ol' fellow down here on Bowling Creek had a bunch of seng dug and dried out and I bought it. I gave him twenty-four dollars for it and I sold it for about forty-eight dollars.

Last senging I ever done I shipped eighteen ounces of it to a fellow in Ohio and he paid sixty-five dollars a pound for it. I don't know what they do with it. I've heard all my life that it went to China, that they used it over there in the tea and some kind of religion.

I trapped down at Athol,* Kentucky, for ten or fifteen years, I guess, then I come back up here and went to trapping. I would average running my traps twice a week. I used good double spring traps; when I got a mink or something it stayed there. I'd set [the traps] and then about every three days I'd run them. [If] I didn't run my traps about every three days, why [the animals would] freeze to death. If [a trap] hadn't been bothered I just shun off away from it and leave it setting right there. Longer it set the better it was. Sometimes I'd set deadfalls† with rocks, make triggers under it, and lay bait on that trigger. They'd get that bait and down come this big rock on them.

When I first started trapping for muskrats I was down in Breathitt County on the Middlefork River and there was some Jett boys. They was trapping and catching a lot and I didn't know nothing about fur. They give me ten or fifteen traps and when I would catch me one they [paid me] seventy-five cents. There was a man lived just above us on the river and his wife's brother was a fur buyer. They came down to our house one night and I said, "Yeah, I caught a few."

He said, "What do they give you?"

---

* Athol is about forty miles from Buckhorn.
† A deadfall is a trap constructed so that a weight falls on the animal and kills or maims it. In this case, the trap contained a lever, or trigger, that secured the animal.

"Seventy-five cents."

"Lord have mercy! They are a-taking your furs. I'll give you two dollars and a half apiece." That made me trap harder.

Gray foxes was easy to catch. I caught them in furrows in cornfields. People'd tend these fields in the heads of hollows, raise corn, gather it and sled it out. When I was small I'd see where [fox] walked these sled furrows hunting for birds and rabbits of the night. When I went to trapping I'd go to them old weed fields and I'd dig a little furrow about twenty foot long. I'd dig [another furrow across] it. Right in that cross I'd set a double spring steel [trap]. Of course, I would bury it completely in the dirt. I have set six traps and caught five [fox] in one night. Then a good mink hide would bring twelve, fifteen dollars. Red fox hides got up as high as forty-some dollars.

You couldn't bait and catch a red fox save your life. They're smarter than I am for one thing. You've got to know your business if you catch one. I've set traps in track roads.* They would follow that track road and they'd get about ten foot [from my trap] and they'd stop there and tromp around a little, go around off the other side. They'd see that somebody had been there and they would shun that place. That's how smart they was. It was a long time before I ever learned to catch one.

[To get a red fox] I'd take and smoke my traps over fire, then I'd carry them in a hunting pack below this track road. I'd cut out [a hole] and put the traps in there, then I'd get damp chestnut leaves to cover the traps. I'd put the same dirt back on it and cover it.

From about the first of February, or a little before, on up to the fifteenth, was the best time in the world to catch them red foxes. They was mating at that time of year and they was in gangs just like a bunch of dogs after a she-dog. I could tell a red fox sign† from a gray one: it was much bigger. Got a foot plime

* A track road is the trail an animal habitually travels to reach his den.
† Footprint.

blank* like a dog and them two front toenails are longer than the gray [fox's].

Them red foxes, [you] didn't want to shoot them, their hide was very valuable. I'd [catch] their toes in a big double spring steel trap; Victor double springs is what I always used. I'd cut me a big forked stick and get down over his neck. I'd hold him with one hand and choke him. I'd feel where his heart was a-beating and I'd take my right thumb and press right down on that. Few minutes he was out. I'd lay him on my shoulder [and he'd] always tip the calf of my leg coming out the hill. I'd skin them down and cut their toenail off with the pelt.

A mink, I thought they's hard to catch but I found out later on they was easier to catch than a rabbit. If I found where one had made a track in a creek or a hollow [I'd set a trap]. Sometimes it would be seven or eight or ten days before it'd come back, but if it come back through there, it was my man. I experimented [with] small fish [or] rabbit's head for bait; [when] one would get that bait he was caught.

I caught nine big minks one season. The least I got was fifteen dollars, and that was good money back in them days. In the Depression they would bring anywhere from fifteen to eighteen to twenty and I have got, I believe, twenty-eight dollars for them. People, then, women specially, wore an awful lot of fancy furs. I've seen red-fox fur, women with them on, have a glass eye, you know. It's awful pretty. The old big red he-foxes, they'd have snow-white on the end of their tail.

I lost an awful lot of traps. People'd find them and steal them. There was one feller up here on this creek,† he's in his eighties now. He was an awful good trapper and he give me a right smart of information when I first started it up and I liked him. He wouldn't bother my traps a'tall if he found one, and about [the] only way you could find one of his was [to] get caught in it. I was

---

* Exactly.
† Squabble Creek at Buckhorn, Kentucky.

on Otter Creek one time and he had a big double spring jump trap. There's a big cliff that went right around the creek about fifty yards long. I got back in under the cliff and a big mink had a little hole dug through that cliff. I allowed I'd catch him for sure. I got out from under there, cut me a little brush to fasten to my trap, and got back in under there. Then I went to rake a little place out with my hand [and my friend's] big jump trap catched me right across [my fingers]. It scared me and shocked me. I was hurt, too.

I set [the trap] back as good as I could. Not very long after that I saw him and was telling him about it. He just died laughing. He said, "I had the biggest mink ever in it." [I] set his trap back and caught his mink for him!

What did you do with the mink when you brought them home?

"I'd always hang them up, skin them, and case* the hides. A fox hide would dry mighty quick on a board and minks dried in twenty-four hours. I'd generally tie them all together, run my twine through where the eye was, and case them in [a] box. The better you case fur and the [better] shape it was in, the better grade you got on it [from] the companies I shipped them to. There was twenty-five or thirty different companies you could ship to, most of them in St. Louis and New York, but Montgomery Ward and Sears, Roebuck was better. You could send a few hides, figure out an order, and they'd ship you things. I have sent a mink to Sears, Roebuck and filled me out a order for shoes, overalls, blue chambray shirts—what I thought my pelt was worth. They would send what I would order and maybe a small check besides. If there weren't enough fur to cover it, they'd send you [the clothes] and a bill.

Did many other people in the area trap?

Lord God, yeah. People had to do about anything they could to make a dollar. You could make [more] money at trapping than

* Cleaning and drying an animal skin is called "casing the hide."

you could anything else if you understood it. [People would] come to me wanting to know how to catch a red fox, wanting to know how to catch a coon, and I'd tell them the contrary way.

I bought furs, too, from other people—when I could cheat them out of it. I never bought a pelt in my life only what I didn't double or triple on it. I fooled with them enough that I could look at a possum hide and tell within a penny what it'd bring.

The year before I went to the army in '42 [hunting] was still good. That winter I caught a lot of fur and had two big mink hides, about as big of ones as I ever caught. Price Turner and Letch Turner lived back in Breathitt.* They'd been buying up fur and offered me twenty dollars apiece for them. I wouldn't take it. I said, "I don't aim to sell to you boys a'tall. I'm going to ship them." I shipped one to Montgomery Ward and one to Sears, Roebuck. I got $5.10 for each one of them. That was when the bottom fell out of [the fur market].

I got up with Letch after that, he was on a mule a-riding. "Now, son," he said, "I want you to tell me the truth."

I said, "I'll tell you the truth if I know it."

"What did you get out of the two big mink hides?"

"Five dollars and ten cents apiece for them." He just died laughing. I never did trap anymore.

In some respects trading among mountain people was—and is— a way of meeting needs without the stigma of charity. When one person had corn and a neighbor had none, the two swapped a bushel of corn for a handmade basket, or a free day of labor. Until the 1930's it was almost impossible for owners of general stores to receive fresh produce from farmers and wholesalers outside the mountains, so they depended upon people to trade their produce for store goods. In the early years nearly every business transaction in the mountains was done on credit of one year's time and it was essential that merchants and craftsmen knew the character of the people with whom they traded. Early settlers

---

* Breathitt County is directly north of Leslie County where Buckhorn, Kentucky, is located.

traded with storekeepers, blacksmiths, millers, carpenters, and other people who did business with the public, as well as with their friends and neighbors. As settlements grew some people made their living solely by trading livestock, produce, pocket watches, knives, guns, and housewares. Swapping still goes on in the mountains among friends and neighbors, children, craftsmen, and some professionals, but it is more informal now. A person who makes his living by trading is rare.

Oscar Kilburn is one of the exceptions. Oscar was born in 1932 and worked in the coal mines near Wooton, Kentucky, but he gave that up in favor of trading, because "There's a little money made in it, then again you don't have to work hard." Oscar lives near Wooton in a hilltop house overlooking his animals. He specializes in trading dogs and horses and usually has twenty to forty hounds on hand. Each one has a name. Lee, Pebbles, Queen, Rufus, Sam, Blackey, Belle, Susie, Bob, and Dan are some of his standard names. Of course Oscar was not born when trading was a necessary ritual, but his trading experiences elucidate an occupation that once was an important way of life.

I learned [how to trade] the hard way. When I was about fifteen all the horse traders met up in the head of Pauls Creek* of a Sunday. Anywhere from fifty, to seventy-five, to a hundred people met up there about eight or nine o'clock of the morning. A lot of them, they'd tell you anything to make the trade. In other words, you [were] just trading the best you knowed. I traded for one [horse] that was supposed to be a seven-year-old, and come to find out it was seventeen.

Some of the old traders was well experienced. They'd know theirselves what they's doing, but they wouldn't let nobody else in on the secret. If you learned anything you're going to have to learn it the hard way. So I ordered me a book [that] told the age of [horses], how to break them, train them, and how to shoe them. That's where I learned the difference between the teeth:

* Near Wooton Creek in Leslie County, Kentucky.

Oscar Kilburn

they hawk at seven and smooth at eleven, and a mare she hawks again at seventeen and smooths at twenty-one. [When they hawk] two of their front teeth on each corner is higher than the middle part, and when it's smooth [their teeth] fit down smooth straight across.

The working conditions of [an animal] counts more than anything else. The better quality they are the more you'll get out of them when you sell them. If you were picking a good farm mule, you'd pick a large-boned mule. Larger the bone of a mule, the slower they work on hillsides. A horse that's been logged with, they're used to pulling a heavy load and having to go fast; then when you put them onto a plow they go so fast that if your plow-hook hits a rock something breaks.

How would you actually begin a trade up on Pauls Creek?

Most of the time a man hollers, "What do you have on hand to trade?" Sometimes if you're really a trader you might have three or four, four or five, head. You start telling him what you have to trade on and then he will pretty well know if he's interested. Generally, the first thing you ask a fellow in a trade [is] how much difference would he give: would the trader give you twenty-five dollars between your horse and his? [Then he will] walk around sometimes thirty minutes to an hour before he'll trade, trying to get the owner to come down. Sometimes another trader will walk in and swap for it, so you've just lost; you'll have to pick out something else to trade on. If ye any trader at all, you'll know in a very few words where ye going to trade, or where ye ain't.

Money is scarce and a lot of people will pay you so much down, so much a week, or so much a month. Just like buying a automobile: you buy a automobile and you make a payment maybe once a month or every pay day. You buy stock the same way. If you sell a mule to a man and he [says] he'll pay you, that agreement holds one year. Then after a year you can go to court if he don't pay you and [you can repossess the mule] if you want to be contrary.

You learn who will pay and who won't pay. If a stranger comes in that you don't know nothing about, most of the time you have to let him pay you off for the horse.

How do you deal with a friend who trades with you and then falls behind in his payments?

You give them more time. If something happens so they can't make their payments—sickness, financial trouble—you just give them an extension.

I have a buddy, Arnold Maggard, me and him have traded a whole lot with one another and helped one another a lot. Generally, one of us sells and the other one bids. We will run it up to make whoever is buying pay the worth of it. Say [I] had one [I] had to have a hundred dollars for. Well, [Arnold would] run it up to a hundred dollars then [when someone else] passes that hundred dollars [he'd] just drop out. You get the price that way pretty well.

[They don't have trading on Pauls Creek anymore because] most everybody in this part has got where they use automobiles to travel. Back fifteen or twenty years ago people mostly used horses. Roads was bad and you could make more time going from the head of one creek to the head of the other on horseback than you could in a automobile. Very few people at that time knowed how to drive a car. About 19 and 60 they started building more roads and a lot of the fellows quit farming and quit fooling with horses and cattle. Now feed's so high you just can't hold them, you have to buy them and let them go. You're better off sometimes if you can make fifteen or twenty dollars on a head and sell it right then, than you are to hold it four or five months and make seventy-five dollars. Your feed bill runs you so much more than the difference would be between them.

If you're much of a trader your name gets ahead of you. If you trade with one fellow he'll recommend [you] to someone else just as long as you're honest and true with them. But if you be dishonest in your trading, and make false statements, you generally run out of business right quick. The dishonest trader we call a "outlaw." A outlaw is a horse that will throw you, kick you, or won't work. You call him the "outlaw of horses."

Sometimes they law* [dishonest traders]. Like you have a real A-1 horse, and somebody comes along with a good-looking [horse] that wasn't no count. [If he] misrepresented the horse and told you false about it, you could put him in court. They call that "swindling" and they can take you to court and you'll have to make satisfaction with them; ever who swindled the other fellow, he'll have to give the horse back or pay him so much money.

I'm forty-one year old and never was put in jail in my life. I won't lie in trading because when you start that you'll just about go out of business. Always tried to tell them the truth.

If you come out with the bad end of the deal you'll just think a whole lot about it and say little or nothing. I always figure if a

* Prosecute.

man was big enough to burn me, why I'd just wait and burn somebody else. An old man by the name of George Stanford burnt me so many times that I was waiting for him to get his burning back. [I had a mule] that took the studs with me. In other words, it stopped and didn't want to go on. That was a stubborn mule, very, very poor in its class. It was a good-looker, and good age, but it was bad quality. I swapped [George] a eight-year-old five-gaited saddle horse to that mule. He got on that mule and took off down the road. I was on my way back home [when he caught up with me] and said, "Now, tell me the truth, Oscar, about this mule."

I said, "I told you the truth: it's a good family mule. When I said 'family' I meant [it] took the whole family to tan her." [George] wound up coming back with a few that looked like they's sick. He laid for trying to get that burning back but he never did.

Trading is the same as gambling. If you are a trader and you buy something, you're taking chances [whether] you're going to make money or not. That's just like these fellows playing cards. When he sets down and draws he don't know whether he's going to win or the other fellow's going to win. You never definitely know hardly unless . . ."

In the 1700's and 1800's corn was as important to the mountain man as it had been to the pilgrim in New England. It was a hearty plant that thrived on the nitrogen-rich soil of the southern Appalachians and was able to grow around roots and tree stumps left in a forest clearing. Corn could be pounded, molded, ground, fried, boiled, or baked into a variety of meals for the family. Corn-fed animals pulled plows and provided transportation for people and produce. Pigs fattened on corn yielded lard for cooking, oil for lamps, and meat for the table. Surplus corn became whiskey, a medicant and source of pleasure for the pioneer.

Corn was a plentiful crop that could often be traded, but seldom sold, locally. In 1900, towns were usually fifty or more miles apart. Roads, where they existed, were poor. Renting a team of horses cost $2.50 a day, and seven hundred pounds of corn was the maximum a good pair of horses could haul. Transporting crops out of the mountains to compete with large midwestern farmers was out of the question, so some mountain people turned to moonshine as a way of converting corn into a marketable product.

Making moonshine, the illegal distillation of sprouted corn into whiskey, was a sensitive, sometimes explosive, issue in the mountains. Few mountaineers objected to paying state and federal property taxes—although it was often difficult to obtain the cash. The $1.10 tax on a gallon of whiskey that cost the farmer only twenty cents to make was another matter entirely. Some saw the situation in terms of corn pone versus corn whiskey: if a man grew a crop of corn, gathered it, shucked it, ground it, and baked a pone there was no government interference, but if he distilled the ground corn into whiskey he had to pay a heavy tax. As a result, the small farmer who generally made no more than a gallon of whiskey a day during a few weeks of the year became a moonshiner and sold his brew to trusted friends or bootleggers.

Distillers who had the know-how and capital to make whiskey on a year-round, large-scale basis did so not only with the knowledge of government officials, but with their blessings, as Dr. Cratis Williams describes. Cratis is a descendant of a long line of legal distillers and whether he would have continued the family tradition or not is a moot question. Prohibition came when he was eleven years old in 1918 and by the time he reached high school his interests were turning toward scholarly pursuits that culminated in 1961 with a doctorate from New York University. In his dissertation, Cratis examined the social and cultural history of Appalachian mountaineers and evaluated the vast body of fiction about them. The sixteen-hundred-page document is considered to be a landmark in its field. Cratis retired in 1976 as special assistant to the chancellor of Appalachian State University in Boone, North Carolina.

He was reared on Caines Creek in Lawrence County, Ken-

tucky, "where people were still living in the eighteenth century during my boyhood." As a child, he played in his grandfather's distillery, where he watched the men work and learned from them the argot, techniques, and art of whiskey making. He recalled:

I was a kind of mascot in the distillery, curious about how everything was done, and no doubt, very much underfoot. I weighed twenty-five or thirty pounds then, but my rugged, two-hundred-fifty-pound grandpa indulged my whims and the workmen respected his wishes. Sometimes, when whiskey had been proofed and was ready for the barrel, Grandpa would fill my little four-ounce bottle for me and Grandma would put some brown sugar in it. The workmen enjoyed cajoling me into treating them to a swig from my bottle and making me feel that I was a very important person.

The Williamses migrated from Copper Creek in Scott County [Virginia] to Kentucky in 1837, and the story is that when they came the ox wagons and carts had the stills, and the brandy, and the whiskey, and the family walked behind. When they arrived, one of the first things my two-greats-grandfather* did was to set his still up, but he was a restless fellow and went on to Kansas after he had been there twenty years or so, leaving only my great-grandfather and a sister. There was great-grandfather's still, my grandfather's still, and my father's still—they were all legal distillers. According to family legend [all the men in our family had a] similar history back to the Whiskey Rebellion. If that's the case, I'm the first in direct lineage since the American Revolution not to have been a distiller myself, though I think I could do it.

From my first recollections, my grandfather would take me with him into his still house to show me what was going on and how things worked. I was extremely pleased with all that and was getting my own little vial of whiskey—of course, weakened suf-

---

* His great-great-grandfather.

ficiently—so I would titillate my ego by carrying that thing around.

The stilling operation was a seven-day, twenty-four-hour-a-day concern. This meant he had to have people on duty all the time. The upstairs of his house had bunks in it in which somebody was sleeping all the time. He had about fifteen people working for his distillery. The storekeeper and gauger* was employed by the federal government and paid seventy-five dollars a month, and my grandfather's portion of his upkeep was to give him room and board. He sat in a little office outside the still house. I used to sit with him, he was a lonely fellow, and I would see him turn these little stopcocks and read the hydrometer. [Distilleries] were inspected periodically to see that they were obeying the little requirements of the law. "Devil" John Wright† was one of my grandfather's inspectors. No doubt the storekeeper and gauger and the distiller sometimes had under-the-table deals.

The whiskey made would depend upon what happened to be in season at the time. Sometimes it was fruit whiskey. My grandfather contracted with old women who had apple orchards and needed to sell their apples. He'd [also] buy the barley and the rye and the corn that the neighbors had to sell, so that he could have the grain whiskey when the time came. A bushel of grain made about a gallon of whiskey, and the quality of the whiskey was unusually good.

The still house itself had an interesting kind of architecture; it might have been eighty by forty feet. It had two stills: one was a five-hundred-gallon still for the mash, the other was what he called his "doubling still," about three hundred gallons. The still house had this fine odor to it that I can still remember when I smell Scotch.

---

* In small legal distilleries, such as the one Cratis's family operated, one man was both storekeeper and gauger. As such, he was responsible for stamping each keg with the date to ensure proper aging, and he worked with the distiller to determine how much malt should be added to the brew to ensure an even quality.
† See pages 58–62.

[To market the whiskey] he contracted with a middleman who gave him prescriptions, or orders, for making whiskey according to a certain formula. This was all delivered to Catlettsburg, Kentucky, where it was bought. Now, he had a license also to sell, but he couldn't sell less than a five-gallon contract. This was to keep the local fellows from buying half a pint and getting drunk, you see. Of course, they were skilled in getting around that. They'd simply make up a group of twelve to fifteen to buy five gallons. If he violated this he could be indicted, which happened to him occasionally. He would sell less than five gallons to some of his friends and sometimes he'd get caught.

These mountain people—many Scotch-Irish among them—knew a great deal about how to make good whiskey and there was nothing wrong with making it from their own point of view. They even paid the preachers with whiskey in the early days and preachers liked that. This is a long tradition with them. If it were easier for small [distilleries] to become licensed this would be one

Cratis Williams

way of boosting the economy in the Appalachian region [today]. I don't know how moralistic people ought to be about those things. Where whiskey is concerned I'm never particularly moralistic as you can understand. I never did think there was anything wrong with taking a drink of whiskey and still don't. I take it when I want it and I just don't share the moralistic view and never have. I've seen some mighty low-down men come drunk on occasion, but people like myself don't do that.

My grandfather, I think, might have been the last legal distiller in eastern Kentucky. His still was closed after the "Act"* became effective. I was a small boy [and] I happened to be present at the time the internal revenue officers came to close it down officially in 1918. I saw them remove the caps from the stills and carry [them] out to a sweet-potato patch to cool off. After Grandfather closed his still officially he put it in the barn loft and kept his oats in it. I used to play in those oats. That was still there when a tornado came through and blew the barn down. Didn't hurt the still, but somebody picked it up and carried it off.

An interesting thing happened [after the family] closed its stills. The country was moving toward middle-class moral standards. Not very [long before] there'd been no awareness of middle-class moral standards in the whole county, but the county seat had become affected by Victorianism. There had been people who had gone away to school and come back with degrees. They had been conditioned in the schools to middle-class morality.

After my grandfather's still was closed officially, within three years the population of the valley had reduced 50 percent, because these three stills had sustained the economy of the valley. The apple orchards were neglected. Trees were neglected and cut down. There was no longer any market. It was eleven miles to the railhead [and] the corn was not worth carrying by wagon

---

* In Kentucky, Prohibition became effective in 1918 when the state legislature ratified the Eighteenth Amendment to the U.S. Constitution.

eleven miles to sell. Although my grandfather didn't pay these local men working in his distillery very much money—probably a dollar a day or less—he kept their family [in food]. The farmers that had white oak on their farms would cut trees for barrel staves; there was no longer a market for that. The one-room country school had seventy-five in it [when] I attended. I went back to teach that school my first year of teaching, 1929; it had thirty-three in it. Three years later when I left it had sixteen.

There was no way for those people to get any money. They preferred to live there, they had their own little farms, little gardens, and little crop patches. They didn't need much money, but now they didn't have any money. During the twenties there was no help.

After Prohibition, did your grandfather go back into business?

He wanted to [but] the license was absolutely out of reach for him, so he could not reestablish his distillery. That would have been 1933 or '34 and the Depression had already come and he couldn't pay [for] the license to reestablish. My grandfather was a very, very independent, stubborn man, and he did just about what he pleased. Afterwards it was very difficult for him to get the kind of whiskey he wanted, so he contracted with a metal worker to make him a small sixty-gallon still which he set up in a cave in the hollow behind his house and he made it whenever he wanted to. He was moonshining then. He felt nobody could make the kind of whiskey he required for himself, [but] he reached the place where the quality [of his own brew] wasn't what it had been when he was a young man. I used to go back from Boone to see him. He would always have me a Christmas present which was a gallon of whiskey he'd made. I didn't always accept it, but I was always grateful.

Where money was involved, doctors and lawyers shared the problems of their neighbors and, by necessity, depended upon trading for a livelihood. From the start, strict "professionalism" was an anachronism in Appalachia and a luxury most doctors, lawyers, and teachers could not afford. Like other people, specialists supplemented their bartered income by farming and when harvests were poor they too suffered. Medical needs were great and country doctors often had to do the work of surgeons, obstetricians, dentists, and veterinarians.

Dr. Charles Gullett began practicing dentistry in his hometown of West Liberty, Kentucky, in 1911 and in 1933 his son Stanley joined the practice after graduating from the University of Louisville School of Dentistry. Practicing good dentistry was important to Stanley before his death in 1975. It was also time-consuming. By 1960 he tired of filling teeth and trimmed his practice by telling patients with cavities to go elsewhere. Later children's dental work, root canals, and bridges were eliminated too, and before his death Dr. Stanley Gullett did only one kind of dentistry: he made false teeth. Making dentures that fit was a challenge and he spent nearly a week in his laboratory creating one pair. The specialty allowed time for hunting and fishing after work and for reading Field and Stream *magazine while the molds set. Stanley's satisfaction with the meshing of work and pleasure showed in his smile (which revealed real, not false, teeth) and he expected to continue practicing dentistry until he was eighty. While dentures were Stanley's chief interest during his final years, he did not abandon cavities completely. In his office was a poster admonishing patients: "If You Can't Brush After Every Meal . . . Swish and Swallow."*

Stanley talked about dentistry as he and his father practiced it and about the Central Appalachian social structure that has little, if any, room for pretension.

[In] 1933 times were hard and my patients were probably 95 percent farmers. They had very little money. When I started practicing the going rate for extracting a tooth was fifty cents, which a lot of people didn't have. You would put a simple filling [in] for a dollar. Actually, you did more extractions in those days because a person felt like they couldn't afford to have a tooth filled. [Abscesses] were harder to treat back then because there was nothing to treat them with [except] salt water. Now you have penicillin. Back then a fellow would go for weeks with a swollen jaw. He could do nothing except [apply] poultices [made of] flaxseed or yellowroot. A lot of people have died from abscesses but it's a rare thing now.

West Liberty has always had a pretty good supply of doctors and dentists. The doctors made house calls. They all had an office, but the office was just a place to load up their saddlebags. Of course, I can't carry my stuff out, the patients have to come in here to get much done, but a medical doctor can carry a world of medicine as well as lances and scissors, and they can go to the patient. I did some horsebacking when I first started practicing. I can remember one time a fellow worked in the log woods and he got his legs broken. He was bedfast and had the toothache. They came to get me with an extra horse, wanted me to go and take out three teeth for the fellow.

My first few years of practice I never failed to go, but, of course, after you kind of get established you get a little more independent, that's human nature.

I have been in [the] office all night long a few times. [Once] I extracted three or four teeth for a fellow and I didn't know he was a bleeder until it was all over. He came back a little after dark and he was hemorrhaging very bad. He came to my house. I come to the office with him and I stayed all night long trying to stop that hemorrhaging. I never did stop it; I slowed it down and the next morning I put him on the bus to the hospital. No pay, [I] didn't even make the charge. He went to the hospital and he had to have a blood transfusion before they could stop that. I was ready early the next morning for my regular work.

My father was a dentist, that's probably [why I became one]. If he had been a blacksmith I'd probably have been a blacksmith. My father really didn't encourage me to be a dentist. You know what he wanted me to be? A banker. He thought that was where

Stanley Gullett

the money was. And it might be, I don't know. It's not [in] dentistry really. You don't go in any profession to get rich on it. That's not the purpose: you make a living, you do a worthwhile service. If I had it to do all over again I believe I'd be a banker.

How did your father get into dentistry?

He tells it like this: He worked on a farm and he had to work pretty hard to make anything. He tried teaching school a while and back at the time the going pay for a teacher was thirty-five dollars a month. He said teaching wasn't too good and it was too hard to work on a farm, so he figured dentistry might be the best bet.

In my father's time there would be some good blacksmiths. They would make forceps, not really forceps, more like pliers, and they'd pull teeth. Of course, they had no anesthetic. You'd just sit down and say, "I want this tooth pulled," and maybe he'd pull that one or maybe another one by it. [It was] against the law even to do it. They were not allowed to charge. It was a neighborly act, relieving the pain. [People were] trying to save a trip to town as well as fifty cents. Of course, those old fellows died out and the younger people didn't take it up. When I first started practicing I'd say there was in this county seven or eight that I knew about; I don't know how many that I didn't know about. [Blacksmiths] would come in and tell me about how they would do their neighbor: "He come in last Saturday night and he was dying of a toothache and he just begged me to pull his tooth and as a good neighbor act [I] pulled his tooth." I've taken out probably hundreds of roots that these fellows had left. I'm convinced that the average person could stand more pain back when I first started practicing than they are willing [to] now.

[Communities] were closer back [in the thirties]. Like I said, the man in this community that would take out teeth, now everybody knew that man. Everybody. You can go in any community now and everybody don't know everybody. There was a time when I knew everybody that lived in West Liberty, probably knew about who lived in which house. Not true now. I don't know 20 percent of the people that live in West Liberty now. The population of West Liberty when I first started practicing was about six hundred; it's about doubled now, I'd say. Yes, people were very much closer together then. They were more willing to help their neighbors then than they are now. They had to depend on each other.

Did professional people keep to themselves?

Oh, no! We were mixers. If you just mixed with professions you would be very lonesome. In those days there were my father and probably two lawyers in town and two medical doctors, so we would have been kind of lonesome. The drugstore was our meeting place. You'd meet there in the afternoon or at night, or you'd go to the ball games. We mixed with the public, or tried to. They had parties, square dances, card parties. The games were different, they played Rook and Flinch and some of them [were] even bold enough to play poker. They had candy parties. Whoever the cook was would cook up a big pan full [of sorghum] and you had to pull it to make it set. They'd lay it on a thin marble slab and then take a knife and cut it into pieces. After it set for a while it's good to eat. It wasn't so good on your teeth, but it was tasty. Then we had quilting parties, house-raising parties, and bean-hulling parties. Whole bunch of people'd get together and quilt or build a house for their neighbor or a barn. That was the neighborly thing and you never hear of things like that anymore. Our people were all pretty much equalized; financially [there was] not much difference.

Until the mid-1800's trading was the basis of the economy in Central Appalachia. For many people, however, the economy began to change about 1840 when industrialists discovered the region's rich forests. Mountaineers responded by using whipsaws and broadaxes to fell the trees and provide the outside world with the region's choice timber. The logging boom between 1890 and 1910 provided mountain people with their first major opportunity to earn cash money and did not completely wane until the 1930's when most of the land had been stripped of virgin timber. Speculators often paid landowners a dollar an acre for the right to fell huge tracts of timber; then sold the chopped oaks, chestnut oaks, beeches, and poplars to lumber companies at a dollar per tree. For many years this was the standard price paid for mature trees, some of which were 140 feet high and had a diameter of 8 feet. The volume of business was tremendous. During one nine-month period in 1909 loggers put nearly 40,000,000 feet of poplar, cut from 20,000 acres of land, into Kentucky's Big Sandy River alone. Farmers also benefited from the logging boom by making railroad ties, staves, shingles, and ax handles, and by becoming lumbermen, mill-hands, oarsmen, and strippers of tanbark.

Logging usually began after the November harvest and continued until planting time in March. Fathers and sons or teams of kinfolks worked together in the forests chopping trees, peeling bark, and trimming branches. Felled trees were chained together and either dragged by men or hauled by oxen to a cliff edge

(Appalachian Photographic

Logging tram road at the mouth of the Terry Branch of Ball Creek in Knott County, Kentucky. c. 1915

(Appalachian Photographic

Rafting logs at the mouth of Beaver Creek in Floyd County, Kentucky, preparing to go down the Big Sandy River to Catlettsburg. At the time (c. 1910), Catlettsburg was the largest hardwood market in the world

where they were pushed with cant hooks to the water below. There they lay in a "log dump" until each tree was branded with the mark of the lumber company that would purchase it and prepared for the treacherous journey downriver.

Working in swift currents and water that was often waist-deep, men bound twenty-five to fifty logs together into a raft using long poles known as "tie-poles" and "chain-dogs," which were iron wedges. When the water was high and the current swift, rafts were floated downriver to mills and lumber companies. In small streams where the water is seldom deep, logs were hurled into the water and prodded downstream with spike poles until they reached a splash dam built of timber and stones. When thousands of logs accumulated behind the splash dam a key wedge was removed and the timber spewed forth. At the mouth of the main river the logs that survived the torrential journey were bound into rafts and guided downriver by oarsmen.

It took about five days to float a raft down the Kentucky River between Beattyville and Frankfort, a distance of 189 miles, and two and a half days to walk back. In 1905 oarsmen were paid two dollars a day for their labor and were reimbursed for meals and lodging received along the way in private homes. However, as Elbert (Ebb) Herald explains, loggers did not always have time to eat and sleep.

Ebb was born on Wolf Creek in Breathitt County in 1911 and now lives about twenty miles away in Lost Creek, Kentucky. He is a retired farmer, well-digger, store clerk, blacksmith, and logger. He is blind now and spends his time preaching in an Old Regular Baptist church and making walking canes out of hickory limbs. To save money Ebb smooths the canes not with a store-bought plane, but with a piece of broken window glass.

Ebb is a good storyteller and one of his best is about his great-grandfather Roger Herald, a farmer who lived in Ireland in the mid-1800's, when people were forbidden by law to work on the Sabbath. Roger Herald obeyed the law until one Sunday his flock of chickens sinned against him. They escaped from their pen and

*tore up his garden. Herald roared after the birds, pelting them
with stones as he went, but a neighbor was watching. Soon Roger
Herald was arrested, tried, and found guilty of "working" on the
Sabbath. His punishment was deportation to America where he
was to be sold to the highest bidder. While Herald waited in the
stockades, his wife sold all their possessions and bought a ticket
on a boat that sailed ahead of his. When he landed on the American shore she was at the auction and bought him for seventy-five
cents.*

I was from a broken family. My father and mother didn't live
together after I was born. I was their sixth child. The same night
that I was born my father took another woman and left. Later on
they was married. [My mother] brought me back up here on Lost
Creek to her family. I was seven years old when my mother died.
In 1922 my father came back from West Virginia where he was
working [and] bought a farm up in Leslie County. I was eleven
years old when I moved to Leslie County. It was a very isolated
country up there, mind you, I said this was in 1922: there was
not one foot of highway, there was not one foot of railroad. My father, he looked around and there was plenty hard work to get
done, and we went to work cutting logs.

There wasn't any saw mill around to sell them at closer than
Beattyville, a right smart piece away. There was a number of
companies we would contact [to] get a contract for so many logs:
Bellepoint Lumber Company, Noble and Hyden Lumber Company in Beattyville, and there was the Lilling G. Bannings and
Reynolds Lumber Company. They would send a man [to] come
and measure logs on the bank and brand them. We'd get the
[company's] price lists and whichever [offered] the most money
that was the one we'd sell to. We'd get maybe twenty-five dollars
a thousand feet, it'd depend on the size of the timber. Some
timber brought more than others. Walnut and white oak at that
time was best. We would get thirty-five dollars a thousand [feet]
for that, but when it come down to beech and smaller grades we
done well to get twenty-five dollars a thousand.

Elbert (Ebb) Herald

Me being eleven years old, there's always something that a eleven-year-old boy can do. My daddy wouldn't let me get on the raft then but I'd [help haul the logs to the river]. When I got to be seventeen or eighteen years old I was big enough to handle an oar. When I got permission to go on the first trip I was looking forward to that and hoping for the tide to come soon. It was in May. We was hoeing corn and whenever there was much rain, and the river went to raising, I couldn't do my work, I *had* to watch the river. It was just something to imagine, to think about.

I had never been down that river before. Later, after I'd made a few trips, I learned that it was work.

There was no fun because there was always a possibility of anything. We [logged] because it was a necessity. Back them days when I was a young man, and during my grandfather's time and my daddy's time, they looked ahead and they seen what they needed to do and that's what they did. My father, he was always lucky, we never did have an accident, a bad accident. I've tore up a few rafts, but we never lost but very few logs. In logging you had to be a strong man and you had to be a man that would face danger.

[We] cut roads through the hills and hauled our logs down to the riverbanks with work oxens and horses. When we got [the logs] to the river we would raft them together and buyers would come along buying. If it was real big logs—anywhere from twenty-four to twenty-eight inches [in diameter]—we would take about sixty-five logs. If they was smaller logs—anywhere from eighteen to twenty-two inches—we'd take seventy-five or eighty on a raft, which would amount to anywhere from eight to ten thousand feet, depending on the length of the logs.

When we would get the logs rafted together and there come a tide of the right depth of water we would get people to ride these logs down. You couldn't turn a raft loose when the water was too high and too swift. If you did you'd lose it; you couldn't control it with the oars. Whenever the tides would get at the right stage we'd turn our rafts loose and sometimes if it was a real heavy raft it took four men to turn it. If it wasn't too big three men would be all right, two men in the bow and one on the back end.

Sometimes it was pretty rough on the water. For instance, one time we were going down the Middle Fork of the Kentucky River. There was a big tide in the South Fork and in the North Fork there was a lot of rain. We would [have tied] our raft up but we couldn't get to land, so we had to stay on the raft that night and it was awful cold. We had a pretty rough time but, fortunately, before we left we had laid some rocks on the raft and throwed some sand on it so we could build a fire. Late in the night we run without fuel and we spent a few hours without any fire at all. It was awful cold. We was hungry and our only fuel was just what drift we might be able to catch. Next morning whenever it began to get light so we could see, we untied our rafts and we just drifted.

We drifted till about ten or eleven o'clock in the day and we hadn't drifted four or five miles when—it was snowing, it was awful cold—we looked down the river and seen a big gasoline boat come. We knowed that was the *Circle B*. [We] tied all of the logs together and hooked his boat to [our raft] and took off with it. He took us on down to Bellepoint and we went and catched the train there and came back.

I don't remember exactly the year, but it was along about '26 the first danger, real danger, that I ever run into on the river. We was a way down the river, not too far from Beattyville, and some people was running up on the bank hollering, "There's a blockade down the river!" A man by the name of Louis Deaton was on a raft in front of us and his raft had hit the bank. It was blockaded. We must have been a quarter of a mile, or a half mile, behind him. We was hoping they would cut it in two and let it out before we got there. One of Louis Deaton's boys, his name was Alex, was aiming to wade to the other side and cut it out. He was an excellent swimmer, but when he got out near the middle of the current the water washed him off. Something happened, I don't know what it was, but he come up one time and they shoved him an oar, but he didn't hold to it. He went down again and he didn't raise.

By this time we was getting up within forty or fifty steps of it. We had to hit it. I was scared but I could swim. My father hollered from the other raft behind us, "Hang to the oar!" I was on the front end; before I could get to the back end we'd already struck it. Lucky for us, our raft sunk but not deep, and the front tie-pole broke. That turned us loose. Later they [found Alex Deaton's body] under the Beattyville bridge.

One time we was rafting and it was an awful cold time. I had a younger brother, you might say a half brother, the same woman wasn't both of our mothers. Farris was six months younger than I was. Me and Jasper Langlan and my daddy was down in the water and me and Farris was using the augers. You have to have augers to raft with, to bore through the tie poles. It was the hardest work in the whole bunch, boring holes. We was rafting with a five-quarter and a six-quarter auger that raft. We'd take turn about. Maybe I'd use one half of the day and he'd use the other one half a day. Along in the evening [Farris] was using the five and he give out or something. So Farris went up on the bank and he went to driving the team and rolling the logs in the water. Well, he wasn't supposed to roll these logs in the water until we were ready for them. Sometimes I would go out and bring them down under the tie pole, and sometimes Jasper would go out and bring them out. This time he let down a big poplar log. After I walked out on this tie pole and went to bring this poplar log down under the tie pole, he turned another one loose and this other log hit the one I was on. That caused waves, and whenever he turned that one loose, why four more appeared! They rolled in, left the water bouncing up and down, and pitched me up toward the raft.

Naturally, I went down. Way down. When I come up, I come up under the raft. Jasper Langlan was watching me and when he seen me go under the raft he grabbed this other spike pole, and when I come up he give me a shove toward the deep water. That way when I come up the second time I didn't come up against the raft, I come out in the water. Well, naturally when I come out in the water he didn't wait for me to attempt to swim or do anything, and I don't guess I could. So, he reached out with this spike pole and got my clothes.

Why did Farris do that? He almost killed you.

There's no one knows. It was two years before I saw him again.

Had you and he had a fight?

No, me and him got along good. He got tired and [he might have been] mad over who would use what auger, I don't know. Farris was that type. You see, Farris has always been a man that no one could ever read, or ever learn. [About fourteen years later]—this is getting plum away from logging—one day he came up where I live on Lost Creek, and stayed all night with us. My father-in-law was working up here at Sixteen* [but] had to meet a man down at Lost Creek, so I went to talk with the man in his stead. Farris went back with me and, you know, when I was talking with the man Farris disappeared. This was in November of 19 and 40 and I never saw Farris again till in October '61.

You and your father quit logging in 1930. Why?

The logs got farther from the river. One year when we bought a boundary of timber up on Grassy Branch, which is now Toulouse [Kentucky], we had to haul our logs about four and a half miles on a wagon. We'd leave home before daylight, we'd get home after dark. So that was hard money and I guess that was one thing maybe enticed us [to quit logging]. My daddy got disabled, and just a single man with no education, why money looked hard to come by. To borrow money to finance something you was starting into then, you just couldn't do it. Nobody had it to loan.

Was logging one of the only ways a man had of earning cash money?

That's right. There was plenty of coal, but no market for it. We had good crops, but if you sold your corn you could get about fifty cents a bushel and it was an awful slow sale at that. Beans and potatoes, you couldn't sell them except in the spring of the

* A coal mine in Breathitt County, Kentucky.

year. If you holed up a lot of potatoes, you could sell several seed taters in the spring of the year; the fall of the year you couldn't sell any. No demand for it. Really, if we run short on money from one season to the other we could go to the merchant and he would supply us with what we needed: meal, flour, sugar, coffee, salt, horseshoes. But in the fall of the year the first tide come so we could deliver a load of logs, we'd settle with him. It wasn't only us, it was quite a few of our neighbors that did that.

Until the coal industry came along, farming played an even more fundamental role in Central Appalachia's economy than logging and was the basis for much of the trading. The first farmers were the eighteenth-century frontiersmen and one of the most valuable things they brought with them was seeds. The seeds were an insurance policy for the future: flax was woven into cloth, hemp became rope, and vegetables provided sustenance for animals and man.

Transforming Central Appalachia into farmland was seldom easy. While the southern Appalachians are actually rather modest "mountains," they occupy 90 percent of the land in some places. There are few commanding peaks, and the land rolls with rugged grace. Hills begin in the valleys and creek beds that lace the region into a geographic unit, then rise steadily to rounded crests or sedimentary knolls. The valleys are narrow; there are few major rivers, and one mountain is likely to begin where another ends. During the early 1900's United States geological surveyors reported seeing at least one farm in the southern Appalachian mountains that sloped at an angle of fifty degrees. It was a finding that lends credence to stories about mountain farmers who fell out of their cornfields and broke bones and skulls.

Early settlers often knew little about husbandry and had few tools, but they approached the mountains with vigor. Occasionally some cleared mountainsides by starting forest fires; more often harrows and hoes were used to upend shrubs, dislodge rocks, and smooth the earth. Corn was the most important crop,

but most families also tried to raise potatoes, field beans, cab-
bage, tobacco, barley, rye, wheat, and oats. Clearing a new
ground and planting crops took weeks; the whole family was in-
volved and the results were seldom long-lasting. Cultivation was
haphazard, and mountains are prone to erosion, so whole farms
frequently disappeared with spring rainfall.

Not everything a family needed could be grown at home and
farmers periodically hauled part of their produce to a general
store to trade garden stuff for salt, soda, baking powder, coffee,
sewing needles, and nails. When possible, they traded for cash
money that was needed to pay property taxes.

Delphia Ramey was born in 1906 and grew up during the
1910's and 1920's when the economy of Central Appalachia was
shifting from agriculture to the coal industry. She and her parents
lived in Marrowbone, Kentucky, near a coal-mining operation.
Her mother and father traded their vegetables and eggs at the
company commissary and not at a privately owned general store.
Transportation was improving throughout Central Appalachia, and
her father earned money by making cross-ties for the railroads.
Unlike earlier pioneer farmers, he let some farmland lie fallow by
annually rotating his crops from one mountainside to another.
Many traditional ways of farm life remained unchanged, how-
ever. When it was time to clear a new ground or to plant crops,
every member of the family helped. Children who were too small
to hoe either amused themselves in the field or weeded rocks from
the garden soil. Between men and women there was little separa-
tion of roles and both were expected to plant crops, hoe, gather
fodder, split rails, and chop firewood.

Delphia lives in Wheelwright, Kentucky, now and has barely
enough land for a small garden, but she remembers days on the
family farm fondly.

Dad owned a farm, it was a big hillside farm, I'd say it was
three hundred acres at the very least. The first thing we did was
get our crop out. Our daddy would have us to clear up a new

ground, sprout it out and clean it up and plant it in corn and beans. We'd switch from one side of the farm to the other one each year, so we had to clean it up. I done a lot of plowing myself. I've plowed a big old-fashioned turning plow that you had to kick with your foot every time you got to the end of a row. We plowed straight around the hill.

[One time] we was all hoeing corn together. Our dog had a groundhog back in the crack of a rock. Our dog was named Ted and I said to my older brother, "Go to Ted and see what Ted's got." The bell was ringing for us to come to the house and he said, "I'm not going." I went and that groundhog was just setting in that hole snapping its teeth. [We knew a groundhog] was tearing the corn down. I broke off a big long limb and made forks to it and I jobbed that in and went to twisting and I twisted in that groundhog's hide and I pulled with all the power I had to get that groundhog out of there. I heard its bones breaking, seems like, coming between them rocks. That was the fattest thing I ever saw. When it come on through the rocks and let go I went tumbling over the hill [with] the dog and groundhog both right on me. We had the awfulest time ever was getting away from that groundhog. I helped the dog kill it. I picked it up and drug it to the house; it was just simply too big to pack. Dad said, "Now you see, boys, look how much corn that groundhog would have eat if she hadn't twisted it out between them rocks." He looked right at my brother Landon and said, "You wasn't too little. You could have helped do it."

The main crop was corn. The corn would feed us our bread and would feed the stock. Of course, one of my brothers had to run the traps every morning when we was raising corn; he was older than me. They'd make little traps out of wood to catch the ground squirrels to keep them from taking up the corn. [Dad] had a very, very big orchard: apple orchard and peach orchard. He had Winesap apples, Golden Delicious apples, Sheep Nose apples—best things ever was—and the Red Delicious, old-fashion Roman Beauty apples, and Ben Davis apples. My daddy

Delphia Ramey

would spray the trees a little but he never could buy the stuff that he really did need because he just didn't have the money to do as he'd like to do.

We raised turkeys and they'd be way back in the valley on the mountain gobbling all over the place. Sometimes Mother would have close to a hundred, but sometimes the foxes would get into them; they would catch her hens, too. We raised a big cane patch every year and that made at least a hundred gallons of molasses.

In fact, that's how I learned to plow. My oldest brother got married and the cane patch had to be plowed out and my dad wanted to go to church. He was a Christian. He said, "Honey, do you think you can do it?" I said, "Well, Dad, I believe I can." It took me two days, but I got it done.

We worked hard. If we needed anything done we did it, such as taking care of the stock, hoeing corn, plowing, and making a garden, raising everything we eat. We hardly ever went to the store for anything except salt, soda, baking powder, and our shoes, if we could get any.

[The older children] helped the younger ones. They put me and my younger sister in one row. One would thin the corn and pull out the weeds while the other one come along and cut up the rest of the weeds and put the dirt to the corn. When we would hoe a round, which would mean to one end and back to the other end, our mother would say to us, "Let's sit down and rest. It's getting too hot now, children." So we'd go under a shady tree and rest a while. The boys would make slingshots, [and] bobwhite whistles out of pawpaw bark. We sat there and played like that till time to get in another row of corn.

My daddy made his plow stock hisself. He'd go to the woods and stay gone all day till he'd find enough timber that would be crooked enough to make the handles of the plow. And then he'd find the beam for the plow and a piece to make the foot to put the plow on.

When the hoe would wear down a little my daddy would take it and an old crosscut saw that was wore out to this old man who worked in a handmade shop. He would cut out some of [the saw] and weld it on to this hoe that was worn out and make it much bigger. He wouldn't try to buy a new hoe. We didn't have the money.

What did you do when you needed money?

There was about five company stores [Mother] supplied with what could be raised on a farm: roasting ears, cabbage, tomatoes, cucumbers, beans, peas, lettuce, onions, squash, cushaws. Other farmers did the same thing. Mother had a one-horse wagon and we would go to the field and pick big sacks of beans. My brother would bring the horse just as far as he could and haul out the big sacks of beans and my mother would go to the mining company stores and contract these beans and sell them out.

Us children had to quit school after Dad lost his eyesight to get our corn laid by. School started in July. We'd go back and stay a little while but then some of the fodder had to be took care of and the beans had to be picked. We'd miss school there. First thing we knowed all the corn had to be gathered and our school was out and we didn't get any school. The schools didn't last long in them days; seven months is all school lasted.

When my dad lost his eyesight we had to sell up our cows, had to sell off a lot of our stock. He walked to Hindman from the head of Marrowbone and had his eyes operated on. There was an eye specialist at Hindman. He had cataracts. We thought that he wouldn't come back alive because one of our family had been in a hospital and we thought a hospital was just a deadly weapon. But he got all right and come back to us.

Were there ever arguments among the children about who should do the work?

Yes, there was in washing dishes. There wasn't any of us liked to wash dishes. We loved to work outside, and we would count our knives and forks, spoons and plates and divide them. We kept this hid from our mother and when one would get its half done, the other one would take over and do its half. Mother would inspect the dishes and if they wasn't exactly right they was all piled right back out. She scalded her dishes often. That kept germs down and we didn't have nothing like we've got of today to keep germs down.

We had the old-fashioned geese that wanted to stay in the water, and when they took a notion to nest they'd go just as far back on the hill as they could go. The goose would go first and then the gander would follow. The gander would stand first on one foot and then on the other and guard this goose till she'd hatched those eggs off. He let nobody come around that nest till she hatched those eggs. But our ducks laid along the edge of the creek. We'd get out of the morning, us children, barefooted, wade that creek, big frost on the ground, hunting for duck eggs.

I've picked a many of the geese [for feather pillows]. We'd spread old sacks over our laps and turn its belly up and turn its wings back behind it and hold it down under [our elbows] and we'd start at the bottom jerking those feathers up and putting it in a barrel. We'd pad ourselves till the goose couldn't bite us. We'd pick and pick, but we'd leave a little bolster right under the goose's wing so the goose could lay its wing back upon that when we set it down.

I can recall another little incident that happened. My mother put me out to sweep leaves out of the yard. We had us a little pet pig and it was pretty good size, and its name was Nancy. Every time I'd sweep up a pile of leaves Nancy'd get around and root in them and scatter them out before I could pick them up. I got mad at her and I hit her across the back with a broomstick. It was a broom that had been hewed down out of hickory, that was what I was getting the leaves swept up with. It's heavy, I couldn't hardly lift it I was so little; but I did hit that pig across the back and broke its back. I was crying and Mother comes out and says, "Oh, my little pig. Something's happened to it." Lord, I stood there so guilty. I didn't tell her [what I'd done] till after I married. Lord no! She'd wore me out. Why, you talk about getting a nettling around the legs, it'd been around my arms.

Our daddy would not allow [us to work on Sunday]. He wouldn't have a nail drove without it was an emergency on Sunday. We went to church and come back home and pulled off our best clothes that we had, put on old clothes and get out and play, jump the rope, and gather up our neighbor's children and have a good time playing.

Dad took in every little strange boy and fatherless girl that was around in the country. He'd keep them as long as they'd stay, but lots of times when he'd make them go to the field and work when farming time would come they'd want to leave and go somewheres else. He'd say, "Now listen, if you leave here you can't come back after my children make this crop."

Now to me that was the happiest time of my life. But after I married [in 1923] I never had very much happiness. I've had a lot of trouble. Our first baby, I had German measles before he was born, and he was born deaf. They really wanted to get rid of the baby and I said, "No, that's a sin," and I wouldn't have that done for nothing in the world. They wanted to perform abortion and take the baby because they said it would be born without any eyes, or maybe without legs, or something like that. He was borned early in the morning, about eight o'clock on the twenty-sixth day of May, and they wouldn't let me see him till real late in the evening because he was double-cleft and one side of his face didn't develop. We didn't learn that he couldn't hear till we sent him to Louisville to a hospital. He weighed twelve pounds when he was born and they didn't want me to even feed him. [They] said he would die anyway and he was just as fat as he could be and his hair was just curly as it could be. And I cried and said, "Mother, it wants to nurse, but it can't nurse." Back then women let their babies nurse the breast, they didn't feed them the bottles. I said, "Send and get a bottle and we'll make the nipple with a hole in it big enough that he can mash on it and mash him out a few drops." And I raised the child. Right there he sets, forty-nine years old right now.

A Culture under Attack

(Appalachian Photographic Archives)

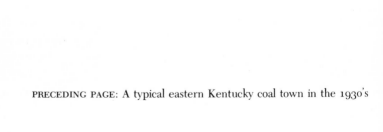

PRECEDING PAGE: A typical eastern Kentucky coal town in the 1930's

4

OUTSIDE INFLUENCES

On the surface there were few changes by the early 1900's except those that seasons bring. Men and women continued to clear new ground, plant seeds hoarded from autumn's harvest, endure droughts, and eye the tassels of new corn. Children attended one-room schoolhouses, memorial services marked the passing of years and people, and trees were felled. Outsiders appeared without fanfare and quietly began the work that would change a region.

As so often happens with decisive moments, the first extraction of coal from Central Appalachian soil is unrecorded. Coal was being mined on Sturgeon Creek in Kentucky's Lee County and hauled to Lexington for sale as early as 1790, but in all likelihood there had been mining even earlier. From 1800 to 1860 a flurry of mining activity was scattered throughout eastern Kentucky and untold tons of coal were shipped to the cities and sold by the bushel for a few cents each. During the Civil War years production waned, however, and did not resume until the 1880's. It was twenty years more before commercialization of eastern Kentucky coal began in earnest and it started with the efforts of men such as John Caldwell Calhoun Mayo, who, by 1910, had spent more than twenty years buying mineral rights and selling them to companies and other speculators throughout the United States. By

1910 many of the investors believed the time, if not the circumstances, was right for unleashing the minerals.

The task of commercializing the coal was overwhelming. Coal officials needed to find thousands of laborers among a small population of farmers, traders, trappers, and timbermen. They needed towns where only small county seats existed. Industry demanded macadam; instead there were dirt roads and worn-out ox paths. Electricity was essential and there was none.

For some speculators the obstacles were insurmountable, so they sold their land and mineral rights to other individuals or to landholding companies such as the Kentucky River Coal Corporation, which John Mayo helped organize. Other speculators who had strong financial backing began building their own towns.

Two factors were in their favor. Their faith in coal was buttressed by the success of speculators in the mines of West Virginia, Pennsylvania, and Ohio; and a lengthy network of railways was already complete. Railway construction had started in the 1870's and it was not entirely accidental that the arrival of rails coincided with serious interest in eastern Kentucky's coalfields. Earlier coal barons had been frustrated in their attempts to ship coal out of the mountains on barges and they recognized that railroads would be a faster, more economical method of transportation. At the time, some coal speculators expanded their corporate interests to include railways while others used their influence to encourage the construction of rails. By 1910 an extensive network of rails was complete and owners of coal seams eagerly eyed their potential. They also eyed the southern blacks and white mountaineers who laid the track and enticed them to stay and work in the mines by offering the dazzling wage of $1.50 a day. Initially many mountain people were unimpressed by the money and the thought of leaving their homes to work in caves, and officials recruited elsewhere, importing immigrants from northern ports and blacks from southern tenant farms. Some people came because of wretched labor conditions on the farms or in the fields and factories of Eastern Europe. Others were enticed to the coal mines by company recruiters who greeted them at the seaports with promises of a better life in Kentucky and Virginia and "free" one-way tickets to the coalfields. Upon their arrival the blacks and immigrants often found conditions to be better than they were accustomed to at home but far less desirable than the recruiters had described.

Educators and missionaries also played a significant role in transforming Central Appalachia from an agricultural to an industrial region. An industrial labor force demanded skilled labor, which in turn required local educational programs. Not finding them, early visitors to the region lamented the absence of schools and encouraged outside educators to uplift the region. Teachers who came served the coal operators by educating young people who would eventually become coal company employees and, in the most progressive coal towns, by teaching the foreign immigrants to speak English so they could communicate with their foremen and fellow miners.

Speculators, missionaries, and educators were all instrumental in bringing a more formal system of law and order to the mountains. Police forces and town marshals were necessary because it would have been impossible to achieve the transition from agriculture to industry by using the old system of justice that Chid Wright described in Chapter 1.

Tourism rather than coal played the dominant role in the history of western North Carolina. As far back as 1885 the Smoky Mountains, which are part of the southern Appalachian range, were nationally known for their health resorts and spas. During the 1910's there was a boom in regional pleasure resorts, fostered primarily by outside speculators. It was a boom that paralleled the growth of coal towns in the rest of Central Appalachia, but when the banks closed in the early 1930's tourists stayed home, elegant hotels and boardinghouses grew seedy, and the industry withered.

The coming of the coal industry and tourism touched and changed nearly every aspect of life in Central Appalachia. People from foreign countries moved into the region, towns appeared almost overnight, police forces were substituted for self-appointed law men, and new social distinctions based on race, religion, and income began to arise. The most far-reaching changes were rooted in the tension people feel when they move from self-reliance to dependence upon something as amorphous as a coal company. For years families had generated their food, clothing, and shelter from the land. When they moved to the camp towns many gave up their land and looked to the coal company for sustenance.

By 1890 the people of Appalachia had been stoking fires with coal from their backyards for years but few had any inkling what value the rest of the country would soon place on their minerals. It was often difficult, if not impossible, for outside speculators to develop the trust and the knowledge of the region's people that they needed to purchase the mineral rights. As a result, development of the coal industry became a joint enterprise. Outside industrialists and speculators generally provided capital and technical knowledge while mountain residents who foresaw the promise of coal traveled throughout the region purchasing rights to thousands of acres of minerals for less than a dollar an acre. For a few mountain men, such as John Mayo, the effort became a lifetime project. Others were less personally involved and worked for large firms such as Consolidation Coal Company. One way or another the mineral and timber resources of southwestern Virginia and eastern Kentucky came under the control of northern and midwestern industrialists in a relatively short period of time. The adverse affects were often not felt immediately because the coming of the coal industry brought jobs, cash, and hope for the future.

The individual most responsible for developing eastern Kentucky's coalfields was John Caldwell Calhoun Mayo. Mayo was born in Pike County, Kentucky, in 1864, the son of a schoolteacher, and after a brief tenure as a mathematics instructor began a career of buying and selling rights to mine the bituminous coal that lay under eastern Kentucky's soil. John Mayo

John C. C. Mayo, foreground, and speculators he was trying to interest in eastern Kentucky coal have their picture taken at the entrance to the Miller's Creek Block Seam in Letcher County, Kentucky

never owned a coal-mining company and he bought very little surface land. His forte was collecting many acres of mineral rights under the umbrella of a landholding company and then selling those rights to a firm that would do the actual coal mining, or to speculators outside the region. In less than thirty years the coal properties initially acquired by John Mayo became the basis for building the towns of Jenkins, Fleming, Wheelwright, McRoberts, Weeksbury, and Wayland–among others. To accomplish his goals Mayo paved roads, built power plants, courted railway magnates, played politics, and recharted the course of the nation's coal industry. In Central Appalachia his success is legendary; outside the mountains he is a forgotten man-behind-the-scenes.

Another key figure in the development of Kentucky's coal industry was Henry LaViers, a native of Merthyr Tydfil, Wales, who came to Paintsville, Kentucky, in 1906 from the coalfields of

Wellston, Ohio. Henry LaViers was a close associate of John Mayo and through him acquired most of the mineral rights he needed to organize Northeast Coal Company and Southeast Coal Company and to build five coal towns. According to his son, Harry, LaViers was a coal operator with a conscience. "Father had very strong convictions about the way he would like for his employees to live. It was a common practice in the mining camps to build double-houses where two families live in the same house. He never built any of those because he said he had lived in them and they were just not satisfactory. All of the family quarrels and conversations went right through one wall to the other. If there was much disturbance in a family he would either move [the man] to another mine or discharge him and get him out of town. He was very welfare-minded for his employees."

Today Harry LaViers lives in Paintsville, Kentucky, where he is chairman of the board of Southeast Coal Company. John Mayo, Jr., lives in Ashland, Kentucky, where he serves as chairman of the board of the town's Second National Bank. Both men were youngsters when John Mayo, Sr., died but his success was their legacy.

MAYO: [My father] went to school in Johnson County; then he went to Kentucky Wesleyan at Millersburg, Kentucky.* He had an instructor there who was apparently quite knowledgeable in minerals [and] it has been said that my father got some inspiration from him to keep on the lookout for coal as being a valuable product some day. As soon as he came back to Paintsville from Wesleyan he had to teach school in order to make a living. I think they paid $50 a year, or $100 a year. Out of that magnificent sum he was able to save $150 [and] he formed a very small partnership with [John W.] Castle and [I. R.] Turner. Captain Castle and Doctor Turner pooled an equal amount of money and they started acquiring acreage—just the mineral rights alone—in

* Kentucky Wesleyan College is now located in Owensboro, Kentucky.

Johnson County. I [would] guess that with the [original] $450 they purchased nine hundred acres of mineral at fifty cents an acre and . . .

LAVIERS: Sold it to somebody for more and it pyramided.

In the steamboat days they used to fire the boilers with wood and then they [discovered] coal. Mr. Mayo's father-in-law [Green Meek], being a steamboat captain, talked about how great coal was for generating steam and from that Mr. Mayo got to thinking, "If it's good for these steamboats it ought to be good for a lot of other purposes, too." Not being a trained geologist or a trained engineer, he just went out and would buy up large tracts of land, maybe sometimes as much as ten thousand acres at a time.

You must understand, he started from a very meager base and to build his empire up into the proportions that it later became it took money, just stacks of money. Every time he would sell a tract he pyramided it by [buying] another one. He didn't start out with some one big company that had a lot of money for him to invest. He started building his own step by step. That's one of the reasons that I have such a high regard for Mr. Mayo. He was a man of vision and he could see what the possibilities were. He was also a very, very persuasive talker. He could turn those bright eyes and you would believe everything he was telling you was just like it was.

MAYO: To coin a phrase, he bought low and sold high. He would get together ten thousand acres of coal that they bought for $5,000 and sell it for $15,000. Then he had another ten to start with, and God knows there was lots of acreage in eastern Kentucky in those days.

LAVIERS: The main reason for his success in putting these properties together and getting operations going was his personality. He had a persistence that, undoubtedly, paid him off in many ways because when he started in on a project he just worked at it day and night. He had a most intense concentration on whatever he was trying to do of anybody that I ever heard of. Mr. Mayo was *always* working.

I think the way he did it was he [went] to the top of [various] companies, introduced himself, told them what he was doing, and asked for their help and for their cooperation with him. He went to Baltimore and got Consolidated Coal Company, which was then and still is one of the largest coal companies, [interested]. Consolidated had been in the coal business in Maryland and Pennsylvania and northern West Virginia for a long time. Mr. Mayo recognized that those were the kind of people that he needed to promote the coal industry in eastern Kentucky and he went to [Clarence] Watson, president of Consolidated, and to those other big companies and simply showed them what he had was what they were looking for. He went to Minnesota [and interested] a firm by the name of Merritt. He went to many places and told these people about the possibilities and got them to buy. When he would sell them one [boundary of mineral rights] he would take that same money, go back and invest it, and put together more coal property.

MAYO: He was instrumental in getting the top men from the railroads to come and look [at the potential for interstate commerce]. He'd probably worn himself out talking to them in their home offices, [so] he brought them here and put together a caravan of buckboards and covered wagons and they made a tour all the way to Jenkins. They would camp and make ten or fifteen miles a day. They had Oscar, who was the chef at the Waldorf-Astoria in New York, as the fellow who took care of the food on the trip. I think, probably, that trip did as much as anything else to commit the railroads [to coming into eastern Kentucky].

He had scouts not only looking for coal, but also for customers and he sent samples, analyses, all over America. [At times] he didn't even have stamp money and he borrowed money to get the postage to send out the samples. He had some periods in there when he wasn't eating regularly. There was a Depression, a very bad Depression, in '93 and there was another one in 1907. Both knocked the socks off of him. When the bad news would strike it would be an almost out-of-business situation.

John C. C. Mayo, Jr.

You mentioned [Leonidas] Merritt who owned the Mesabi iron-ore range in Minnesota. He interested the Merritts in fifty thousand acres and they agreed to pay him $200,000, I think, for these rights. He took $100,000 in cash and he took the Merritts' notes for $100,000. Shortly after he got back to Paintsville with the Merritts' notes, they were bankrupted by John D. Rockefeller, Sr., who held a mortgage on the Mesabi range and they could not meet the mortgage payments. So this note that he had was absolutely worthless.

LAVIERS: Of course, as now, politics was mixed up with a lot of business transactions. There was no accurate surveys; [deeds] would just say, "up a [certain] ridge and down a stream." They overlapped in many instances so that people that were living on large farms, maybe a couple thousand acres, were not sure where their boundaries were. Mr. Mayo ran into all kinds of entanglements about land that had no taxes paid on it and you couldn't get a clear title because it was all messed up in heirs. So he went down to the Kentucky legislature and, with the assistance of some people that he had made friends with, [got] a law passed which may have been subject to some criticism at one time but was a very appropriate bill where the state of Kentucky escheated a lot of this land and [gave] title to the present owners. In that way, the people could make a valid deed for which Mr. Mayo would pay them.

In meeting with the legislators he naturally was at Charleston, West Virginia, and in Frankfort, Kentucky. Clarence Watson was president of the Consolidated Coal Company and the Elkhorn Coal Corporation and he was from Frostburg, Maryland. At that time the state legislators elected the United States senators; it was not by popular vote. Clarence Watson decided that he wanted to be the senator from West Virginia so he came over here and told Mr. Mayo what his ambitions were. Mr. Mayo had been dealing with him, and Consol had been here in a big way, so he went to Charleston and with the aid of some friends that he had in West Virginia he was able to get Clarence Watson elected senator from West Virginia. One of those fellows up there said, "It beats hell that a coal miner from Kentucky can come over here in West Virginia and elect a Maryland citizen as senator from West Virginia."*

You had to have some genius to get that accomplished. It was a good thing for everybody concerned: Senator Watson went on to use that office to promote the coal industry, not only in Kentucky, but West Virginia, and in Maryland. Through Senator Watson the B & O railroad built two lines up here to Van Lear [and] up Shelby Creek to haul coal from Jenkins to Elkhorn. That's how Mr. Mayo accomplished what he did: he got the right people to work at it.

MAYO: Politics was almost his lifeblood; it had to be. You

* Clarence Wayland Watson represented West Virginia in the United States Senate from 1911 to 1913. He was born in Fairmont, West Virginia, and lived in Frostburg, Maryland, for many years.

couldn't have made any tracks in those days of any size without being on the right horse politically. He was instrumental in bringing back old Governor McCreary* for a second shot at the governorship, which he won thirty-two years after his first. He was instrumental in having Camden† elected to the Senate, instrumental in having Watson elected to the Senate, all for the very purpose that he needed here: to clear titles and to enact legislation that would be favorable.

I know for sure that there was not a year that went by from 1907 [until his death] that my father was not asked by the Democratic party to either be a candidate for the governor, or senator, or congressman, and he refused in one great big fat "NO." He was not interested in politics for politics' sake, only as it would help him. His influence in politics, of course, was personality and money. I would suppose in his lifetime that my father probably contributed more dollars politically than he had at the time of his death.

I would suppose [my father] organized thirty different companies, maybe some of them with no more than two or three thousand acres of coal, some with as much as ten, twenty, thirty thousand acres, and the vast percentage of this was barren of coal. Some of those natives out there who was supposed to be "stupid" because they sold their mineral rights didn't *have* any mineral rights.

Why did he organize so many companies?

MAYO: When you got a sufficient amount of minerals together you would form a company around that and dispose of it in what-

---

* James Bennett McCreary was governor of Kentucky from 1875 to 1879 and from 1911 to 1915. It was during his second administration that the state legislature passed a law which invalidated the Virginia land grants and gave titles to the current owners.
† Johnson Newland Camden, Jr., was a native of Parkersburg, West Virginia, and represented Kentucky in the United States Senate in 1914 and 1915.

ever way you saw fit, or hold it, and then you'd go on to another one.

LAVIERS: The other thing was that when you sold a company like Consolidation fifty thousand acres of coal you don't go back next week and try to sell them fifty thousand more. If he got more acreage he'd try to find somebody [else] to mine that coal. There was another reason for it. Most of these companies wanted to have some assurance that their title was good. He just couldn't run the title down on all of this acreage at one time. Maybe he'd put his lawyers to working on one group of acreage and if he found out there was some vacancies on it, he'd send somebody to [buy the outstanding mineral rights]. Then he could put that all into one company and be sure that it had reasonable good title. So he had to put what he could into a company and then work on another one.

MAYO: One of the most interesting contacts that he had was with a fellow named Booker Mullins in Pike County. He was a tough egg. He was twice the man as "Devil" Ance Hatfield. Bill Ward, who was the driver for my father, drove the buckboard up to the foot of the hill under Booker Mullins' house and my father walked up the hill. Booker was sitting on his front porch and Booker was suspicious of everybody. I'm certain there was a still in the backyard, maybe two, but he was ready to take issue with my father for trespassing. [My father's] first remark was, "I'll give you x number of dollars to let me talk to you for five minutes." He came down the hill with ten thousand acres which was involved in that particular transaction.

LAVIERS: Can you imagine that approach, just going up to somebody and saying, "I'll give you so many dollars to just let me talk to you"? You know when he'd get in New York or Philadelphia he had no trouble getting in to see somebody with that kind of an approach.

MAYO: One time when he got back from a trip to New York, which had been very successful, somebody here in Paintsville said to him, "Aren't you afraid that those city slickers are going to take you [in] and then kick you out?" He said, "They may do it, but my back pockets are going to be lined with their money and it won't hurt very much."

LAVIERS: The man was a genius, there's no doubt about it.

What would be your reaction to people who say John Mayo took advantage of mountain people by paying only fifty cents or a dollar an acre for their mineral rights?

LAVIERS: Mr. Mayo never exploited any of those people. That's just not so.

MAYO: It would be very interesting if those people knew what a very small percentage of those acres had any coal at all under them. If you take a fellow like Booker Mullins who had ten thousand acres of land, [he] probably didn't know where his next meal was coming from. If he could pick up $5,000 in those days, this was a fortune.*

John Mayo made a great deal of money. Why didn't other mountain people note his success and begin doing the same thing?

LAVIERS: [People here] didn't *see* him make money. There was no evidence of it until the railroads and companies come in here, and that was too late! His success was not evident so that anybody could be inspired by it. Mr. Mayo was not a pretentious fellow. He's not one that would flaunt or would show his affluence. He was very plainly dressed, plainly spoken.

MAYO: Harry, you may remember the statement Joe Creason

* The Elkhorn seam of coal, which is an extraordinary ninety inches deep in some sections, lies underneath the land around Jenkins, Kentucky. Consolidation was anxious to mine the seam and Mayo acquired most of the property for the firm before approaching Booker Mullins, who owned the key lands. John E. Buckingham, an associate of Mayo's, recounted in an unpublished biography that Mayo wooed Booker Mullins by offering him $1,000 in new $5 bills for the privilege of merely talking to him about the land. Within ten minutes Mayo had the property deed and Mullins had $10,000. Soon Mullins left the mountains, moved to the Kentucky Blue Grass section, bought a farm, and became inconsolably homesick. He returned to the hills, bought another farm, and spent the remaining days of his life pining the loss of his old homeplace.

made many years ago in *The Courier-Journal:* he told a story about my father and said that he lit a cigar with a twenty-dollar bill. Now this was the most stupid statement that a man could make.

LAVIERS: That was a blatant lie! John Mayo would never light a cigar with a twenty-dollar bill. He'd throw you out of the room if you did.

MAYO: The thing about it was, when anybody saw any physical evidence of the activity in the coal business, it was too late. He had it already corraled and there were very few opportunities to go anywhere else. Besides that, big corporations are lazy. If you can come up with a proposition that they like the looks of, they'd rather for you to go and get it together for them than try to do it themselves.

As far as the Big Sandy country is concerned, there were not an awful lot of people of substance and certainly [none] with any vision that'd undertake the same thing. As a matter of fact, a lot of people had him tagged as a visionary, and some people went as far as to say he was a lunatic, because he was trying to put together something that didn't mean anything. What the hell! All they'd ever done was dig some coal out of the side of the hill and cook their Sunday dinner. That's as far as their foresight took them.

LAVIERS: Of course, there's another reason for it, too. The communications in those days were very poor. There were no roads. The access to this part of the country was extremely difficult. Mr. Mayo was a native here, he rode horses and buckboards all over this back country on very primitive roads. Nobody else was willing to do this, or had the burning desire to do that. In addition, Pennsylvania and Ohio coalfields were at their best then. They were furnishing about all the coal that was necessary for the steel industry and for the utility industry and they didn't want any competition. [Also] most of those companies up there were unionized then, and the South was non-union and paid lower wages.

The coal companies in the North bitterly fought the development of the coal companies in the South and had it not been for the desire of eastern Pennsylvania anthracite [operators] to get into another type of coal, a good portion of southern West Virginia and eastern Kentucky would not have been open for twenty, twenty-five years. The use of anthracite is limited to home-heating stoves, so they wanted to get into a field where they could make coke, which was bringing a pretty high price then. The Pittsburgh Coal Company and the New York Coal Company and Lorraine Coal, they tried their best to keep the Big Sandy from being opened up. Mr. Mayo had to overcome all that.

The answer to Mr. Mayo's success in putting these companies together was that he thought, and worked, and dreamed, in a big way.

MAYO: I would say that he was not only ambitious for himself and his family, but for his associates and for his part of Kentucky; probably "for his part of Kentucky" might be rated at the top of the list rather than at the bottom. I think he showed that all through his life in what he did for his community, and for his state, and for his family. It was his ambition to help provide as best he could for bringing eastern Kentucky out of the wilderness situation and more on a par with central Kentucky.

LAVIERS: Mr. Mayo, as far as I know, had no burning desire to accumulate a fortune. None at all. I'm sure that Mr. Mayo was just as concerned about eastern Kentucky as his son is, or I am, or any of these people that are trying to do something here [are], probably more so, but he did not have time to take a fatherly inspection of anything. I think those monuments that he built are evidence of his desire for the people. You must remember, he didn't have an opportunity to do too much. I think the greatest tragedy of the whole thing is his untimely early death [in 1914].

MAYO: [I have little recollection of my father] for the simple reason that he was away, I would say, a total of eleven months of the year. Some of the trips that my father took, they would be gone months and [be] completely out of touch with the world. No media of any kind reached into the wilds here. [One time] when he got back he found out there had been a very severe panic in the year 1907 that had caused him an awful lot of trouble, but he didn't know about it until he got back to Paintsville.

[My mother] was very, very helpful to my father and she actually went into the mountains of eastern Kentucky with him. On many occasions she wore a dress specially designed, I would guess, by Pogue's in Cincinnati that had linings all the way around inside the skirt with little pockets built in that you could drop in twenty-dollar gold pieces. The natives at that time were still pretty wary of greenbacks. Gold was a language that they understood. She rode with my father into the mountains and was the bearer of the goodies.

He started building the [family's home] in 1904 and he realized that he was going to be forever getting finished so he built another house to live in while the big house was being finished. Seven years later the big house was completed. The interim house was regularly referred to as the "Buckingham House." The main hallway of the last house had a tremendous fireplace in it and it was his assembly room [for] friends and business associates. The main stairway going upstairs came off of this room and there was a back stairway. If you didn't have sense enough to go up the back stairs when there was a group of men in there discussing and looking at maps, why I think he wouldn't have hesitated to [tell] us to not mess him up, but he never had the occasion to because the women in the house knew how to run a house in those days.

My grandmother was the disciplinarian of the family and she did, I thought, an excellent job. She did not hesitate to lay it on if she felt that my sister or I had it coming to us. She was sort of a major-domo.

How often would you see your father in an average month?

Maybe none, maybe none in six months and [then he] would be just like a complete stranger coming in. He was just not there, he was out doing his thing wherever he had to be: in the fields, or promoting the properties in the East or the Chicago area, or Pittsburgh, or what have you. As far as I know he never spent five minutes of his time, never "wasted" five minutes of his time as he would have put it, in relaxing.

The only conversation I can remember [having with him] is of no importance whatever. One day he asked me to go to the store, Oppenheimer and Flax, to get him a collar button. When I got back he said, "How much was it?" I said, "I don't know, I just told them to put it on your account." He seemed to be a little bit disturbed that I had not taken the trouble to find out what the collar button cost. It [was], I judge, ten cents, maybe fifteen cents. It was certainly not gold.

LAVIERS: I think John has been a little modest about his father. He was one of the most interesting people that I ever knew and I was only fourteen years old when he died. I was around the house with John a good deal of the time and I have very vivid recollections about Mr. Mayo. He had the brightest piercing eyes. It seemed to me that he was looking right through me all of the time. The other [recollection] is that he very seldom laced his shoes [and] he had a big cigar that was constantly with him. He also didn't go to bed until two or three o'clock in the morning and I wondered how he would get enough sleep. My most vivid recollection was he was gone most of the time. He was in New York, or Chicago, or Cincinnati, or Louisville, or Charleston, or somewhere.

I think he was one of those in a million that come along who have a great vision. He laid out the town of Paintsville. He put the original sewer system in about 1904 or 1905. He had the streets paved. He did a good portion of this out of his own pocket, but he was able to persuade the local authorities here that this ought to be done. He built this big mansion which is really a sight to see today. He went to New York and got a crew of

Italian stonemasons, brought them here, and provided living quarters for them and their wives and children while he was doing the foundation of the house, the commons, the stone church. The man was very farsighted, much more than anybody else that I've ever come in contact [with].

MAYO: The last trip that he made was to South America. In 1912 he made a trip to the Argentine and it was not a pleasure trip because anybody who had sense enough to come out of the rain would not go to South America in 1912 for a holiday. It just wasn't that kind of a place. When he came back he was very enthusiastic about what he saw there: the mineral resources of the country, the timber, cattle, everything. He [made] the statement that he was going to seriously consider moving the family lock, stock, and barrel to the Argentine because he thought the future there was fantastic. I imagine by that, he had about decided that he had done most everything he could do as far as eastern Kentucky was concerned.

LAVIERS: He may have neglected some things he oughtn't, but my father-in-law always said he was in church every Sunday he was in town and he told me what seat he sat in. Always the same place.

How did John Mayo die?

MAYO: The diagnosis was acute Bright's disease. He took ill along in January of 1914 and was taken to the Jewish Hospital in Cincinnati and underwent treatment there for several weeks. There was no improvement in his condition and he was then taken to New York and was living with the whole family in the old Waldorf-Astoria Hotel [when he died].

LAVIERS: What killed Mr. Mayo, he burnt himself out. You can't go day and night at the pace he went, rack your brain and push your body to do the things that he did without burning it up. A normal person just don't function that way.

MAYO: At the time of his death his estate inventoried at $600,000. He is listed in a hundred different documents as a multimillionaire. That just was not so. This was the sum total of his business at that time. Of course, $600,000 in those years was a lot of money.

Warren Wright was born in 1920 near Burdine, Kentucky, in the heart of the Central Appalachian coalfields. As a youth he gave little thought to the land, people, and heritage which were his but all that changed in 1961 when coal company employees said they intended to strip-mine his land. Warren sided with the land and eventually saved most of his property from the strippers. Since then he has completed an intensive study of the coal industry's history that focuses on the role of early speculators such as John C. C. Mayo, Sr.

Warren talks about the coal industry and explains how it naturally followed Appalachia's late-nineteenth-century logging boom. He discusses some of the people who developed the industry and describes the questionable methods speculators often used to acquire land and mineral rights.

In the headwaters of the Big Sandy River the exploitation of the timber was well under way perhaps two decades ahead of the mineral exploitation. The first active buying of land in Pike and Letcher counties was in 1887, roughly two decades from the end of the Civil War. The [logging] facilities [were], of course, cruder and more obtainable and companies could start exploiting that marvelous stand of timber earlier than they could get commercial mining under way. You understand they were only cutting what would now be the priceless stuff—the choice white oak, the black walnut, and the yellow poplar. By use of mountain oxen and mountain men they could cut, and begin to float, a vast amount of prime timber out of this mountain down the Big Sandy to the Ohio at Catlettsburg.

The coal industry demanded many more people, many more buyers, more expertise, more legal [personnel]. Even then they were already understanding that the coal was everywhere; that anywhere you bought land you'd be getting coal and probably other minerals [as well]. I'm persuaded that these people had the education and background and experience to know that it would take hundreds of years to exploit this field and its vitality.

A significant proportion of the speculators and potential exploiters were our own people. You do have to recognize that some of the mountain people got in on the first floor and have been just as active in exploiting us ever since as the larger majority which came from the outside. As big as [John Mayo] is in the area right here, he still isn't big enough to change the generality; that there [was] a horde of outside, good American speculators that fell upon this area. [Mayo] saw this vision of capital and of what capital could do in the mountains, and he began to buy on a small scale, and then larger, and larger, and larger, and I mean holdings large enough to reach into three or more counties! Finally, he got to the point where there were about five dummy corporations which he owned. They were "dummy" in the sense that they did not have an existence of their own outside of someone who establishes them. You can contrast them to holding companies inasmuch [as] the holding companies were usually incorporated outside the area and were set up to hold the riches that they meant to get, and to steal, here. I'm sure that Mayo understood that these corporations would cease to exist, as they did, just as soon as his end power was aggregated and pulled together. The largest of these was Northern Coal and Coke Company, to whom flowed almost all that Mayo did accumulate, and then as Northern Coal and Coke Company was not intended to be an operating company they transferred [their holdings] to Consolidation Coal Company when Consolidation came into this area about 1911.

Mayo really dedicated the larger portion of his productive life to pulling this empire together. He is Mr. Consolidation Coal Company because he literally prepared the way for Consolidation Coal Company in this area. He was said to be worth perhaps $10 million when probably $10 million was the equivalent of $100 million at this time. He died, of course, outside the region. He had no interest in the region at all except for what he could get out of it, although he was born in Pike County [Kentucky]. We really honor our exploiters here, we mountain people do. Almost every town in this area is named for some bastard from outside the region who gutted it.

Basically, I will tell you how [speculators] got the titles. They would walk up on one of these ridges. They'd look down into the watershed and see a little curl of smoke coming up from some cabin. The people living in this cabin might own by patent twenty-five, or fifty, or even a hundred acres around them. [They] might have a possession claim by having lived there five years, or [they] might be a renter, [or] a squatter. Once that speculator had seen that curl of smoke, he'd go down and buy that watershed from that man and woman who usually were not able to sign their names. He would buy all that they claimed they possessed and also all that he wanted them to sign a title for, and get their signature, or in about 80 percent of the cases, their marks.

[The mountain man] didn't even know *what* he was selling, especially if it were a surveyed deed that said "sixteen and a half poles north by northeast," and such-and-such. Of course, it was a truism that he also didn't care what he was selling. You must understand this if you want to understand eastern Kentucky. This is not by any means [an] isolated case. The isolated cases are those where some damn company actually bought a true and honest title; where some men had a patent for fifty acres, valid, perfected from the state.

What was the reaction of mountain people to these outside speculators?

It generally was not negative. Visitors and strangers here, even when the mountain wars were going on, were generally accorded good treatment. Once that it was established among families, or in an area, that you were not there to do them harm, they gave you the best treatment they had. So there was not a background of distrust to confront these newcomers. Once their purposes were known the mountain people were either too ignorant to care what the outcome might be, or else they thought that business and enterprise was the best thing that could possibly [come] to an area or to an individual. They went along. For one thing, there was no money economy and so even a small amount of money represented quite a bit to them.

We are beginning to suspect that in some cases there was coercion, where [speculators sometimes] frightened people about their own status. Of course, no speculator was going to openly threaten a mountain individual very often. They were shrewder and better psychologists, and they also had a better respect for their hides than that. Around Jenkins,* Kentucky, [the coal companies] had a prominent mountain man who was feared and respected in this area and we believe that when any difficulties ever arose in regard to getting signatures, and getting deeds, they had recourse to this mountain man.† I'm sure that this gen-

---

* Burdine, where Warren Wright lives, is on the outskirts of Jenkins.

† Warren was referring to John Wright, who was described by his son Chid on pages 58–62. Chid described his father's involvement with coal companies this way:

"When these fellows started looking around for somebody that could buy up this land and deal with these people that owned it, they turned to what they thought to be the most influential man and that's where [Pap] came into it. Everybody knew him in a thirty-mile radius and I guess John Mayo wasn't any exception. [Mayo] got G. B. Vaughan and John Wright and B. F. Johnson and William Henry Potter [to] work in buying up that land. They all were, I guess, the brains back of the beginning of the [coal] deal. They made their headquarters at Pap's house because that's where everybody made headquarters when they came to [this] section, whether they were lawyers, or doctors, or land buyers, or surveyors.

"Some people would sell the land *and* the mineral rights. I think they were willing to sell it and glad to get rid of it. They didn't have any idea about what they were selling. Not a bit. All the people knew how to do was take a pick and a little black powder and shoot out enough coal to last them through the winter.

"Pap stayed connected with [Consolidation] from about 1900 to 19 and 25. He sold all his land to the Northern Coal and Coke Company and then he was kind of a steward or guardian over it. He had several hundred, maybe a thousand or two acres of land that he looked after."

Warren Wright

tleman felt that he was doing great things for his country in promoting and in preparing the way for Consolidation Coal Company. Incidentally, he was so effective in this empire building [that] to the end of his life we understand Consolidation pensioned him.

Let's give the mountain people credit for one thing: they had no way [of conceiving] the technological and social and physical effects upon the region that had to follow what they were doing. Many of them felt that the particular stratum [of coal] that they may have seen or utilized on their farm was the only one that there was. They couldn't even imagine a power shovel, to say nothing of one working in their backyards, and they had no way of knowing whatsoever. So when we read about how happy they were with this new way of life, if we don't remember that they didn't know what it was, we can't properly study it. I think they did see, probably, that there would be a bigger money economy, that they would be able to purchase things which they had not purchased. I think they saw one of their benefits in the coming years to be work itself. I suppose, just like all Americans, they took a good view of that commercial aspect.

What were some of the other changes brought on by the influx of outsiders?

The companies were very helpful in regard to religion. The coal companies were glad to see the churches established. They contributed to buildings. Half of the old churches still standing in the Jenkins area were built by company labor and with company materials. The company has always been rather glad and willing for preachers to be employed. They'll see that a preacher gets work because they know that ordinarily mountain preachers are going to be so totally absorbed in doctrine, they're not going to deal with social conditions and, as a matter of fact, they're going to inculcate the thing that "this is not a place for the church to be involved."

The towns and the county seats began to grow. They built hundreds of houses all at once, so you have those big towns springing up with the problems and with the needs that towns have. More interesting, I think, is the development of the county seats where one finds the mass of attorneys. They controlled largely at first all of the county elective offices. They did it automatically through control of the money. Whoever holds the money has the power and the legal system, that's obvious, but they did exercise also a direct control on all of the county courthouses and always have ever since.

I suppose controlling the great number of ignorant votes was a big factor in the early control of county politics. You see how important it was for them to control the office of tax assessor, and I'm sure to some extent they did that for many years. They needed sympathetic people—or their own people. In Letcher County, particularly, the image [of the coal companies] has always been paternalism; it's quite different from other towns. No machine guns, not so much of the thuggery which was really prominent in other places. I do understand, however, that among the black people and ethnic people who first came here that there was quite a bit of civil oppression. The blacks were required to work. They had such things as "shack rousters"— officers of the law [who] would come around Monday morning and find out if you were not able to work. If you were nursing a hangover you got the hell out and went to work just the same. With our southern blacks in their uneducated state, and the state of peonage in which they came here, conditions were pretty rough in most of the mining camps; weekends were [especially] rough. So officers actually did control the working habits of a lot of these newcomers. At that time, of course, they could put you out of their houses on short notice, or no notice at all.

As I grew up of course we counted Negroes inferior. The mountain people looked at them that way and there's no doubt in my mind that the ethnics also, though probably out of European oppression and hard living themselves, soon looked at them in the same manner.

Why did the coal companies go out of the region and recruit blacks and immigrants to work in the mines?

I suppose it was expedient, or at least it was convenient for them to bring in those people whom we would ordinarily think of as subservient. The real factor was the scarcity of population: there simply were not enough mountain men. Had they re- cruited every available working man in the mountains, the work force would have been far undersupplied. Everything was done by hand and they just had to have more people. For instance, had Letcher County been the only mining county, they would have drawn on the nearby counties, and the Virginia people, and have gotten the work force. Being as the exploitation began at the same time [in] almost every watershed there was simply not enough people.

All the miners were poor people, of course. Mountaineers

were rather contemptuous of foreign people and it took years for that to be almost totally eradicated. I'm reluctant to say these things, but at that time they were [called] "Hunkies," "Wops."

"The foreign people was not discriminated against at all," said Steve Tomko, *"only sometimes the American people would get mad at some of them and they would call them 'Hunks': 'Old Hunk, why don't you go back to the foreign country where you came from?' They called me Hunk, but I didn't pay no attention because they really didn't know what a Hunk meant."*

The men in Steve Tomko's family began coming to the coal-fields of southwestern Virginia in the late 1890's. At home in Austria-Hungary they had been tenant farmers, working from sunup to sundown for the "big-shot" landowners with little hope of ever saving enough money to own land themselves. Shortly after Steve was born in 1900 his father migrated to the United States in search of a better life in the coal lands. Two years later Steve and his mother joined him.

(*Appalachian Photographic Archives*)

Steve Tomko in 1937

Steve talks about their lives as immigrants in the coal town of Glamorgan, near Wise, Virginia. He alludes to conditions that made a miner's life not as far removed from the fields of Austria-Hungary as he would like to believe.

I heard my mother telling about working in the fields, that she and my father worked for the "big-shot" farmers. They were poor people, that's all, they was just as poor as they could be. They had to do whatever their employer told them to do whether they liked it or not. If the wages wasn't sufficient enough, they'd just tell them they could go somewheres else and there wasn't much where else to go to back during them days. Naturally, when they heard of America they wanted to get away from there to come to a country where they could do as they pleased.

[My father's three brothers] had come here first. When they got here they wrote letters and told what kind of place [it was], and how much money . . . Money was something, you see. They didn't know what money was back during them days.

Steve Tomko in a recent photograph

Mostly what they worked for was to get their food and clothing. When his brothers wrote and told him how much money they was making and what kind of work it was, why it wasn't till he accumulated enough money [that he came].

The foreign people in that first two or three years stuck together pretty close. They didn't know the American language and therefore they didn't mingle around much with the American people until they got so they could understand each other better. For years and years they held to their own customs, they didn't go with American ways. The biggest majority of them were Catholic people [and] they didn't go to the American church. There were so many of them here the company finally had them a church built on Hunk Hill. The priest would come over here from Stonega, Virginia, once a month and hold mass for the foreign people.

During them days foreigners, they were all good workers. They was after making money and they would work hard. When they got started in the mines [the foremen would] say, "We want you to load ten cars today." They'd go ahead and load the ten cars, regardless of how long it took them. The other men, they couldn't depend on them. They could tell them load eight, they might load four.

They took care of the foreigners during them days. They had one place up there where all the foreigners lived and anything they wanted they'd get them. Say, if they needed something for their home, they'd help them out and get it for them. About once a month they'd let them have big parties, drinking parties. They'd have a big time, [but on] Monday morning there wasn't one of them that wasn't right on the job.

What made the foreign people such good workers?

Because they had to work hard in the foreign countries. They was nearly like slaves and they wasn't making nothing. When they come here and found out the conditions and everything, that give them a good heart to work.

During the First World War [companies] needed a lot of coal and a lot of coke [and] they didn't have enough men here. They was drafting men for the Army and they got a shortage of men, so [coal companies] got transportation agents to go to these places in Alabama and get these black people. They would give them enough to bring them here and set them up, and give them a job and start working. Them that fell for it, they come. I don't know how many carloads they brought here. [Transportation agents] would tell them what the mining conditions were, but they didn't understand plainly what it was till they come. They thought it was easy work and they could make money easy, [but] when it come to showdown, that they had to brute for it, they didn't like it. When they'd take off [the agents would] go back and get another transportation in to try to supply their needs for their coal.

[The coal company] had a section they called Hunk Hill, which was for all the foreigners. I imagine there would be about twenty houses there. They wanted all the foreigners together, they didn't want them mixed up with the Americans. The colored people, they didn't want them mixed up, they had a separate camp, Smokey, for them. They had the best location of all because it was right at the commissary door. There were about fourteen homes for colored people, besides they had a colored people's church, they had a colored people's schoolhouse, and a colored people's boardinghouse. [White people lived in] Greasy, and Sawmill Holler, Powerhouse Holler, and Red Row, and Happy Hill. They named it Happy Hill because the people there would have big times, and blowouts, and things.

Back during them days conditions in the mines was unbearable. You see, when [the foreigners] come here they were all greenhorns, they didn't know anything about mining. Mining at that time was hard work, real hard. How many of the foreigners that come here were killed I don't know.

[The worst] conditions of the mines were, at that time, air.

Breathing. They didn't have enough ventilating systems to keep the fresh air circulating through the mines and that's what really got all the miners: breathing that old coal dust, and poison mixture of air and no oxygen. I remember times when I worked in there that the conditions got so bad that my carbide light—it takes oxygen to burn—wouldn't burn. Still, we had to work under them conditions. You'd tell the foreman, "I just can't stand it up there anymore. There's no air in my place." A lot of times they'd tell you, "Well, there's a barefooted man outside waiting for your job if you want to quit." Times was so bad that if you quit other places was as bad.

The quest for scenic beauty, not coal, brought outsiders to western North Carolina during the early 1900's. Shortly after the Civil War, pleasure seekers had discovered the beauty of the Smoky Mountains and numerous hotels and tourist homes were opened, primarily in the Asheville area. Later mineral waters were discovered in the area and health spas became an added attraction, especially to persons suffering from tuberculosis. Soon the baths became a haven for patients and scores of sanatoriums were built.

One of the most significant efforts to attract tourists to Asheville—and certainly the most spectacular—was made by Fred Loring Seely and his father-in-law, Edwin Wiley Grove, who built the Grove Park inn, which flourished for many years as one of the nation's most lavish resort hotels. Seely was born into a Port Monmouth, New Jersey, working-class family in 1871. By the time he came to Asheville in 1910 he had invented a machine to manufacture medicine tablets and developed another machine that molded, counted, and boxed the pills; became a leader in the quinine development field; and founded the Atlanta Georgian, *a newspaper that competed successfully with the Atlanta* Constitution *and the* Journal *for six years until Seely tired of crusading journalism and sold the paper in 1912.*

Shortly after Seely died in 1942 the inn was sold and since then it has become a convention hotel. Memories of the Grove Park inn's heyday remain much alive in the memory of Seely's youngest son, Fred Loring Seely, Jr. Fred is a retired navy lieutenant who designs elaborate needlepoint patterns. He lived in Asheville near the Grove Park inn until 1975 when he moved to Tryon, North Carolina.

My grandfather came here in 1905 and Asheville at that time completely relied on the tubercular-sanatorium complex. In fact, that's why George Vanderbilt came here; he was tubercular. It was almost like a leper colony in those days. I know Mother would think many times about even allowing us to go into a movie because, of course, they thought tuberculosis was far more contagious than it is. The wave of it was really gone [when I was young], but the fear remained. The only thing they knew to do was to rest, be in the altitude, breathe clean air, and drink clean water. Many fortunes were made in these sanatoriums and a lot of them were very luxurious.

My grandfather, "Doctor" E. W. Grove, this was my mother's father, had been a pharmacist in the Confederate Army and after the war he went back to Paris, Tennessee,* and by accident he suspended powdered quinine in a fluid so it could be taken with a spoon, which had never been done before. They used to have to take it in powders and it would choke children. This was about 1890, and my father was with Parke-Davis, so they sent him to Tennessee to see what my grandfather had done and he recognized what he'd done. Inasmuch as quinine [was used] just like penicillin today, this grandfather with a third-grade education in a matter of four or five years was worth millions of dollars. He was a genius, completely uneducated, but an absolute financial genius. Anyway, he came here and fell in love with the country, the mountains, and he realized that the tubercular installations were going to prevent tourists from coming to Asheville.

* Paris is about halfway between Nashville and Memphis.

[In the early 1890's] my father had gone to Peru and took the first cinchona bushes, the bark from which they get the quinine. Peru was very unstable politically, so my father went out with my mother in '93 and he established the first quinine plantations in Java and they lived there many years. In 1905 [my grandfather] sent for him to come back.

My father had very little education but he got into architectural school at Princeton and studied architecture for [a while] and came back here with my grandfather and they started buying up Asheville. Mr. Vanderbilt was here already and they made an agreement that [Vanderbilt] would not buy anything north of the railroad tracks and they would not buy anything south of the railroad tracks, so they wouldn't be in competition with each other and run the prices up by bidding. Then everything in the north of the city, which is now mostly fine residential areas, was just all farm land. They went to work and bought this stuff up at fifty cents and a dollar an acre.

Then my father drew the plans for the Grove Park inn, and it's still said to be one of the most unique pieces of architecture in the world. It's built on the side of a mountain, with a golf course dropping down below, of native stone boulders that were quarried about ten miles from the site. The average weight of the boulders is about a half a ton and it's so built that you can't see any mortar between them. In the lobby there are fireplaces at each end that are twenty-four feet wide. One boulder forms a mantel over the tops of the fireplaces, and those averaged sixteen tons. It was just magnificent.

The only thing they had to work with were chain hoists; they didn't have any modern equipment. He brought about four hundred colored men here from Atlanta and Charleston and they set up a regular army camp—mess tents and everything—and he rented hundreds of these klieg lights that they used to use in theaters, and set them up. They worked twenty-four hours a day on it. They brought a whole family of tile masons from Italy [and] they were here so long I thought they were part of our family I was so used to them. Every floor, even the boiler room, was handmade, porcelain tile. They had their opening banquet in December 1913, eleven months after they broke ground.

As this progressed my grandfather and father bought every tubercular sanatorium in town and burned them down, because they knew that no one would come here as a tourist, or industry wouldn't come. So they substituted one industry, if you can call the tubercular thing an industry, for [another]. Tubercular interests moved to Arizona.

They had a complete plan. The first thing that they would create would be the finest resort hotel in the world—and that's what the Grove Park inn was known as—to attract the extremely wealthy. Even in those days he was getting $25 and $30 a day for a room, which was like $150 now. People would come from Atlanta, and Charleston, New Orleans, Mobile, and Birmingham, and they would spend the whole four months of the summer. They'd send their saddle horses up on the train, the grooms, bring their own maids and chauffeurs, and ship their cars on the trains. They would settle down for four months and every morning there would be forty or fifty beautiful horses lined up to the hitching rail by the front door, and they would ride horseback, [or go] to the tennis courts, golf course, bowling alleys, and billiard rooms.

It was run exactly the way he wanted it run. The main valves were in the boiler room and at ten-thirty the flushing system and the toilets were shut off so nobody could be disturbed by a toilet flushing. At ten-thirty they closed the gates of the driveway, so if you were out in your car you had to leave your car and walk down so you wouldn't disturb anybody. Ladies were not allowed to smoke except in parlors. Every night it was white ties for dinner and evening dresses. We had a permanent full-time organist and Galli-Curci would come to sing for a week, and Caruso came six or seven times to entertain the guests for a week, and Madam Schumann-Heink, who was quite an opera star. They had huge movie projectors and there would be a movie one night in the lobby. And the food was just unbelievable. Of course, people ate, in those days, seven-course dinners and would take two hours to eat.

The waiters in large part were Cherokees my father had trained. They have the Qualla band of the Eastern Cherokee Nation forty miles from here. These were the fierce ones who hid when Andrew Jackson moved the Cherokees to Oklahoma and were eventually allowed to remain. Of course, now it's become extremely commercialized, but in those days it was just that, a Cherokee nation, and he thought it was a good thing to do for them. They made excellent employees.

[The inn] was the center of attraction of America. Just about every President from that point forth stayed there. Mr. and Mrs. Coolidge used to come and the Hoovers came repeatedly. They had a tubercular son and my father established him in a cottage on the mountain with one of our local doctors who cured him. Mr. Roosevelt used to come down. My father, when he was at Princeton, lived next door to Woodrow Wilson, who was a professor at Princeton, and they became great friends and he managed Mr. Wilson's campaign for President. So, when the war came the inn was taken over by the government for the French Army and was used as a recuperation center for the wounded French officers. It was called Camp Green and I can vaguely remember the blue uniforms. The reason I mentioned this was that he and Mr. Wilson became firmer and firmer friends. As you remember, soon after the armistice, which wasn't known to the public or to the government at that time, Mr. Wilson had a stroke and for months Mrs. Wilson signed his name to all the government documents brought to the White House [and] said that he couldn't be seen but that he was lucid, which he wasn't. This has all been brought out since. Actually, where he was, he was hidden at the Grove Park inn, he and his daughter Margaret in one of the cottages. As soon as he recovered a little bit, which was about three or four months, they smuggled him back [to Washington]. The Congress and the Senate and everybody in Washington thought he was in bed in the White House.

[Henry] Ford had been my father's roommate when he was in Detroit. Every summer Mr. Ford, Mr. Edison, and Mr. Burroughs, who invented the adding machine, and Mr. Firestone, of Firestone tires, would meet in Detroit and Mr. Ford would supply them with about fifteen Model T Ford touring cars. They had colored drivers and cooks, and these cars were packed with all kinds of camping material and tents. There were practically no roads and it took them two weeks to get from Detroit to Asheville and they would camp every night along the road. A lot of times they would have to drive across fields for a day, they couldn't find a road. They would come to the inn and stay about a month every summer. Those who played golf, played golf, and Mr. Ford used to hike all the time, and then they'd take their two weeks' trip camping back to Detroit. They did that for years and years.

From there my father and grandfather laid out a plan and they started buying up downtown Asheville. There was an old hotel called Battery Park, which was built right after the Civil War on top of a mountain right in the middle of town. I'd say the mountain was about nine hundred feet high. Originally a Confederate artillery battery had been placed on this mountain. They bought the mountain and the hotel, and burned the hotel. It took them three years to level [part of] the mountain. The only thing they had was black powder and mules with drag pans and hundreds of men. I think at one time they had four hundred mules working.

Why did they want to level the mountain?

To bring it down and establish it as the center of the town. They brought the mountain [partway] down and they built a ten-story hotel, which was about as high as the peak of the land they had removed had been. Battery Park in those days was really not a resort hotel, [it] was to serve the commercial needs because they had plans for industry and we had no first-class commercial-type hotel.

It was an uncanny thing, this was in 1924, but they had the whole concept of a shopping mall and they built this building right in front of Battery Park. It was called the Arcade, and it had all the gift shops in one building with a mall interior. Then they had all the good doctors and dentists on the second floor. There were great ramps going up to the roof and they were going to build an apartment hotel on that and then put a bridge across to the Battery Park so that people could go across to the restaurants. They put a two-hundred-car garage in the basement and people thought that was the most ridiculous thing: "Why would anybody in the world use building space for cars with all this parking space?" Now, of course, there isn't any parking space.*

[My father and grandfather] went to Washington and spent about six months and got the government to put the new post office right across the street from the Arcade because they knew the post office would always draw the town. It was a planned city concept, which had never been heard of before. Then they started tearing down the old store buildings and building uniform buildings. They got one finished, which is now Ivey's department store. [That night] my grandfather came up here and went into the kitchen late at night and opened the icebox and got a can of oysters out, which was kind of a dangerous thing in those days. People died because the solder was reacting with the seafood and it was full of botulinus. He ate this can of oysters and he was dead in about an hour. The next day the whole economic world collapsed and he wasn't here to steer what he owned.† The St.

* In *Look Homeward, Angel,* Thomas Wolfe, a native of Asheville, remembered the tearing down of the old Battery Park hotel another way:

"In the center of town, there had been a beautiful green hill, opulent with rich lawns and lordly trees, with beds of flowers and banks of honeysuckle, and on top of it there had been an immense, rambling, old wooden hotel. From its windows one could look out upon the vast panorama of mountain ranges in the smoky distances . . . It had been one of the pleasantest places in town, but now it was gone. An army of men and shovels had advanced upon this beautiful green hill and had leveled it down to an ugly flat of clay, and had paved it with a desolate horror of white concrete, and had built stores and garages and office buildings and parking spaces—all raw and new—and were now putting up a new hotel beneath the very spot where the old one had stood. It was to be a structure of sixteen stories, of steel and concrete and pressed brick. It was being stamped out of the same mold, as if by some gigantic biscuit-cutter of hotels that had produced a thousand others like it all over the country."

† E. W. Grove's death on October 28, 1929, came just hours before the great stock market crash.

Louis Union Trust Company was the trustee and they took over everything and liquidated a lot of his holdings.

[Asheville] had the highest per capita loss of any city in the United States because we only had one bank and they were in collusion with the city and county government and these land frauds. The [bank] president and his brother drilled out all the safe-deposit boxes and took everybody's securities and jewelry, everything that was not in cash in the bank, and sold them to get cash to keep the bank open. A friend of mine who had the Gulf Oil Company here told me not long ago he went to bed one night in October '29 worth five and a half million dollars and when he woke up the next morning the only thing he had was a hundred and fifty dollars in the cash drawer of one of the filling stations, because it was all on paper.

They'd ridden this terrific wave—this instant millionaire wave—and all of a sudden they went down and it was a Depression you just wouldn't believe. If things had gone on it would have been great, but when the end came there wasn't any money, it was all on paper. This is all true. The mayor jumped out the window of the courthouse. Cashiers at the banks killed themselves, and insurance companies were paying people fifty dollars a month to stay on in these huge mansions to keep vandals out. They were destitute; they had to have fifty dollars to eat. The trust companies liquidated so many things for ten cents on the dollar to get out of paying taxes that today would be worth millions and millions of dollars.

Fortunately, we didn't lose anything except through the bad judgment of the trust companies, but it wasn't [really] bad judgment. They liquidated a lot of stuff [because] nobody thought that the world would ever come back. It was over. This town absolutely disappeared in the Depression and it didn't come back until after the war, and then it came back with a real bang. Now, within the last three years, Asheville has grown more than it had in the preceding twenty-five years.

[In] 1925 my father had realized that the town could not live on the tourists alone. He felt it was unsound to have one base of the economy. The poverty level was terrible in the mountains here. They were living on what they could produce in great part and he felt there was a tremendous source of untapped labor which could be made skilled. He also realized that our water here was so pure that many chemical processes could be carried out without even filtering or distilling the water, which saved millions of dollars. That was the big selling point to bringing the American Enka Rayon plant here because they had to have absolutely pure water to make these viscose fibers. So he got them here, and he got Champion Paper here for the same reason: the labor and the water for making pulp paper. Within a couple of years there were five or six thousand mountain people employed who'd never really been employed before. Those bred other industries, and now we just have anything you can name: electronics, Gorham silver, Beacon Blanket, which is the largest blanket mill in the world, Sales Bleacheries. They just evacuated New England and brought their plants down here because the labor conditions are ideal and we're not organized. When the

Fred Seely, Jr.

day's work was done this fellow would go up that cove, and they never had any time to foment labor trouble. They were being paid on a scale that they'd never even believed possible, so everybody was happy. They were used to just the bare living wage. I know up at the castle* they had eight gardeners who would get there at six o'clock in the morning and work until six for a dollar a day, and my father was very much criticized for paying them that much money. The wages he paid at the Inn were commensurate.

The industry tapped a huge source who were not benefiting in any way from the tourism, so it balanced our economy. Then, of course, all these people coming here from the North and discovering Asheville brought thousands of their friends. The people would come through here on their way to Florida in the fall and then on their way back in the spring. We had two booming seasons at the hotel of people stopping off to see their friends from Rhode Island, Massachusetts, and New Jersey, who were down here with the plants. Then that bred the retirement business. People came here as tourists and came back here to retire, and that became an industry in itself. Then [during the 1940's] the attractive facilities brought the religious assemblies, which was a multimillion-dollar business. Each sect has huge installations within twenty miles of where we sit. Billy Graham and the Baptists are Ridgecrest, Lake Junaluska is the Episcopalians, the Methodists have a huge one, the Presbyterians have Montreat, and the Lutherans are right up almost beside of us here. It's a tremendous business and it's sort of a tourist deal actually, but they're here for a cause. In some ways it's hurt the other tourists businesses because they very successfully have kept the liquor by the drink out of here, which is very attractive to tourists.

What were some of the positive and negative influences of the tourist trade and the new industries on the people of Asheville?

On the negative side, it took quite a bit of education to cause the local people to accept the tourists. This was one of the most

* Fred Seely, Sr., built a castle near the inn for the family's home.

provincial areas that you can imagine. They resented these Northerners coming in here: they were strange people, they didn't speak like they spoke, and they didn't dress like they dressed. They looked on it sort of as an invasion. And another thing, they were mostly Yankees. You'd be surprised how long the memories of the Civil War lasted; they lasted well up into this period we're talking about. I can remember in my own life, my father's father was a colonel in the Union Army and my mother's father was a major in the Confederate Army and she could never have them both visit at the same time. Now I'm talking about when I was twelve, fourteen years old, and they were men in their eighties, and there'd be a fight.

[In the early 1900's] the people of Asheville didn't care about growing. The town was completely secluded by the mountains and it was mainly Scotch-Irish ancestry, people of seclusion [who] didn't desire big business or a lot of wealth. They owned their land and they owned their houses and they were content with what they were making. There was a lot of poverty in the mountains but those people didn't recognize the poverty. They were living like their grandfather lived in Scotland and Ireland and they didn't realize their children were full of rickets. Maybe they were right and maybe aren't too much better off now, I don't know.

There was a lot of educating [to be done] and it was badly handled at first. The paper mills would come in and just evict these people. When the TVA came and started putting in these power lakes, they had to physically remove these mountain people from their cabins. They paid them well for everything and built them beautiful cottages with electric lights and everything. These people, hell, they didn't want that. They wanted to be left alone.

All these things were very big in the mind of the local people. This was their little town and these were their mountains, and if somebody wanted to make corn liquor, by golly, he had the right to make it. It was a frontier town and all of a sudden it was not.

They were frightened, really; there was not as much resentment
as there was fear. No one understood what was going on. Fortunately, in my grandfather's case, and my father's case—my grandfather was a hill man from Tennessee, and my father was a man
who understood everybody—when they came they got right in
with them. They knew how these people wanted to be treated
and everybody worshipped them. In other words, they didn't
come in and run over them as the boss. They came in and gradually established an employer-employee relationship and these
people would do anything in the world for them. You had to
handle yourself so they would accept you, or you would never get
anywhere with them, you're liable to get shot. These were people of extreme poverty and great dignity. I know many times
when I've been hunting in years past back in the mountains and
you'd come to a cabin and they'd come out and say, "Stay for dinner," and if you didn't you would insult them, but you would
know that while you're eating probably two of the family waiting
on table weren't going to have anything to eat because you were
eating it. That's the kind of people they were. They didn't want
you messing with them.

These people were so closely intermarried that they developed
all the genetic debilities of intermarriage. Sixty percent of the
mountain people in my childhood were composed of ten Scottish
family names. So the Stuarts would marry the Stuarts and they
developed a tremendous number of clubfooted children, and that
was my father's great project in life: finding these beautiful mountain children with clubfeet and having them operated on to correct it. I don't know how many thousands of mountain babies he
had corrected. When he died he had files and files, which nobody'd ever seen—which I'd never even seen—of pictures of
babies before they were operated on and after they were
operated on. I don't know how many hundred thousand dollars
he must have spent. It was a simple thing to correct at a very
young age. He was just obsessed by it. He would have to go and
talk to the families and practically beg them. They had a deadly

fear of surgery in a hospital. He would have them sent to that Shriners' hospital in Oxford, North Carolina. The reason he did that, a lot of these people had brought their Masonic ties with them from Scotland and they trusted the Masons. He was able to tell the mountain father that his brother Mason was not going to do anything to hurt the child, that he was going to be among Masons, and that was about the only way he would sell them. They wouldn't let the local doctors touch them.

He was such a complex man. For instance, this architectural thing was just unbelievable. He came out of an eighth-grade education and would first of all make himself a chemist and the most prominent man in the world in the quinine development field, and then go three months to architectural school and come back and build the finest piece of architecture of its kind in the country. [Frank Lloyd] Wright and people like that would come down here to see it. Then he got obsessed about the chain-gang labor system in Georgia, where you or I could hire [a group of] convicts from the state for twenty-five dollars a day and keep them chained and feed them if we wanted to feed them, or not feed them, and do hard labor. If they died, they died, and that was all right. So he went to Atlanta and started a newspaper, the Atlanta *Georgian,* and he sold it to Mr. Hearst, who was a great friend of his. He became an editor of one of the most successful newspapers in the South with no experience, and fought this chain-gang labor system and got it declared illegal, and then lost interest and sold the paper.

What do you think Asheville would have been like had your father and Dr. Grove not come here?

I think it would have remained a small mountain town. Mr. Vanderbilt until their arrival was the controlling interest. He had this 175,000-acre tract, he was doing a lot of good, he was training the mountain people in weaving and they had schools for the crafts. I think had they not come, Mr. Vanderbilt would have kept this town about the way it was because he wanted it as a hunting preserve for himself and his friends. At that time the Biltmore House cost $7 million to build. It had 365 rooms and the whole thing was stocked with every kind of game and fish you could imagine. The last thing he wanted was any industrial odors or congestion of tourists. Now, paradoxically, the house is one of the biggest tourist attractions in the country. The grandchildren have opened it to the public and they had a million and three quarters people through there last year at $3.50 a head.

[When my father died] we sold the Battery Park. The man who bought it from us milked it, and he sold it to a man who went completely under, and now it's just standing there. It's a shame. But now we have a huge Hilton, a big Sheraton, and we have five Holiday Inns, and a Rodeway, and a Ramada. Great Western has three here. It's all proved out in the end what [my father and grandfather] foresaw in the beginning of this century. They opened the way for others who have come and done what they did.

Even before outside entrepreneurs such as Fred Seely, Sr., and E. W. Grove began fashioning Asheville into a tourist town, local residents were opening their homes to people who came to escape the heat and humidity of southern summers. The most famous was, of course, Thomas Wolfe's mother, Julia Westall; another was her neighbor, Julia Elizabeth Dean Shuford. Mrs. Shuford died in the thirties, but her daughter Dr. Mary Frances Shuford continues to live in the family's rambling old home on Asheville's Orange Street, where she has practiced medicine for nearly forty years. A septuagenarian with a droll sense of humor, Mary Frances is apt to say ruefully before barging into a full afternoon of the calamities that patients bring: "I've got twinges in my hinges and don't get around as much as I used to."

Everybody in the South was poor. It was after the Civil War, and 1900 wasn't so far after, either. We didn't have the people that were on the seaboard—princes, and the lords and the ladies—we had workaday folks. In 1898 there was a panic and my father's business just collapsed and he lost all of his savings. When Mother got into this big house it was just natural for her [to do] as other owners of big houses did: she took in boarders.

People who stayed here through the winter were usually business people [and] schoolteachers. The people who came from the outside—we called them the "tourists" or the "summer people"—were more affluent and they could afford a summer's vacation. There was a big difference in the purse and consequently Mother made a big difference in the price. She didn't make any difference in service or food.

Daddy didn't pay [the tourists] any mind a'tall. Sometimes he'd walk home from his [law] office for dinner in the middle of the day, but usually he was late. As I think on it now, I think he was always late on purpose. Mother would serve dinner on time. All the boarders would eat, they'd go to their rooms, in the yard, on the porches, do what they wanted to do. Then Daddy would come in and look around surprised, "Dinner ready?" Mother would serve his plate and sit down at the dining-room table with him. I think he liked that close companionship and liked to have her there, and he didn't care about all those others. If dinner was cold, he never complained.

It was all just such a homey affair. The [tourists'] children romped and played across the yard, played in the sand pile, played on the swings. [The adults] sat on the porch and they rocked, and they talked, and they laughed. They did embroidery. They'd walk downtown to the ice-cream parlor or to the drugstore and get a chocolate sundae, and they would get up a game of bridge. They didn't need much to do. They weren't hikers, they weren't nature lovers, they weren't scouts, they weren't explorers. They came for the scenery and the coolness. It's hot down in Georgia and it's hot down in Florida. There was no air conditioning then.

There were a lot of places where they took in tuberculosis patients. There were a large number of sanatoriums, especially up

Mary Frances Shuford

on this mountainside here. You could hear those poor folks coughing all the way downtown. Sanatoriums were run very much like boardinghouses, but they didn't influence Asheville much, I don't think, because we were afraid of tuberculosis and we just didn't have anything to do with them. They hurt Asheville a good deal because it became known as a place for tuberculosis, as a health resort. Mother took no sick people and most of the big boardinghouses made that same distinction. The sick people had to stay in the sanatoriums. In that day and time we took illness just as something sent from the Lord and we did the best we could with it. It was a doctor's concern, a doctor's business. Every now and then the businessmen of Asheville might express a concern about Asheville becoming known as a health resort instead of a tourist resort. The tourist business paid better than the tuberculosis patients did.

Do you think the tourists changed the town very much?

The change in Asheville was brought on by the Smoky National Park. It's the park that has brought all these roads through here: we've got the cars [so] we've got to have some place to go. The tourists never did change Asheville [to] an industrial town; they changed it from a little country town, an agricultural town, to a tourist town.

The park is a federal project. We had to fight against Tennessee [to get it]. They wanted the park over in their state, but they put it here because the mountains were already here. They're still savage mountains, too; we haven't conquered them. You can go out and get lost in them and you could fall down them, and you just can't play too much with them, they don't take any monkey business. One of the finest men we had in Asheville was a great hiker and he went up a mountaintop somewhere in the Smoky Mountain, zero weather, ice everywhere, and he was just thrilled to see that mountain section in the ice storm. Well, he slipped on the rock and fell to his death. The mountain didn't give him any quota a'tall. Children have been lost along that trail,

they get lost in the laurel thicket. It's just as wild and just as
rugged and impenetrable as it ever was.

How did your mother feel about Mrs. Wolfe's boarders?

She didn't know them, she didn't pay any attention to them.
They were not so affluent [and] they would have for their
boarders railroad people. We associated more with the Asheville
people. You see, my father was a judge, he was an outstanding
lawyer here, and my mother's people were prominent in Georgia. We didn't know the boardinghouse keepers like Thomas
Wolfe's mother, that sort of crowd. They weren't in our set and
yet Mrs. Wolfe came from a fine family and a very intelligent
family, the Westalls. They were certainly worthy to be friends,
but the Wolfes, Mother didn't know them, didn't have anything
to do with them. That was one of the things that made Tom
Wolfe so bitter toward Asheville. He was from good stuff but his
mother was stingy, she was mean, and his father was a drunk.
His family was looked down on, really, but it wasn't because they
took boarders, it was because she was just mean, that's all, stingy.

I've read parts of [*Look Homeward, Angel*] and I had a complaint that my father made about a book once. He said he didn't
like the ending. I said, "What's wrong with the ending?" He said,
"It's too far from the beginning." [Thomas Wolfe is] very wordy,
but everyone says it's literature and I take their word for it, but
he really gave Asheville a blow and a knock.

In the 1910's and 1920's the hills of Central Appalachia be-
came more accessible and it was not long before missionaries and
educators were attracted to the region. Warren Wright, who ear-
lier described the ways of some coal speculators, is a theologian
and has studied the role of the mountain missionary. He said
there were basically two types of missionaries: those who adapted
to the people's culture and lifestyle but had a compulsion, "which
I recognize is supreme, to make the name of Jesus Christ known
wherever we possibly can, and those who were so imbued with

their own political and social heritage that they immediately [started] to change the natives."

Regardless of how history will judge the Reverend Samuel Vandermeer's activities during his fifty years as a missionary in the mountains, there is little doubt that he and his wife, Nola, cared deeply for the people in Kentucky. Sam's nephew was former Cincinnati Reds player Johnny Vandermeer, the only person ever to pitch two consecutive no-hitters in major-league baseball. During his career Johnny Vandermeer earned a great deal of money and was lavished with gifts from fans, but after retirement he told his Uncle Sam, "I think you've fared better pitching for Christ than I have pitching for the Cincinnati Reds. Fame is very fleeting." It was a tribute that remained close to Sam's heart until his death in 1975.

I was brought up in Paterson, New Jersey, and one day there came a missionary to our church and he spoke about the fact that there were many areas in our own country still untouched with the gospel. I was tremendously impressed by what he said. That night I went home and talked to the Lord about it and said, "If there is some area where there is a special need, would you just open the door and let me go there?"

A friend of mine with whom I was working amongst the colored people in Brooklyn, New York, her church, Lafayette Avenue Presbyterian, had a mission station in Buckhorn, Kentucky, in a very isolated part of Perry County where Witherspoon College was located. She invited me down for summer vacation and I went in the month of June [in 1923] and hoed corn in the fields with the boys and girls. On Sundays Dr. Murdock, who was president of the college at that time, asked me to go to some of the little outlying Sunday schools.

Summer was coming to a close and I thought a summer vacation should end [but] Mr. Murdock said, "We need help so badly," so I finally agreed to stay on a little bit longer. Then Mr. Murdock asked me if I would help out with the high school

Sam Vandermeer

at Buckhorn because he had to go to New York, so I took some of his high-school classes. When he returned from New York he asked me to go to Cow Creek in Owsley County. I went over to Cow Creek and taught for a month, taught subjects that I hadn't even studied.

Then the people on the Freeman Fork of Long Creek said, "Can't you teach our children? Our school has been closed. We will board you." The little schoolhouse was terribly dilapidated: it had been made of undressed lumber, and green lumber, so there were cracks in all the walls, cracks in the floor. The roof was terrible and there was just one pot-bellied, which was cracked, for heating.

I began teaching there in September and I was in a different home every night. Of course, the houses were very primitive, many of them didn't even have a kerosene lamp. We'd eat by the light of the fireplace. Many had no windows and the door had to be kept open in order that there be enough light in the room for eating. Sometimes we slept five in a bed because [there were] maybe two rooms for that large family. It was interesting to see how they managed. You see, a lot of them at that time had no outhouses and when you went to visit them, well, you were sort of stuck. I remember going home with this man one time and I saw only this one room with two or three beds in it and there were a couple of women there. I suddenly realized that I was going to have to sleep in that room too and I had never done that kind of thing. I wondered how they were going to work it out. When it got to be bedtime the man of the house said to me, "Let's go outside and take a walk." When we got back the women were in bed. Worked very nicely.

The wonderful thing about it was that you never felt crowded. The welcome was always so genuine. There was always an abundance of food no matter how poor they were. Now it wasn't always the right kind of diet, but was substantial and there was an abundance of it.

[Soon] the fathers and mothers said, "Can't you teach us, too? We'll come at night." So in the same little schoolhouse the fathers and mothers came at night. We had Sears, Roebuck's catalogue, we had Calfey's rural arithmetic, and we had the gospel of John, those were our textbooks. These fathers and mothers in the night school amazed me by their ability to learn and I realized the potential of the mountain people. There was one grandmother who was seventy, named Kate Helton. Kate came every night, her eyesight was poor, but she came up that creek. Kate would try awfully hard and it was a thrill to her when she learned to add one column of figures on the blackboard, and then two columns of figures, and then we got into subtraction. I'll never forget the night when we started long division with these adults. Poor Kate she pushed her glasses in every conceivable position and she took the piece of chalk and she chewed on it and she looked at the problem and said, "Sam, I've gone as far as I can go. I can't do this." I said, "Kate, you've done all the others, you can do it," and she mastered it.

At the end of the school I had the thrill of being at her home. She said to her husband, John, who was the postmaster, "John, I want you to go down the creek and measure that log. I want you to tell me how long it is and how big it is through the butt." He measured it. Then she said, "Now, get me a paper poke." John brought her a paper poke. Kate fished in her pocket where she carried her revolver, and her twist of tobacco, and she pulled out a little piece of pencil and she chewed on it. She told him exactly how many board feet there'd be on that log. [Then] John measured the wagon bed and she told him how many tons of coal it would hold. John was just amazed: "Where did you learn that?" She said, "I learned that at the night school. You laughed at me for going."

When February came I felt I should still go home. I had a little service in the schoolhouse and they said they were going to pray me back, and they did. I came back but I got a little cabin for myself. I had one teacup and one teaspoon and folks brought in things. Somebody brought in a rocking chair and I had corncobs for candles. I put an umbrella over the stove when it rained so that I shouldn't get too much water in the soup. Then I read in the Bible one time that it's not good for a man to live alone, and I decided that if the Bible said that then I better be doing something about it. One day my travels took me over to Leslie County and I was introduced to this young nurse, Nola Pease. We got to talking and then we made the mistake of walking down to the post office together. Some lady saw us and had a dream that night that this young man who rode in on horseback and this nurse were going to get married. We'd heard about the dream and rather than have that woman going through life not believing in dreams, my wife proposed to me. But [I] always liked to do a little courting before you get married and it was thirty-five miles horseback from where I lived to where she lived. I'd have to ford the Kentucky River twice, cross two mountains, and go through a place called Hell for Certain in order to get to Wooton Creek, near the mouth of Cutshin Creek. John Fox [Jr.] wrote a book about that, *Courtin' on Cutshin.* I always said he never did it because his book is too tame. To make a long story short, we did get married and I took her over to Morris Fork.

My reaction when I first went to that community was that I had come to a tired country. Mothers were tired, the children were tired, the men were tired trying to make out a living on those steep hillsides, and the cattle looked tired because they weren't getting the proper food. Even the houses and fences were beginning to look tired because the land was so steep. And the land itself was tired because it had raised corn year after year after year with no crop rotation.

Right from the very start it seemed we were accepted. One of them said to me, "You talk proud, but you don't act a bit proud." My language, see, was different, and we just went on from there. There was never any sense of trying to break into the culture. I did some things that were queer, and they did some things that were queer, and we both understood that. We never went in with the idea that we were teachers, we went in as learners because they had much to teach us, and so often I was amazed at some of the profound statements some of them would make.

For instance, at times I'd get sort of lonesome for people of my similar background. I had no access to good books, there was no radio, of course no television, and I know just one time I was feeling a little sorry for myself. I went to this little schoolhouse and there was an illiterate mountain preacher talking. He was the father of twenty-three children and he had a set of artificial teeth that were three sizes too big. When he talked these things would bob around in his mouth, and his lips would be pulled back, and you'd see these huge white teeth. He was short of stature and just as homely as a mud fence, but he was very sincere. This particular Sunday when I was feeling sorry for myself and sort of low, that man in his message made a statement that has stayed with me all through these years: "The man who has the spirit of God within him, has a flesh controller." That was exactly what I needed because the spirit of God was within me and here the flesh was manifesting itself in loneliness. It was a rebuke to me and I accepted it as a rebuke, and I profited by it. Now, where did a man like that get that? He absolutely couldn't read a word and yet he made that profound statement. This is what amazed me all the time with these people.

You see, the thing everyone has to remember is that every community is different. Mountains were barriers and what was true in one little community might be absolutely untrue in another community. People forget that, and that's why I resent blanketing the mountain people as being the same. The people in Buckhorn felt that they were just a little bit better than the people at Morris Fork. The people down at Morris Fork felt that they were just a little bit better than the people down at Elsom Creek, and if a mother was provoked with her child she'd say, "You act just like them Heralds down there." The Heralds lived down in Elsom Creek, you see. There was that caste system almost, but it's not peculiar to a mountain people. The more I was with the people, the more I realized that they basically were just like anybody else, only thing is they hadn't had the opportunity. Then I was amazed at how far they had gotten without the opportunities that most of us had.

I found out that because of their confidence in us, they accepted. You see, we had put [in] a robed choir, we did it partly because the children came in overalls and the colors clashed. Of course, nowadays that's the style but at that time we'd built this lovely little brown rustic church and to see the children come barefooted in overalls with these bright colors or frayed collars . . . We made just simple white robes and so they all came in looking alike. We also made a rule in the church that people were not to walk in and out; that they were to be reverent in the house of God. There wasn't to be any drinking [from] a bucket of water on the communion table; they were to drink before they came in. There was not to be any whispering in the church. One man said, "You know, you're doing a heap of queer things around here, but we know you're working for our good and for the good of our children. Now you all keep ahead and we'll try to follow." Wasn't that a fine tribute? There was confidence and they knew it was for their own good.

When we were getting John Morgan from Berea College in for a week [as a] recreation specialist to teach us how to play games, Jim Cornett stood up in church and said, "Now, Sam, I've gone along with you on everything but this business of bringing a man in here just to learn us how to play, I just don't go along with that. What we need is someone to come in here and show us how to work." I said, "Jim, all we have to do when the man is through here is furnish the mule to take him on to the next place." He said, "Yes, and we'll get that fellow here and we'll be stuck with him the rest of our lives."

When John Morgan arrived I said, "There is one man who thinks your coming is useless and I want you to make a friend of him." Jim Cornett had an open mind and he was a very wonderful person. After a week of seeing the people playing together, learning these songs, Jim Cornett said, "I hate to see him go, but he can borrow my mule if he needs one to go to the other place."

This was the attitude, even if it was strange: we'll go along with it because [we're] so tired of doing without. They'd gotten to the place where they were ready for change and I think God sent us in just about that time. I think this is important: to start where the people are, get their confidence, and then you begin to build on that. We gradually introduced the better hymns; this couldn't be done at once, it had to come very, very gradually over a period of years. They were singing songs like, "If I could hear my mother pray again," songs about the graveyard, mournful songs. That was their level and that was as far as they could go. We began there and then we introduced the Christmas carols and they learned to love them. We would take hymns that were not too difficult, not too far removed from their particular culture, and gradually introduce them. We started the folk games and the singing of some of the new hymns at the same time, and so up the creek the children were playing a little game they called "Holy, holy, will you skip with me?" We had taught them this mountain game of skip and we had also taught them the hymn of "Holy, Holy, Holy," and they put the two together. Of course, it sounded sacrilegious to us, but we knew they were only doing what [was] right.

There hadn't been any church weddings; [people would] just go to a town preacher and be married at his home, on a porch, or anywhere. Never anything about the beauty of the marriage ceremony, it was just reading the license and a few words. I understand one preacher wished them "a long life and a greasy spoon."

When we finally did have [a church wedding] several of our people came and said, "We feel like we've never been married. We didn't know marriage could be so beautiful." We always gave it the works. I am very artistic, I love architecture and interior decorating and landscaping. We had paneled walls stained brown, and we had the open truss work, and then we had homemade chandeliers with tall white candles. I always had beech leaves that were treated with glycerin up against the brown wall so they looked like a wood carving. My wife would play the organ. I'd always have a candlelight service at the close of a wedding after the vows have been taken. I'd take a tall candle and light it from a candle on the altar and present it to the bride and groom. I'd say a little bit about what marriage is, and the sacredness of marriage, and then I'd say: "I'd like to have you take this candle with you into your new home and when the next anniversary comes around light the candle again. Maybe the bride will put on her dress again and reach across the table, and hold hands, and look into each other's eyes and take the vows again. Or when a baby comes into the home it might be nice to light the candle, or maybe the husband gets a raise in pay, light that candle again, or in times of sickness light the candle." It is always a very moving experience. You can do those things but you have to begin very, very simply and you have to build up to it.

Our work with the church was the main reason we were [in the mountains], but we felt as a Christian they should have every area of life developed to give them what we would call an "abundant" life. We did health work and we worked with the schools, but we still didn't have any roads. We couldn't get electricity until we got roads, and so we'd go to the state department at Frankfort with delegations trying to get roads. They'd say, "Why do you build those churches and schools in out-of-the-way places, then expect the state to build a road to them?" I'd count up to ten and then I'd say, "Well, you know, they happen to be Kentuckians." I [told them about] a little boy who stepped on a rusty needle. We tried as quickly as we could to get him to Lexington so he could have the shots for lockjaw. It meant taking that little boy on a stretcher over into Owsley County, and the creeks were swollen, then taking him on horseback to Booneville where we could get a car, and then to Lexington. That little boy died just on the outskirts of Lexington. The father and mother came back with that little boy's body in a little bundle on a pole and they wanted me to say that this was God's will when I knew it was the highway department's fault.

We'd go up to the highway department with these stories. Finally the man who was running for governor, we managed to get him into one of our community fairs and he was so amazed that these people were doing all this without roads. In his campaign speeches he stressed rural roads and he cited this as an illustration. Then the next year he said, "I want you to get the highway commissioner in to make a speech." Well, they were due at our house at six o'clock for dinner; they arrived at ten o'clock at night. The men who drove the jeep were state police and they had driven in the war, in the battle zones; they said they never encountered anything over there like they did trying to get to Morris Fork. Pretty soon we got a gravel road from Booneville over toward Buckhorn and yesterday I had a thrill of riding over some blacktop. It just came in before the election.

You had to work at every area of their lives. The interesting thing was, when the government started coming in with all these programs—the VISTA program, the in-service training, the adult education, the health program and improvement programs— every program we had done with a very limited staff, with a very limited amount of money, and of course in just a limited area. These are the things we were doing because the church realized these were the things that needed to be done.

In spite of the fact that there was the poverty, and the lack of facilities, and everything else, I never saw more beautiful living in my life. For instance, I went home with little Arnold Hilton one night. Arnold was a sickly boy and I had never been in his home but I went up this long, rough creek with this boy, with boulders that were as big as this desk, and you either had to walk in the creek or you jumped on these boulders. I was just amazed that the child could get to school, but I got there and had a wonderful welcome from the grandmother and the grandfather, and his mother and his father. I forget how many children there were in the family living in two rooms. This was late in the fall and it was already getting quite cold and the grandmother had made a cake in an iron skillet under the coals in the fireplace and they had a big pitcher of creamy milk. We sat at that table with snow-flakes coming across the table while we were trying to eat our supper, and then we went into this other room which had two or three beds in it and the fireplace. The old grandfather sat in front of the fireplace and told the children stories about an imaginary place called Popcorn Creek. In Popcorn Creek there were ice-cream cones on trees, there were hams and meat hanging on those trees, and apple pies. While he was talking he would take cornstalks and make the kind of animals that there were on Pop-corn Creek. He built a little corral out of cornstalks to fence in the animals and the children sat there spellbound. The old grand-mother sat by her spinning wheel with a pipe in her mouth, spinning wool to make socks for her family. The mother sat on the other side of the fireplace with a little stringed instrument called an autoharp, and she was singing a little ballad:

There was a time I know, when in the Book of Heaven
An old account was standing of sin yet unforgiven.
My name was at the top and there were many sins below,
But I went to my Keeper and said, "I settled long ago."

There was the firelight, there was the whirring of the spinning wheel, there was the grandfather with those children, there was the mother singing softly. I thought to myself, "This is as near to heaven as you can get." The next morning I thought, now you can feel sorry for these people but you can envy them at the same time. I found that in home after home where they were so beautifully adjusted.

Another thing that always appealed to me about the mountain people was their gentleness. You never felt like they were poor white trash like you do sometimes in the slums of a city. These people had nobility. I'm sorry that so often this is not mentioned when they talk about our mountain people.

This man that I mentioned talking to his grandchildren about Popcorn Creek, I wish you could have seen him when he lay in his casket. You could have taken somebody in the room and said he was president of Columbia University and they would have believed it. Anywhere you go you can make caricatures of the extremes, but that doesn't mean they are all that way. I have a high regard for the mountain people. I have met many who, despite poor English, a lack of education, were refined gentlewomen and gentlemen.

Did you ever have any problems with the mountain preachers?

No, fortunately I was able to get along with them. I was always very sympathetic, I never laughed at them. [One time] I was having a funeral service and Uncle Bill Combs, to the surprise of everybody, walked in. Uncle Bill had moved to the coal mines up at Combs, Kentucky, with his wife. It was a completely new life for her from a farm at the Middle Fork of the Kentucky River to a coal camp where she sat all day alone, no friends, while Bill went to work. Bill came out to the service and, as is the custom, I asked him to speak. He got up and said, "Children," that's an expression mountain people use, "I know you're all surprised to see me, but when me and the old woman went to bed we laid still a while and then she said, 'Bill, honey, if I was to die where would you bury me?' I said, 'Honey, let's not talk about dying.' She laid still another spell and by-and-by she said, 'Bill, I want to know: if I was to die where would you bury me?' I said to her, 'Now, hush. We're not going to talk any more about dying.' She laid still another spell and said, 'Bill, I want to know.' [I] said, 'Why, honey, you know when you die I'd take you right back home and I'd bury you on the hillside right behind the house.' We laid still another spell and by-and-by she said, 'Bill, honey, would you just as soon take me there alive as dead?' Children, we got up out of the bed and we packed our plunder and we came home."

Now that was psychology, which she'd never studied. He couldn't resist that. He was also one who couldn't read, but he'd say these lovely things in service every once in a while and I always appreciated him. I never felt that he was any less sincere than I and I knew he was doing just as much good as I was doing in his own way with his limitations. But he had advantages I didn't have. You see, he was one of the people, which I wasn't; I was the outside.

.

5

FROM FARMS AND HOLLOWS
TO CAMP TOWNS

Throughout eastern Kentucky camp towns grew rapidly, as did the population. Between 1910 and 1920 the number of people living in Harlan County increased nearly 200 percent, from 10,564 persons to 31,546. Other Kentucky coal counties, such as Floyd, Knott, Perry, Letcher, and Pike, were similarly inundated with newcomers and new money. By the 1920's the rolling land around Jenkins, Kentucky, that had once been "Devil" John Wright's cornfield, housed more than 8,000 people in nine hundred new homes.

The first miners and executives lived in camp tents pitched on earth so rich with coal a fine black powder often permeated the topsoil. Building more permanent, self-contained towns was necessary, however, because industrialization would not tolerate a work force that was scattered among hills and hollows. Stores, post offices, physicians, policemen, sanitation facilities, and schools were needed to attract masses of people to the coalfields. Coal companies with sufficient capital and social conscience also provided hospitals and movies, civic centers and libraries, baseball diamonds and churches. New houses appeared by the thousands and there was a vast difference among them from one coal camp to another. Some were flimsy tar-paper shacks with green wood underpinnings; others had sturdy exteriors, windows, electricity, and closets. Regardless of quality almost all the miners' houses looked alike and were constructed row after row after row around the tipple. Officials' homes were different. In the wealthiest mines they were hill-top mansions, beyond the reach of coal dust and most mountaineers.

Transforming the hills of Central Appalachia into America's power plant demanded, among other things, a new economy. Trading as Oscar Kilburn's forebears knew it was an anachronism now that cash was available and men were paid according to their value to the coal company. Coal miners seldom saw much actual cash because the new industrial economy was based on scrip. Scrip was manufactured by individual coal companies and usually was a metallic or celluloid disk bearing the firm's name and a monetary value. On payday, which came once or twice a month, men received federally minted money. If employees wished to draw on their earnings betweentimes—and by necessity most did—they received not cash, but scrip. Frequently families came to the coal camps with little or no money and began drawing scrip immediately after the man completed his first work shift, which meant there was rarely any cash on payday. Scrip had to be spent within the camp and was seldom accepted by private merchants or other coal companies if the employee moved elsewhere. In essence, scrip was a means of keeping miners at home and forcing them to patronize company-owned businesses, such as the commissary, movie house, and soda fountain. From a business point of view it was also a canny way of insuring that most of the money a company spent to meet its payroll would soon be returned through its own profit-making sidelines. The same philosophy carried into other aspects of camp life and deductions were routinely made from employees' checks for rent, electricity, mining explosives, medical care, and insurance. Most of the money went directly back to the company.

When mountain people began moving to the mines, the miles between their farms and the camp towns were deceptively short.

Most could be physically crossed in a day or two, but for many people the emotional transition took years. How a person adjusted to life in the new town depended on the nature of the farm he left and the nature of the coal town he migrated to. It also depended on whether he was a man, woman, or child, for each faced a different set of problems as well as the communal one of a rapidly, drastically changing family life. No longer was the labor and rest of families governed by the sun and seasons, and how could it be when the mines know no daylight and remain a moist sixty-five to seventy degrees year round? When men became miners they left home in the dark of morning and returned at night. Their women rose with them and at night they waited, heating water for the tub bath that signaled the end of a miner's day. Children seldom saw their fathers from one Sunday to another and rearing the young ones became primarily the woman's responsibility. Spinning, weaving, canning, milking, and hoeing—labors of the farm— were now replaced by daily skirmishes with waves of coal dust that fouled every floorboard. Once the soot was beaten away, women shopped at company stores and visited with neighbors who were both a blessing and a worry. Farm life had been lonely and neighbors filled the void pleasantly. Their proximity was also an invasion of privacy and their presence instilled fear: Are they like me? Do they want for their children what I want for mine?

Children reacted differently. On the farm they had worked from dawn until dark through most of the year; in the coal towns there was little land to till and their lives became easier. Neighbor children were now as close as the barn had been and the potential for fun—and mischief—was inhibited only by the imagination. As youngsters discovered soda fountains, marching bands, and movie theaters in their midst the mystique of court day and trips to the mill began to fade. In the end, many adjusted better than their parents and for them the coal towns became home.

Rebellion against farm life and the need for work led Melvin Profitt to the Kentucky oil fields in 1919 when he was fifteen and then to the coal mines in 1921. The farms Melvin grew up on were unlike those Alice Slone, Delphia Ramey, and others remembered fondly in "A Simpler Time," because his father was a sharecropper who worked not for himself, but for landowners. During the latter part of the nineteenth century and well into the twentieth between 19 and 40 percent of all eastern Kentucky farms were operated by tenant families who gave the owner of the land they farmed a sum of money, or share of the crops, for the privilege of tilling his soil. In return, landowners provided tenants with clothes, housing, seed, and tools. No doubt there were some good landlords, people who did not take advantage of their tenants; it just so happens Melvin was seldom acquainted with them.

From the time he was a child Melvin has dedicated himself to having a good time and, if necessary, to making life difficult for bumptious bosses. As a youngster he delighted in planting the landlord's seed corn in hollow trees; as a miner he was occasionally paid by unwitting companies for loading more sandstone than coal. Today Melvin lives in Hazel Green, Kentucky, not far from his Wolfe County birthplace. His life is simple but irreparably marred by the black-lung disease that is his gratuity for a career in the coal mines. He endures it with grace and humor by composing songs and writing stories about the charmed and bedeviled life of a most likable fellow named Mountain Mel.

My grandfather died young; he took bone scrofula. He had bought a farm over on Johnson Fork of Lacy Creek.* He paid for his farm and he had a wife and five children. This old doctor that was doctoring him had to have a new kind of medicine, which he said cost three hundred dollars. [My grandfather] had to mortgage the farm to get this three hundred dollars. He takes the mortgage to the doctor. My grandfather died and my grandmother couldn't raise that amount of money. [The doctor] closes this mortgage and set these kids, and that woman, out on the

---

* Near Hazel Green, Kentucky.

road. Well, there was no handouts in them days, there was one chance and one only with a mother and a bunch of kids: she would just have to take these kids and go across the county and hunt homes for them.

It's heartbreaking to think about. You're hunting homes for these kids, you'd rather give them to somebody than for them to set there and starve. My father, at that time, was nine years old [and went to live with a landowner]. Now, this old landlord will say, "I'll take that boy there, he can do a whole lot of chores. I'll board him, and I'll clothe him till he's twenty-one years old and at that time I'll give him a young horse, bridle, and saddle." Now imagine, this kid would maybe work ten years, maybe eleven, for a horse, bridle, and saddle. I mean for that amount of time, that long, and he'd made a slave out of him!

I kind of hate to discuss [the landowners], I mean it almost made an outlaw out of me. When I was young we lived on these landlord's places and these tenant children wasn't thought any more of than a hound. They was as afraid of these landlords and their wife as they was a copperhead. Actually, I formed a hatred for them when I was a small kid and it just growed on me. The tenants was actually just slaves, white slaves.

[One landowner my father worked for] had a daughter about sixteen when I was about eight, and they had a boy about the age of me. They'd go to town on Saturday, take this boy along, and this girl would come out and holler at my mother to let me go stay with her till they got back. Soon as [I'd] get there she'd start finding out what I'd like to eat. Oh, she's so good to me, I just loved her. A lot of times she'd just look straight at me and I knew that she was in the deepest sympathy with me. Still in all, we'd hear that wagon coming back from town, I doubt if you could have took enough rope to have tied me in there because I's getting away. [Later I learned] a tenant boy and a landlord's daughter couldn't have company, unless they done it on the sly. And in case they did slip away and marry, this landlord would go and will the boy or girl out of his estate.

Melvin Profitt

This landlord, he'd bind this tenant to work for him for fifty cents a day, five pounds of meat, or a bushel of corn a day. Of course, now, [he] did furnish a house, I mean a roof to go over their head, which I should give him credit for. The first one that I remember there wasn't even window glass in it. It was built in the edge of the woods and under a tall tree. There was a shutter window on the back. In the summertime you could open that for air, sunshine, and in the winter you could shut it to keep the cold out. There were two chairs, a step stove, wood beds, a table, and a brass lamp. We made out with it just the same as a man would with one of these thirty- or forty-thousand-dollar houses now.

We didn't have any extras. We'd have a costume that we'd wear a little special when we'd go to church or when we went to school, and the other that we wore around home would be something like a fly net: just a bunch of strings. There were so many different things that looked to me [like] a child was cheated out of everything. It was impossible for a sharecropper to school his children [properly] for the simple reason we didn't have but five months of school and it commenced the first Monday in July. Seasons was actually a little longer than they are now and blackberries was ripe [in July] and we had to put those blackberries up. Here would be potatoes to pick and fodder to save. There was so much stuff that kept these kids from school, they didn't have a chance of going.

The landlord's children and the tenant's children, they didn't care too much about each other and they were taught that, naturally. We was [all] Democrats and Republicans and we'd go to school. The Democrats would play ball agen the Republicans, we would have spelling bees, Republicans agen Democrats, and we'd have fights. I was one of the Republicans. [The landlord's children were] Democrats.

My dad was always a mighty independent voter. I knowed of him voting against one man because he offered to pay him for his time for going to the election. My dad was very independent, but the majority of [the tenants] wasn't. When it come up elections the landowner would go around and he'd whisper in the tenant's ear who to vote for, and that *must* be done. No way out of it. They've always sold votes in this county and I guess they have in yours. [Selling votes] was a cash crop and is till the present day.

My dad was an awful hard-working man and an ambitious man and I never knowed a time when there wasn't food in the house, and I have knowed a lot of folks that didn't have it. The tenant farmer could have one cow. He could have a couple of hogs, maybe, but he was allowed all the chickens that he wanted to have, which played a big role in the family in them days. There was always a sale for poultry and eggs. Nearly all the families would raise a bunch of turkeys for the Thanksgiving market. They would take this money and buy clothing for their families for winter.

When I was a boy my dad had three or four cows but you couldn't have bought a gallon of milk from him at any price. He would *give* that away, but you couldn't have bought it. You couldn't have bought a bushel of apples from [him]. He'd give you all you wanted, but you couldn't buy them. Actually, I'll tell you what makes a right smart believer [out of] me: when apples quit bearing out here, nobody had none hardly, we used to have them every year.

The landlord, he would furnish the team, he would furnish the seed corn, and the plows, and what they needed to farm with [and get half the tenant's crop in return]. I was a very small boy, I guess I was seven years old, when we left this one farm my dad had stayed on ten years. My dad didn't have no team and this [landlord] comes in and told my dad, called him "D" for short, William David was his name, "I'm going to furnish everything like I have been so you can farm this land the same way, [only now you'll have to] give me two thirds."

My dad said, "I'll see you in hell!" That's the nearest I ever come to hearing my dad swear in my life. [The landlord] went on away and my dad, he goes to Hazel Green and he rented a house from J. T. Day, the richest man, I guess, at that time in the county. He paid a dollar a day for labor and he furnished these men work year around. My dad moved away from that farm and that was the first time that I had ever been to Hazel Green. There was coal on this farm and in the wintertime he couldn't work in the ground, he would work in [the man's] mine. He dug this man's coal for fifty cents a ton. A lot of times when he wasn't in the mines they made rail fences. He'd cut, split, and lay up a hundred rails for a dollar.

After I got older and got to thinking how ignorant it is to just think about wanting to kill people I kind of repented. But I hated them, I just hated them. I'd think about my grandmother when she set out there on the road with little children and nowhere to go and nothing to feed them on. I think it was unfair all the way through, that's one reason why I slipped away when I was fifteen year old and went to work in the oil fields. I thought if this is the best there is, we ain't got nothing.

World War I, now that was the beginning of the division in the people. Before the war these hollows was full of tenants. When this war come up, then work started booming: coal mining, railroads, factories, oil fields, and everything. One man would sneak out and get him a job in an oil field, or in a coal mine, which my dad was one. He comes back home every three or four weeks and his neighbors would find out about it, maybe get them a job so they could follow the same pattern. The mines [near] us here were hiring everyone coming along and they was making a good wage scale. The family that was back [on the farm], of course, was not raising much, not having labor. The landlord missed this man very much. So it comes up winter and this land-owner had a barn full of stock and he didn't have much feed for it, so he'd have to sell a portion of his stock to feed the rest. In 19 and 18 when this war got hot practically everybody that was drafted passed the examination. Well, this made it a lot tougher on the landowner. He just about had to rake and scrape bottom to make it through. Well, by 19 and 19 he had sold practically everything in the world that he could rake and scrape in the way of stock. He had nothing left but his dirt, his real estate, and when the war ended in '18 these boys started coming back. Well, this man had one chance and one only, that would be to sell them a hunk of his dirt. These tenants was ready to buy that, and did buy it, which equaled the people up more than anything. Now, that done my heart good.

These GI's come back, they looked good in these costumes. About that time them automobiles come around, they called them "joy wagons." [Young people] liked to ride then as good as they do now, and the boys [would] slip them girls out. They pretty soon got to marrying right straight off. It just got out of reach of the landlord, he just absolutely couldn't will them *all* out of his estate. I guess they decided that they wouldn't use this farm after they died and they'd will [it to their children]. That is what equaled the people up in Wolfe County and about all the other counties in eastern Kentucky. They all become, you might say, just one. There was no big "I's" and little "yous," they's all about the same class. There was a lot of men lost their lives in World War I, but there's not a doubt in my mind it was worth everything that it cost. Now a lot of people wouldn't agree with me, but it's that way.

I went to the oil fields when I's fifteen and I stayed down there till about '21 [when] I slipped away and went into mines at Jeff, Kentucky, and got a job at Kenmont Coal Company. I'm going to tell you I's as big as any man then, don't think I wasn't. I'd go down through them mines with my head throwed back. I felt good, I'll tell you.

Actually, I went in the mines when I was six year old. My dad was a miner [for a landlord]. I would go in there and this coal was tall enough till I could chase around in there, hand him a file to file his auger with, or a pick, or something he needed from the outside. I could stand up and run from one place to another where he would had to run on his knees. I guess I was quite a bit of help to him and I really enjoyed it. A lot of folks say we don't inherit [a love for coal mining], but I'm going to think awful strong that we do.

Now these companies all they cared for was a man being a brute and if he was, he had a job; if he wasn't, he didn't have a job. If you was a brute and could do a brute's work, which I could, I got anything I wanted. But I've seen old men go in there and they'd cut a place twenty-four foot across, six foot deep, back in that vein of coal and you had to load that out in a day. You had to clean that place up before you come out at night regardless of what time it might have been. I come out one night, I guess it's at least nine o'clock, there was one of them little jack-legged bosses standing there and [he] looked over at me, said, "You clean up?"

"Yeah, I cleaned up."

He looked at [this] old man, poor old fellow, I was in sympathy with him. "No," he says, "I didn't."

"How many cars do you lack?"

He said, "I guess there's four more in there."

"Well," he said, "you get the hell in there! If you can't get it out let somebody in who can get it." He run that old man back in there. It's either go back or lose his job. My nerves run as high as a pine tree many times like that.

In another mine that I worked at, in Knott County, this was during the Depression, there'd be anywhere from seven to fifteen men every morning begging for work. They'd be turned away. There'd be old people there and I've give my lunch away many a time. They'd lay out in the hills and some of them could barely walk, old people.

I think about as bad hurt* as I ever was in my life was at this same mine. I was supplying track one night and I went up in this place and [the roof] sounded like it was ready to fall. A boy by the name of Fields, about sixteen years old, [was] cussing me when I got up in there to bring him some track. I said, "Son, I'll

* Melvin is referring to an emotional hurt, not a physical one.

get it to you right away, but you don't need no track in here. What you need is timber and if you don't get you some timbers, you're going to be dead."*

"By God!" he said, "I know as much about this rock as you do. I's raised in here."

I said, "I don't dispute that now, but I tell you this is going to fall in." I went back out for some reason, I don't know why I done it. I looked at my watch as I went out and in exactly fifteen minutes from the time I went out the motorman told me about that boy getting killed. That slate had fell on him. He's just mashed in a jelly. I couldn't hardly make my mind up to go back to work next day. It's awful.

I guess I passed up death several different times, or at least I felt like I have, in mines. I don't know how many times I've run out from under rocks and they'd fall in. Once I was totally fastened to two hundred volts of electricity for two or three seconds. Never knowed of anybody to live over that except myself.†

I signed up at Consolidated Coal Company on Smoot Creek in Letcher County the first day of November of 1926 and I stayed there till late in December of the year 19 and 29. Then we come back here and stayed a while.

Why would anyone leave a job during the Depression?

[The mines] wasn't running enough to keep the family and something else . . . They charged you a dollar for a dirty car.

---

* Timbers supported the ceiling, or "roof," of a deep mine and were used to prevent the coal and slate from caving in.
† In *Night Comes to the Cumberland* Harry M. Caudill explains why electrocution was a ubiquitous danger in many mines: "Within a few years after the mines were opened electric locomotives began to replace the horses and mules which pulled the underground trains of coal. Power for these machines came from naked cables suspended from the tunnel roofs. The wire was never more than a foot or so above the motorman's head; many motor operators accidentally touched it and were electrocuted. Other miners straightened up at an unfortunate moment, or stumbled over cross-ties, and touched the deadly cable. The consequence was [almost] always death or serious injury."

This coal was in two different veins and there was a streak of "jack rock" [between them]. Jack rock [is] just rock, something like flint rock. They couldn't sell that dirty coal, it just wasn't clean. It wouldn't burn, no account for anything. I was right smart of a coal hog. I would shoot that [vein of coal] up so hard that I'd just get in there and scoop it all up. Get my car pretty well loaded [and put] clean coal [on top]. I got by with it for a long time; then they sent these men up from headquarters, which is Pittsburgh, Pennsylvania, to watch [them unload coal at the tipple]. [I] had a nice car of coal as far as could be seen, but when it went out here on the tipple and they dumped that car of coal into the railroad gon* for shipment it wasn't so very clean. Each man had a certain number that's drove inside [his] car. They've got your name and number in the head house [so] they know whose car that is. It's not to guess for them.

Eventually, it got so tight that they put on what they call the "shot foreman." You'd drill your holes, have to furnish the powder, then this man would come and he'd shoot your coal for you so it wouldn't be shot too hard. Well, here's what I'd do: I'd drill my holes and then I slipped me a stick of dynamite right in the back of that hole. He didn't find that, so he'd tamp his [dynamite] right in on it. You had to learn to be shifty.

In other words, you put one stick of dynamite in the hole, the shot foreman came along and put another stick in, and when the coal exploded you had a bigger cut to work on than the next miner?

Exactly right. Of course, I got plenty of sport out of it and plenty of hard work, too. Most all of them, they'd clean this hole out, then they'd wait till this man come along and shoot the coal. He didn't shoot it half hard enough and they'd dig theirselves to death trying to get it loose so they could load it. My coals always shot up in fine shape. I got in such a habit [of] loading that [jack]

* Gondola.

rock that in two weeks they charged me thirty-five dollars for dirty coal. Then to head it off, there was a man come through here, a lawyer. He was charging these guys five dollars to get their money back that they'd been charged on this dirty coal. He takes their five dollars and [we] never did hear of him no more. I had to do something, [the mines were] only running about half of the time and I just couldn't make a bread check. I decided then to come back and live on the farm.

In '30 I went to the Wisconsin Coal Company in Knott County. While I was there I'd buy two weeks' supply of groceries with this A & P outfit, which was about 50 percent of the price that we'd pay in a commissary. Pretty soon there was a bunch of people that got to doing the same thing. The superintendent come down through the mines and he hollered at me, "Melvin, I got a paper here for you to sign."

I said, "I've signed all the rest of them, I guess I just may as well sign that one." [They'd] take up contributions for sick people, you know. I'd always sign it, so I said, "Let's see what it's about."

He said, "Everybody that works at this mine is going to have to trade at the company store."

I said, "Now, Saul, that's saying a great big word. I'd rather trade at the company store, lot rather to do that if you fellows [priced] groceries there like I'm buying them."

He said, "We can't."

"Well, then I can't buy them." We argued around a long time. [He said] they's going to lay everybody off that didn't sign the paper.

Finally, he was trying to get the best of me. He said, "Melvin, you know we furnished you a lot of extra work here." When they run slack I would get a lot of extra time because I was a brute and that's what they's looking [for].

I said, "Yes, I admit that. Appreciate it very much, Saul, but on the other hand, did my work satisfy you?"

"Yes," he said, "there was no kicking on the work."

"That was my money, I worked it out, and I have the right to trade it where I want to trade it." I never did hear no more about it.

After you married why did you continue mining instead of going back to the farm?

I had to do that in order to support the family. I had to get away from Wolfe County. In Wolfe County there has been a number of people to starve and almost went naked. Where I worked on one of these farms for seventy-five cents a day to [buy my] bread and meat, well I was making seven to ten [dollars] in the mines. I didn't love to leave, but I was almost forced to. I knowed a number of people that was married before I was [who] wouldn't leave their wife and family for any reason. I would rather been away from them and see them eat a little higher on the hog, and had more clothing, than to have stayed there and worked, and sweated, and maybe couldn't pay my bills like a lot of other people.

I boarded in the camp most all the time and my wife, until we got a house, she stayed with my parents. I'd come [home to Wolfe County] maybe once a month and mail money back home. I worked like that until 19 and 26 and at this time I took a job at Consolidated Coal Company [on Smoot Creek] in Letcher County and rented a house and [we] moved there. That was the hardest mine I ever worked in, in my life. Of course, I was strong. The average for the mines was three-and-a-quarter tons to the man, but I don't remember ever loading under ten.

The living conditions was terrible. Now I want to tell you, it was terrible. It was filthy, in other words. Sanitation was out. Maybe five or six families would draw water from one pump. There was many houses close together. They had outside toilets between these houses and these toilets was too bad to even think about. They had boxes they'd scoot under there to catch the droppings in and then they had Negroes that would take them out and haul them away and empty them and bring the boxes back. It'd been pretty hard to tell, actually, how people existed, but they did.

It was no good to raise kids. Them kids would run together, they fought, they done everything. Actually, them coal camps, about all of them were just made up of outlaw people that cared for nothing. I knowed two men there that swapped wives just like swapping horses. One of them had three kids and the other had six, I believe. Saturday night, payday night, these people got drunk. Lord, lord, lord, gambling, drunks, went on every night.

I made pretty fine money all the time and rent wasn't too high, I think about two-and-a-half a month. Utilities wasn't too high, wasn't nothing like as high as it is now. They didn't charge much for coal, either; they delivered it for about three dollars a ton. And you didn't pay much on your lights, either.

There was no doubt [some] couldn't pay it. The company would shut down maybe two or three days a week [or] a month. There was all these people there in that camp and they'd just work today and they'd go draw that out in scrip tonight at the office and spend it at the store. The next day, the next two days, they was on starvation, just about the whole camp. It never did happen [to me], but I was always watching for them times. My wife had a nail drove in the side of the house [and she hung a bucket on it]. She'd put scraps in that bucket and I've seen kids come up there and get them scraps out of that bucket. It's heartbreaking. I told my wife, "By golly, let's feed them if we can. Let them little fellows come and get them something to eat." I never missed anything by it and I was always lucky enough to make pretty good money.

Actually, miners is about the closest people to each other that you'll ever find. As for myself, if there are two people running for office here in Wolfe County and one of them's a miner I have a little closer feeling for him than I do the other guy because I do know what he went through. It's an unknowing question, actually, to say why, but they'll just about go the limit. I lived in one camp a while and when they shut down a lot of these older heads would always lay up food. These other folks hadn't laid none up, they would just divide that. As long as one eat, they all eat. I don't know why they are so very close to each other, but they really are, more so than any group of people that's ever met.

Actually, I like the camp better [than the farm], to tell you the truth about it. I'd go out there to work and I didn't have a lot of stuff to worry about. I'd put in my shift in the mines; then I could go in and take a bath and go to bed and sleep like a baby and not have a lot of stuff to worry about. When I was back on the farm a cow might be getting out, or the hogs breaking out. It was a little tougher on the farm, actually, than it was in the coal camp.

In the coal camps the people who had the best homes with the plushest surroundings were the mining executives, engineers, and accountants. Not surprisingly, the persons who filled these top positions were often imported from outside the region along with the blacks and foreigners who were on the other end of the economic totem pole. Among the outsiders was Francis Marion Addis, a mining official in Wellston, Ohio, until 1910 when he moved to the coalfields of Van Lear, Kentucky. Addis belonged to a small cadre of executives who migrated from one place to another establishing new towns and companies. As a result of the travels, his daughter, Frances Addis Turner, was reared in a variety of Appalachian coal camps. She was born in 1911 and from 1918 to 1921 her father was superintendent of the Elkhorn Piney Coal Company in Weeksbury, Kentucky, which was a showplace among camp towns. Later, when she became an adult, Frances chose to remain in eastern Kentucky rather than migrate out and has spent her career teaching English to Appalachian high school students. Today she is still teaching school and lives in Price, near Weeksbury.

During her childhood Frances observed the day-to-day life of a coal camp from a rare vantage point. Her family lived above "Silk Stocking Row" and her father's position in the company allowed

her to mingle with people from all parts of the camp. The oppor-
tunity was not wasted, for Frances is a keen observer.

The home that my father occupied at Weeksbury as the assistant superintendent my mother liked very much, but when my
father was promoted to the general manager of the company, the
last step up the ladder, we had to move into the superintendent's
home because whoever was below Dad was waiting for that
house. Our home in Weeksbury had cost, in 1916, nearly a
hundred thousand dollars. It was built originally for the [com-
pany] owner for a summer home. This home, which we lived in
for four or five years in the early twenties, was probably seventy-
five feet long. There was a full-length attic which was destined as
a ballroom. There were six bedrooms and three bathrooms and a
beautiful conservatory where my mother kept her flowers. The
master bedroom had plate-glass mirror doors [and] its own beautiful fireplace with marble. There were six rooms in the basement, which included the furnace room. This whole house was
heated by steam radiators. The janitor was paid, the light bill and
the coal bill was paid [by the company], but it was charged off as
part of the superintendent's salary, which no doubt was another
tax break for the company.

The houses that would be one step down the ladder would be
[assigned] to the bookkeepers, the chief accountant, the doctor,
who was by no means top man on the social level because this
was retained for engineers and executives. This row of people
[was] called "Silk Stocking Row" because they usually were somewhat younger people than the top executives' families were, and
of course, there was more social life because there were more of
them and they met for parties and picnics and card games. I
remember hearing the older women speak about, "Well, wonder
what went on down in Silk Stocking Row over the weekend?"

Then, of course, there were some [laborers'] houses more desirable than others. I believe that these houses were given out to
various people on the basis of the man's efficiency; what he was

Frances Turner

worth to the company. If he were a coal loader who produced a great deal of coal in a day, or if he was an electrician who was doing an excellent job, if he was valuable to the company and would be hard to replace, of course he was someone that the company needed to hold on to. As he showed that he was a desirable worker he was promoted, maybe not money-wise, but he was moved into a better house in a better part of the camp. Actually, there were entire parts of the camp where the houses were four rooms. In a better part they were five or six, there were larger lawns, some were fenced, some were not. The houses that were the center of the camp were often considered more desirable because this is where the social activity went on.

Usually the camp was segregated not only as to the quality of the housing; it was also segregated as to ethnic background. The Italian camp at Weeksbury was called "Yellow Flats." All [the] houses in the camp were painted in a variety of colors—pink, green, white—to break the monotony, but these little stucco cottages [where] all of the Italians lived were all yellow. Then, there [were] the Polish, although it embarrasses me to say that the Polish for some reason always carried the name "Hunkie" and the

Czechoslovakians were thrown in. I'm sure it was our ignorance, that we weren't even aware of the difference [between] the Hungarians, the Czechoslovakians, and the Polish people.

The Italians always seemed to become a tightly organized group and cling together more than the other three groups. I would assume that the Czechoslovakians, the Polish, the Yugoslavians, the Hungarians, were a [larger] group and they probably integrated with the natives more quickly than the Italians who were more clannish by nature. They adopted our customs much more slowly. They held to their own festivals, their own religious services, their own foods much longer than the other groups. I knew of very little, if any, friction in these coal camps although I would have to admit that each ethnic group provided more or less [its] own amusement, unless it was the theater, or a band concert, or something that was open.

The Negroes came in a little later and they, primarily, were all from Alabama. They also had their own camps. I remember very little fraternization other than many of the black women [worked] for the officials' wives, certainly not because they had to because they had the same advantages as anybody else as far as the opportunity to make money. They could do anything, but I never ever remember seeing them in the soda fountain, and they had their own church, and their own school, also provided by the company.

There was always in every camp I ever lived in a movie house. The whites sat in the left section, the middle section, the balcony; the Negroes all sat in the right section. Usually the company did not operate the movie house themselves; it was given as a little fringe benefit to the superintendent who in turn re-leased it or hired someone to operate it. So, there were movies in the coal camps far earlier than there were movies in the local towns. This was a way of keeping these people content and happy because they did not want to lose labor.

The company also employed the doctor and had its own doctor's office [with] all the emergency equipment in it. It was better equipment than the local hospitals [had] because, again, [it] was maintained by the company. The doctor was on twenty-four-hour call. The only thing the miner paid him was two dollars a month and this included medical expenses, medication, child delivery, the whole package. Many excellent doctors came into eastern Kentucky who were just out of medical school because it was a good way to get yourself out of debt and move on. We're being used the same way now, not that I have any criticism of that, but it was being done in my childhood also.

The coal camp schools were owned and controlled by the coal company officials. They interviewed the teachers, they hired them, they paid them. They were probably much better than the schools that were controlled by the county because they did have libraries, and whatever aids there were up to that time, and they were comfortable buildings. These schools were not exclusive because on the fringes of every coal camp there is always going to grow up the junction towns and these children attended [company] schools, also. As a consequence, people who had no connection with the company—independents, merchants—were compensated by these schools.

This business of the company controlling the school went on until at least 1930; then gradually the county board began to pick these up and take over part of the expenses. Of course, then they had control. But the coal company, through its influence and its money, retained the choosing of the teachers because they controlled the purse strings. If the school needed something new, some goodies, then the county board could depend on the better coal companies coming up with this money because, of course, it was tax-free. As a result, they were able to retain control at places like Wheelwright even into the Depression years because the county needed that money they were rather free-handed with. The first football uniforms that Wheelwright ever had were bought entirely by the coal company in the late thirties. The baseball equipment was bought by the company, the band instruments were bought by the coal company.

The companies would employ men who could play baseball and could do something in the coal camp, [and] I'll have to admit that many of these jobs were more or less what we would call "made" jobs. There was a great rivalry with baseball teams, competition became great and there would be pressure put on the officials: "Why don't you hire so-and-so, he's a good player?" and it was done. I can remember when Drift [Kentucky] had a baseball team that hardly [had] a native on it. It was equally true of Wheelwright, Weeksbury, or any other coal camp.

Now on the fourth of July at Weeksbury they always had some kind of extra entertainment. The company provided the very expensive fireworks in the center of the town at night, then there would be all of the ice cream and watermelon, the band play, the festival activities, and even a speech or two in those patriotic days following World War I when we were making the world safe for democracy and all that. All of this would be provided by the company.

The company provided usually at least two stores [that] handled furniture, hardware, clothing, as well as food. The [trip] to the company store for the women of the coal camp was probably the social event of the day that men were not in any way mixed up with. Where modern women might go to a discussion club, or to an afternoon bridge game, or to a matinee, or to an art museum, these women got "cleaned up," I remember they called it, and they went to the store. They managed to spend quite a bit of time there. They saw people from all over the coal camp in different parts of the store and it was a social occasion as well as a business affair.

[Nearby] there was another building which included the community hall [and] the fountain which sold sandwiches. Adjoining that was a barber shop, and adjoining that was a place that no lady would have ever considered looking in as she passed in those days: a poolroom. Also along this row of businesses there was the private bank. So the company provided you with housing, electricity, hair cuts, a school, a doctor, a theater, a poolroom, bank.

You could be born, live, and die in one of these camps and really never have to leave it.

There was [also a] clubhouse maintained primarily for the unmarried accountants, bookkeepers, engineers—officials, in other words. It was not frequented by the laborer because they had separate quarters for the unmarried laborer, or laborer who couldn't have his family with him, and these were called "boardinghouses," and believe it or not they were segregated. All of the foreigners [stayed at] what was called the "Hunkie boardinghouse," and all of the Anglo-Saxons frequented another boardinghouse. There would be a boardinghouse in each area of the camp, probably as many as three, and they were huge buildings. It was considered a [plum] for a man if his wife could [be] the boardinghouse [manager]. These families were [carefully selected] and if he worked in the mines they could double their income. That was a choice tidbit to be permitted to operate one of these boardinghouses. But the clubhouse was for visiting officials and unmarried officials of a little higher echelon because, believe me, there were strict social lines. For instance, I remember that all of the officials' homes in every camp I'm familiar with were built on the hill. It was a matter of apparently looking down on the rest of the camp. I don't think they were really built for that, but I'm sure a lot of that went on. Not with my family, but I'm sure that the bookkeepers' wives . . .

[Today it seems] highly amusing that people would feel either superior or inferior on the basis of the housing or on the basis of the money that was made since people's attitudes have changed completely. Everybody's attitude didn't have to change. I grew up in a home where this was considered ridiculous to feel superior to anybody because your father happened to have a little better job or you went to school a day longer. We would have been punished for such thinking. One of the few spankings I ever got was for calling a colored woman who was ironing by her given name. I was told that she was older than I and she was entitled to a title just as much as anybody else was.

A man once advised my father that another employee would get beneficial results if he'd rub his belly with a blue flannel hat. This type of thing, of course, faded with a professional doctor, with professional equipment, with schools. Even movies I would say spread a new kind of culture to eastern Kentucky. I'm not saying it's a better kind of culture, I'm only saying a new kind of culture. We will have to grant that railroads, schools, doctors, recreation, and better housing was beneficial. But, of course, we are back to where we began. [Comparing] what went out of here in the wealth of eastern Kentucky would only be like stacking a penny against Fort Knox. Economically, of course, the tragedy is when the coal company no longer could show a profit. These people, especially those who were second-generation miners, knew nothing about how to make a living except at the mines and there were no more mines. When I came back to the coal mines to teach school [in] Wheelwright in 1934 many of them were more or less helpless. They had all their life been able to conduct all their business through the company and to be totally on their own was a new experience. They had no skills other than mining skills and many of them were approaching middle age. You can see this created a dreadful situation because they were like abandoned people through really no fault of their own.

Now many people did not live in the coal camp itself. I must say that the spirit of independence was still alive somewhere in eastern Kentucky because I have known many people who never lived in a company house. Let me speak for myself. We were married thirty-seven years [and in that time] my husband was never off of a coal company payroll as an accountant. We never lived a day of our married lives in a coal camp or in anything that belonged to a coal company.

People bought small homes, they paid for them, and if it was impossible to drive to work often they lived in one of these boardinghouses from Sunday afternoon till Friday evening and then went home to the family. Living in one of these coal camps

Marvin Gullett

was a step higher type of living from the comfort viewpoint than struggling to pay for a home to go back to, although that seemed to [be] a wiser thing in the long run.

Marvin Gullett was also born and reared in a coal camp, but his was a different town and a different way of life. He was born in 1918 in Perry County, Kentucky's Blue Diamond mining camp, and as a child his gymnasiums were abandoned coal tipples, not converted ballrooms, and his father labored inside a deep mine rather than in an office building. Marvin never lived on a farm until he was an adult but his parents and kinfolks had been farmers and even as a child they urged him to look beyond the world of Blue Diamond.

Most people felt they was going to paradise when they moved to the mining camps. It was a way of life that they liked. The wages was so low on the farm you couldn't make more than a dollar a day, or fifty cents a day. [In the mines] they would make seven, or eight, or ten dollars a day and you could buy some of the comforts of life that you couldn't afford on the farm. There was a feeling of neighborness. Everybody lived pretty close to one another [and] there was a great population. I guess five thousand people [lived] at Blue Diamond at one time. Once they was in close proximity to one another they become like a tribe. They loved one another and got along pretty good. There might have been a few violent men around the camps that would drink pretty heavy and some people would get killed, but as a general thing the people got along good.

It wasn't boring, not near as bad as some people think. The men, they'd get out [on their] days off from work and talk to one another on the commissary steps and they'd play horseshoes, have wrestling matches. I've seen men gather on a little village green and the best wrestler, the one that won, [would] be the hero of the camp. They had socials and they'd visit one another a whole lot.

The men were the breadwinners in the mining camps and when [a man's] son got big enough to work he followed his father's footsteps. Back in those days nobody thought of being anything but a miner when he was a young man. At sixteen years old if [a boy] could pass the physical examination, he was ready to go to work. All he had to do was sign his name on the book in the company store and he was a miner.

The worst thing about living in the mining camp, one was always in constant dread. Many years ago the mines were very unsafe. The company wanted all the production they could get so the safety rules wasn't too grand. You couldn't be confident about when the top was going to fall in. Only God above knew. Many a time I'd go to bed and I'd lay and worry whether Dad would come back alive or not. I'd heard them talk in the miners' jargon about what mining was and I realized it was dangerous. I've seen men going around on crutches, all they'd do would be hang around the company store. [Where we lived] the company wouldn't put him out of his house because he got hurt in company service. [Other] companies were pretty hard. He'd have to move, go back to the farm and finish up his days.

Sometimes great tragedies come upon whole families. Many a whole family [was] caught in one section, killed. That poor widow, if she didn't marry again, would have to take in washings to raise the family up. Most of the mining people, though, would give her all the work they could to help raise her family. They had sympathy from everybody. When a miner got killed everybody loved him and revered his memory, but the man was gone and he couldn't provide for his family. There was many lonesome graveyards owned by the mining companies. Sometimes four and five men [were] buried in a day, killed in a mining accident.

My mother, she was very happy around the coal camps. She was a miner's wife and she was brave. Mother was the mainstay at home. She made everything go as far as it could. We always made a little garden stuff in the mining camps; it was company land, and we let out stock run out in the woods. [We] didn't have to buy much out of the store, maybe a sack of feed every now and then, but there was a great comfort [in having] this store.

I was very happy. Although we didn't have many toys our mother and father was always close to us. We couldn't be lonesome, there was so many kids around the camp. Many miners had ten, fifteen children. Everybody felt a common kinship because they all had to work and fare together the same way. There was even a commonship between the mine operators and the men at one time, before the Great Depression. [If] you got out of work the boss would say, "You won't be laid off. I'll let the commissary carry you."

Back then [children would] listen to their parents better. Whatever the mother and daddy told them, they believed it.

There was some rough elements you had to stay away from, they was called "outlaws." Some of the kids would try to steal out of the company store and you had to stay away from these boys. Some kids would have to go down to a place called Greendale, a reform school, [where they'd] put them over a barrel and whip them and they'd come back and make good miners. I knew a boy back when I was a kid that got sent to the pen for stealing a pie. He was hungry and he went to his uncle's house and there was a pie sitting on the window and he got it. He had to go to Greendale for a year. Of course, he came back a better boy.

You always worried about [your children] because they might get hurt somewhere. It was harder to keep track of them because there was so many things they could get into in the mining camp. I know many days I worried my mother. We'd climb all over the old tipples. Of course, if I'd fell I would have been killed. Sometimes they did have tragedies like that. Many a day when I was a kid I'd go and watch the mine motors pulling the coal around the sides of the hill, watch the tipple, watch the men run a slate buggy. I remember Dad whipping me pretty hard for taking steel bearings out of the mining machines and making marbles out of them. On days that we weren't going to school we got to go around the old tipples, crawl through them. They had a chute you could slide down through.

We lived pretty close to the tipple and you couldn't keep anything clean in the house. It would seep through the windows, it was on everything. A woman could work from dawn till night and never keep it too clean because you just couldn't get rid of all that dust. The kids would get out and play in that coal and they'd look just like a miner when they come in. Then sometimes these old slate heaps would catch fire by themselves through spontaneous combustion and if you had to live by one of these burning fires it was terrible to have to breathe [those] sulphur fumes.

Any miner's wife would get bored and sometimes that caused a lot of trouble. Through the winter there was nothing to do [other] than keep the house clean and get the children off to school. The miners worked ten, fifteen hours a day and [women] was left alone a whole lot. People [would] gather and talk through boredom and get some tale started and cause a fight between husbands. It was a pretty dreary life in some ways, although that was all people knew. Back at that time they was better satisfied with it than they would be now.

Many marriages broke up. [Miners] knew a woman from the country didn't mind hard work and was used to hardship and they'd go out in one of the hollows and court some old farmer's daughter, [marry her and bring her] around the mining camps. A woman lots of times wouldn't be satisfied. She'd be used to a pretty clean, independent way of living and she'd try to get the man to quit his job and go back. Say you leave a place out in the country where the air was clear like wine. You go around to these old dusty, dirty coal camps and you could tell the difference and some people wasn't satisfied with it, though most people settled down to that way of life [for] economical reasons. They could make better money around the mining country, is why some followed mining, not that they liked it too good.

Many times I'd not see my father even on Sunday. When the work was good, sometimes he worked seven days a week. The miner made such low wages he had to work nearly night and day back before the union came in before he could have any money left. Of course, in those days he was a young able-bodied man and the hard work didn't get him down. He said mining was in his blood and he wasn't afraid, [but] he always told his children never to become a miner. He'd say, "Look what I go through, I'm not much better than a slave." His hands was skinned and broken and he'd get pretty tired. Sometimes he'd come out of the mines and he'd be wet all over [from where he had] worked in water and ice [had formed] on his clothes. When he'd take his clothes off they'd stand up. But he was young then and able to take it. People wasn't soft. They'd been raised on the farm and they was tough mountaineers and they adapted to coal mining very well.

In my life I've observed that all mountain people like to be alone. They like to get as far up in a holler as they can, be independent. If people tried to intrude on them too much they'd call them "foreigners." They'd say, "I don't want no trouble with a foreigner because he's not my kind of people." The farmers [sometimes] reacted very violent to [these outsiders]. They kept the tradition [of] the Ku Klux Klan alive to keep the foreigners out, what they called "Jews," "Wops," and "Dagos." The Jews were very much hated people. They peddled goods and mountain people thought anybody [who] wouldn't get out and work by the sweat of his brow and breath was terrible. There'd be some shifty lawyer come in and try and cheat the men out of compensation when they got hurt around the mines and some doctors [would] swear to the companies against the miners that got disabled. They hated men like that. If [there] was somebody they [didn't like] the Ku Klux would lay switches at his door, give him a warning. If he wouldn't improve they'd burn a cross not far from his house. The night riders [would] whip on him and sometimes made him leave the country. That was the mountaineers' way of fighting back foreign intrusion.

When I was young sometimes they'd kill a foreigner. Most of the time the court stood for the Englishman more than they would for somebody else because the judge was usually Anglo-Saxon. Justice in the courts wasn't too good at that time: the judge could be bought; the lawyers was crooked most of the time, you couldn't get good representation in court. The courts was run by the coal companies and they had the power to elect whoever they wanted and the "will of the people" wasn't what we call it nowadays. Back then the "will of the people" was the man that had the money, that big operator, coal baron. They had absolute authority on their own property, you had to do what they said.

The Appalachians always had a surplus of labor. No matter how many got killed they could always replace them. Somebody'd come in and say, "I need a job." He was hired. If he proved to be a good worker he could stay there as long as he's able to work.

When he got too old to work he's condemned by the company doctor: "John, I'm sorry. You've done all you could do for the company and we appreciate it, but we have to send you home. You're not able to work anymore." Most of the time they had big families and somebody'd take care of them. Sometimes they went to an old people's home [in] the Bluegrass. [The] Masons had homes for disabled miners that belonged to the lodge. Some of them saved their money and they was able to pay their way after they quit work. From 1922 to 1928 was good years around the Appalachian coalfields. People worked hard and some of them laid up some bank accounts, but after they lost their money in 1929 most of them didn't bother to save anymore. After the '29 crash many miners went bankrupt [and so] did many companies. The steel on their machines rusted away and their tipples rotted down and they went to the hands of the receivers. I've seen many an old abandoned mining camp and there's nothing more desolate. People began to drift around like vagrants during the Depression. They went begging for work and they couldn't get it because half of the mines were shut down.

[In] 1912 when the first railroad was built from Jackson to Hazard, it seemed that people just changed overnight from a rural farming settlement to an industrial community. At the time the Hazard coalfield was opened up it was said to be the greatest coalfield in the world. It covered several thousand square miles; every mountain was full of coal. Up to that time goods was brought up the river in a pole boat and when the railroad come along it brought in new supplies and new people. Thousands of people [came] to work in the mines from other places, people they'd never seen before. Many people come out of Tennessee to eastern Kentucky to open up the coal mines and they brought their talented men with them—bookkeepers, superintendents, and supervisors. Naturally, they wanted to have schools for their children, so they built schools. Prior to that time there'd been no systematic way of education in the mountains because people just met in one-room schoolhouses and they didn't learn very much. After they came in it was a great benefit to the people. There probably wouldn't have been any roads in here if it hadn't of been for the mines.

[Mountain people] had a reason for being worried. After the coal operators come they swindled them out of a lot of property. The mining camps went up but a lot of times they lost the legal right to the property; the mining company owned it so they had to do what the mining company said. The free way of life of Appalachian people was lost. You had to know how to hold your job; just one word said to the company that they didn't like, they would fire you. If they fired you and wanted to blacklist you, you couldn't get a job with any other mining company. You had to do what they told you, pay whatever rent they charged, and [accept] whatever wages they paid. In a way they was like tenants on their own land.

When the rush to the coal mines began, some mountain people stayed behind because they were wary of the new industry, too old to enter the mines, or hesitant to leave the familiarity of home. Dock Burdine Franklin was among them. He returned home from World War I, resolved that a coal digger's life was not right for him and decided, instead, to compete with Imperial Elkhorn Coal Company's commissary in Sergent, Kentucky. In 1920 Dock borrowed a thousand dollars and opened the D. B. Franklin General Merchandise Store in Sergent. Today it remains the unique store it was in the twenties. Dock's general merchandise includes boots, miners' lamps, diamond rings, Real Kill roach spray, deep-sea fishing reels, flea powder, pearls, Fine Arts Complexion Soap, tennis shoes, cemetery wreaths, notions, over-the-counter drugs, plus a full line of groceries.

A narrow path leads from the front door halfway back through the store to Dock's counter and cash register. He bought the cash register when he opened the store, thinking every merchant needed one, but soon found he was mistaken. Dock keeps cash in his pockets and drapes jewelry on the cash register. Just inside the front door is the Sergent Post Office, a testimony to the good luck and political connections that helped Dock become postmaster of Sergent soon after he opened the business.

Sergent was a small town even from the start and Imperial Elkhorn employed only fifty miners, enough to support a general store or a commissary, but not both. A. J. Laverty, the coal company's mining superintendent, resented Dock Franklin's competition.

A. J. Laverty kept after the men pretty close about trading with the commissary. He'd tell them it might mean their job if they didn't patronize the company store. The union would [later] put a stop to all that [but we] never had a union down here. Of course, I didn't approve of him trying to keep the men from trading with me and he didn't approve of my trading here, so naturally we didn't have anything much to do with each other.

They wanted all the business themselves because they had a store and they had to pay the salaries of the store [personnel]. Every time I sold one of their customers something their company failed to make any profit on that sale: it went in my pocket in place of the company's treasury. [The miners] didn't like the way they was trying to drive them around, but they didn't say too much. They thought they ought to have a right to trade where they wanted to. A lot of them would do their trading at night after the commissary had closed, you see. They'd just trade with me because they felt they could save money, and they could. They didn't make anything much and the commissary was high. I didn't have any overhead; just done my work myself.

I think [telling the men not to trade with me] was the biggest thing that they did to me. Cutting prices didn't hurt so much because you could cut a few items and go ahead with selling your other merchandise. Some of my customers traded at both stores and they told me [one time that the commissary] was under me about a nickel on pork chops. We was selling them for about fifty cents and they cut a nickel. I cut them to forty. They cut them to thirty, and I cut them to twenty-five cents. They cost about forty cents [wholesale]. We kept cutting back and forth and we got them down to about twenty cents a pound. That was competition personified. I was a little man, they was a big company, but I stood my ground.

Of course, they had a bigger buying power than I did, because I was in debt when I started October the twentieth, 1920. I owed a thousand dollars to the First National Bank of Fleming and didn't have a thing to start with. The commissary had a bigger store and they had plenty of money to buy with.

They opened about eight o'clock and stayed in until about five. I opened about seven o'clock and stayed open until after dark. Sometimes I'd still be in there till ten o'clock. After I quit having sales, I'd take my one-horse wagon and deliver all over the county. They didn't deliver anything.

The Imperial Elkhorn Coal Company fought me pretty hard. [When I first started out] they enjoined me from completing the store. They had one of their carpenters plant some stones right above my store building and pretend like they were going to build houses. They sent a summons up here on me to appear in court. I was in a hurry to get it tried so I could finish my building. We went over to Pikeville and Mr. Williams, the engineer for the Imperial Elkhorn Coal Company, was their main witness. I asked my lawyer to ask [Williams] if they don't have plenty of room to build all the houses they'll ever need without using my property? He said they probably did, so that clinched that.

[Another time] I had a car of hay come in one night from Jackson, Michigan. The conductor on the train called from Whitesburg and said the [mine] superintendent wouldn't let them have siding. Siding is where they load [coal] from out of the mines. He could have just brought [my hay] up here and shoved it in that siding and I could get it off when I wanted to. The conductor said, "Mr. Franklin, we got your car of hay from Michigan, but we can't get siding for it." "Well," I said, I called him by his

Dock Franklin

name—they thought the world of me, the railroad men did—"if you'll bring it up I'll have men there to unload it in thirty minutes." So I went down and got my men and we unloaded that car in thirty minutes. We threw it off on the railroad right-of-way, next to the tracks on both sides. I didn't get to haul it all up till the next day. I was just lucky it didn't rain on it.

[Laverty] was scared of his job and he thought anything [he] might do would help the competitor . . . They might find out something about it at headquarters and it might hurt his prestige with the company. Of course, he naturally [had to] protect his own position and you can't blame him for that.

I had a farm up here and [once] they asked me if they could come out up there and empty the water out of the mines [onto my land]. I told them to go ahead. They had ponies and everything in there, and dirty mine water, and I let them come out with it. My wife had the flu and we didn't have much coal at that time. I said, "Mr. Laverty, could an outsider here get a little coal?" He said, "Mr. Franklin, we've got to cut the outsiders off from everything."

I came up from carrying the mail [that evening], threw my mailbag down, got me a big sledgehammer and mashed that pipe up, stopped the water from coming out. I've always been sorry of it, but I haven't really regretted it too much. He made me right mad at the time.

In late '24 the mines run slow. The [company] couldn't pay men and I couldn't pay my bills. I got to checking up and I owed over $20,000. Naturally, I got into deep water, didn't think I'd ever get out of it. Huntington Wholesale Furniture Company had a man that I loved very much. He's a wonderful man, Arthur F. Chambers. Every time he'd come he'd have on a red tie. I got in debt about $1,500 to him for furniture, refrigerators, and radios. I owed over $20,000 to the wholesale companies and to the banks for real estate. I had assets to cover it, but nobody could pay me. The companies would begin to get restless and this man in West

Virginia said, "Now, Dock, don't you worry about us, you pay us as long as you can." I had another man that [I] owed $1,200 for hats and caps—I don't buy hats and caps anymore—he said, "Now, Mr. Franklin, don't you worry about what you owe us. We ain't going to fret."

Several large accounts got to lawing me. They placed it in the hands of the attorney at Whitesburg. I didn't know what to do. Well, little Jim Combs was sheriff of Letcher County at that time and I went out in front of the old courthouse—got a new courthouse there now—and talked to him for a few minutes. I said, "Sheriff, I'll give ye a mortgage against everything I got if you'll give me a chance on these excuses here against me. My hands are tied. I just can't do anything now. Can't pay them but I mean to pay them." I talked to him for a while and he said, "You don't need a mortgage. I don't need anything but your word. You ain't going to beat nobody." That give me a relief, you know, and I was able to roll up my sleeves and give business a little harder knock. In 1930 I wrote a check for everything I owed.

How did you make up that money?

[People] begin to get jobs other places and pay me on what they owed me. I had a little property that I sold off and got the money out of it. And I worked like a dog.

In 1928 the [company] went broke. I thought when the mines quit operating here that my business would be doomed, but really, I reached out and got business from all over the county, practically. People'd come seven, eight, fifteen miles to trade with me in them days.

[Credit has] been my biggest trouble since I've been here. I've credited everybody all over the county. The last time I checked, over twenty years ago, I had over $60,000 out, and I guess I got $75,000 now that I never expect to get. I've lost my shirt; doing a good business and worked awful hard, but I've lost a lot of money.

I know people that's traded with me for years [and] I just don't like the idea of saying no to them. They'd come and open an account and then they'd trade for two weeks and when payday [came] they'd pay it off, some of them would, and some'd pay a little on it. They'd trade on and the first thing ye know they'd get in [debt] maybe a hundred dollars or two hundred dollars. Once a year one or two customers [who have] been gone twenty-five years come back and say, "I owed you some when I left here and I wasn't able to pay it. I got my Social Security the other day and I want to pay it all off." Seems like they want to get even with the world. I always figured that if a man traded with me a year, paid me $1,200, if I made 20 percent I'd make $240. If you left owing me for a hundred dollars and I never seen [you] anymore, I still made [$140 on your business]. I've operated on that theory, but it's not a good one, not good business.

Never garnisheed a man in my life, never lawed a man. I've written letters and asked them to pay me, but if a man is going to pay you he'll pay ye without too much dunning. Sometimes you can drive a man clear away by hounding him to death about an account.

In many cases I just trust people too far; I had too much faith. My wife always told me, "D.B., you have more faith in the human race than anybody I ever saw in my life," and she was a college graduate and [had] traveled around quite a bit. I've never regretted losing where I thought there might be hungry [children], because it could have been me. I could have been an outcast myself. The good Lord has blessed me wonderfully, gave me my wife, a good companion for forty-eight years. I've had a good life and I think that I owe people something, so I've never turned anyone down that I thought [was] hungry.

I know people look at [the store] and say "Ye don't have any system a'tall." A man came in here one time from Pike County, a feller by the name of Burke. He was selling tobacco for the R. J. Long Tobacco Company. I had on my old work clothes and waited on the trade and he stood there with his arms folded and shoes shined. Looked like a gnat would fall off of him if it hit. Shiny and clean as a pin. He told a feller, "How in this world does this man find anything in here?"

He hadn't been there for two or three months and I had him a nice order wrote out for four or five hundred dollars. After I waited on the trade he came up to the counter, laid his order pad down, and said, "What can I sell ye, Mr. Franklin?"

I said, "I had a short order list here but if I decided to buy an order from you it might fall over behind that stuff I don't know I've got and I'll never find, so I don't believe I'll buy anything." He was beat. I did it more for a joke, but I didn't buy any tobacco. He came back in about two months and I did buy. He said, "Mr. Franklin, I didn't mean that the way you took it."

I said, "Yes, you meant it just the way I took it."

People always think [I] don't know where anything is, but when I go in there at night to get anything I hardly ever turn the light on if it's dark. I've been awful bad to save juice all my life; don't like to burn up electricity because I'm afraid it might give away.

Dock is still not certain why he, rather than an Imperial Elk-horn employee, was named Sergent postmaster in 1920, but he was delighted with the appointment because he knew customers would inevitably combine mail call with buying general merchan-dise. What he did not anticipate was the impact of a Miss Lonely Hearts on his trade.

A lady moved into Sergent and she'd write [hundreds of] let-ters. There was a lot of people all over the country, what they call "lonely hearts," [that] wanted to get a companion, men and women both. Some of them would write and tell her they was [to] inherit and, of course, that would be quite an attraction for the opposite sex. They'd send her a dollar, or two dollars, or maybe sometimes five dollars. She'd get an awful lot of mail. You've seen these first-class mail pouches, haven't ye? Some days you could hardly pull it together at the top to lock it; some days first-class mail was that much. She'd buy maybe fifty dollars' worth of stamps a day.

They based my annuity on the sale of stamps and the more stamps I sold the bigger my salary was. If I didn't sell many stamps, I didn't get much through the year. [When she came] the post office went from a small fourth class to a big third class. It over doubled [my salary] and made my annuity grow.

Did you have anything to do with her coming here?

Well, I always thought I did. I'll tell you why. We didn't have any church here and my wife and I decided to build a church. You know, the Bible tell ye, "It is more blessed to give than to receive." My wife and I put over $12,000 in it ourselves. I thought that was responsible for this woman coming. I felt the good Lord was smiling upon our work, and our efforts, and you couldn't make me believe anything else.

[By 1963] my retirement pay far exceeded my salary. I wanted to get rid of the office and I wanted it appointed to Mrs. Tubbs, the lady that's working for me in the store. I hated to give up the office because I didn't want [it] to leave the store. I thought it helped make it a sign of attraction for my business.

Archie Pathes, the undertaker here at Whitesburg, [was] over here at the cemetery one afternoon and I said, "Archie, I want to retire. I'm losing money."

Archie said, "Well, Dock, I'll see what I can do about it." [He was] a United States marshal at that time; he went to Washington quite often.

One morning our congressman, Carl D. Perkins, called me up and said, "Is this Mr. Franklin?" I believe he called me "Dock."

I said, "Yes, sir!"

He said, "I understand you want to retire from the government service there as postmaster."

"Yes, your honor, I'd like to if I can get everything fixed up right."

He said, "Well, I called you this morning to let you know that if you want to retire we'll fix things any way you want them fixed." He was a Democrat and I was a Republican, but I voted for him ever since and I'll vote for him as long as I live.

I said, "Yes, sir, your honor. I'll send my request in for retirement today."

The Post Office Department, they were awful nice to me, awful nice. The inspector came in here one morning; I knew he'd come to check me out. He says, "Mr. Franklin, you've made us an awful good postmaster. We're awful proud of ye. I hope your retirement years will be as good as your service to the government." When he got ready to check me out he said, "Here's a penny that don't belong to the government. This is yours." I should have framed that penny.

In the camp towns miners seldom had time to enjoy whatever social amenities existed because their lives were bound to coal. Most laborers left home before daylight and walked to the mouth, or portal, of the mines which was little more than a gaping hole in a mountainside. Once inside the mouth they entered a tunnel that had been hewed by the miners before them and began moving toward the face of coal. Where the tunnel was four or five feet high miners walked to the face in a hunchbacked position. Where it was two or three feet high they crawled on their knees. The distance they walked, or crawled, from the mouth to the face varied, ranging from a few hundred feet to more than a mile.

Monroe Quillen began digging coal from a seam near his family's home at Whitaker, Kentucky, in 1920 when he was ten. At thirteen he accompanied his father to the underground mines and learned the skills that would later make him a highly respected coal miner. In 1948 he retired from mining and began selling Chevrolet cars and trucks, again with considerable success judging from the score of manufacturer's trophies and plaques displayed in the Quillen living room. While he was selling automobiles in Whitesburg nearly everyone Monroe knew bought a

Chevrolet from him. Only one friend was a stubborn holdout.
That was Dock Franklin, the Sergent merchant and supersales-
man, who according to Monroe "will always have the mistaken
notion that a Dodge is the better car."

Monroe talked about digging coal before the mines became
mechanized. He describes what the mines looked and felt like,
how coal was blasted from the earth, and how it was transported
out of the mountain.

A big coal mine is similar to walking into a hotel. You're on a
certain floor, you go down the main corridor for a ways and then
you'd turn off on a wing. Well, that [wing is] what we call "sections" in the mines. Then when you turned little places off [the
section] that's your "rooms." You're assigned to a room just like if
you go to a hotel and register you're assigned to a room. You go
in there and you go to sleep. The coal miner goes in there and he
loaded him sixteen ton of coal in that room.

The temperature is about sixty-eight, seventy degrees year
round. You have a moisture period in July, August, September—
what you call your "sweaty months"—same as you'd have in the
basement of your home. It's just like being in a cave, only the
cave doesn't run smooth like a seam of coal. That seam of coal is
absolutely smooth. Mines in this big Elkhorn seam of coal usually
run on a level grade; you don't go down or up much. I have
walked from here to Haymond, three miles up the road, through
the mines if it was raining, rather than walk [outdoors]. I enjoy
working in the mines, myself. I never was afraid in there. It's not
a place to take a vacation, or loaf—it's made to work in.

I thought to myself a lot of times: "I've been somewhere today
nobody ever went before." In the mountains I've scooted up
under rocks to stay dry [and] I've wondered a lot of times there,
too, if anybody had been there before. There's a possibility of
that, but not when you clean up a cut of coal in a coal seam. No
man has ever been that far before.

I started working in the coal mines for Southeast Coal Company at Seco, Kentucky, [on] the date of my sixteenth birthday, August 29, 1926. My father was working in the same section that I worked. It was dangerous to put a man in the mines that didn't understand shooting, testing roof, putting up timbers to make it safe. To send a man in there the first day that had never done that would be very dangerous. But an experienced miner, he shows the man how to stand, how to drill with his breast auger the first thing of a morning, how to get dust out from under this cut of coal, and he shows him how to take a pick and bump it against the rock top and tell [whether] it's loose or not, and where to set a timber. After you've moved the coal out from under a rock you beat on [the rock] with a coal pick or a hammer. It'll sound hollow like a board if it's loose and you've got to put timbers under it. If it's tight it's got a keen ring to it, just like hitting on anything solid. I never seen a rock that I wasn't afraid to lay down and go to sleep under because I know [I've] propped it up [correctly].

You had no safety precautions back in those days other than what you learned yourself. They didn't care if you didn't put any timbers up in the mines. They'd never come around and say, "You've got to do this or that about making yourself safe"; they left that up to you. They was interested in one thing and that's a ton of coal. The percentage [of miners killed per number of hours worked] back then was much greater than it is today. Now they've got it up to about a million hours per man killed. They didn't keep statistics back then, but a little mine like Acme Hill [where] my father was mashed up one time, they worked about thirty men and I'd say they averaged two men a year killed in the mine.

The first mining I done, I worked on what we call the day shift. We would arrive at the portal about seven o'clock and we'd walk approximately a mile and a half to what we'd call the working place, [where] we loaded the coal. Each entry would have from twelve to twenty-four rooms and every man had his own room to work in. When you arrive at the working place the machine men [would have] cut a little trench under the bottom of the coal with an electric cutting machine. It's hard to explain what a coal-cutting machine is. You've seen a chain saw that saws trees? The coal saw lays flat, the chain saw goes up and down. We'd take a long-handled shovel and shovel this "bug dust" out from under the coal. [Bug dust is] the fine coal, or the cuttings from the machine that crossed your face. It's what they call "carbon coal"; they fire steam furnaces with it.

The method [of drilling coal] was very crude. In the early days we used what we call a breast auger. The breast auger is a crooked auger as any drill would usually be and out at the end there's a couple of points that a blacksmith sharpens and makes a twist to them. [On the other end] is a double crank, similar to an old car crank. Then there's a steel plate that goes across your legs with a socket welded on it. You stick the end of this auger in [the coal] and you push [the steel plate] with your legs, turn [the crank] with your hand. A good stout man, back in the days when they drilled with them, could drill a six-foot hole in about six minutes, that's if you didn't rest. If you was older and weaker it'd probably take you twelve minutes to drill a six-foot hole. They had one mine foreman for each mine back in them days. The coal loader, he didn't need any boss. If he didn't load coal, that's his business, he didn't get any pay.

The first coal I worked in was about sixty inches high. We'd get our breast augers and drill us about three holes and then we'd put two to four sticks of dynamite in each one of these holes. Back in them days you'd drill a hole for each ton you wanted to shoot, charging it with approximately four sticks of 40 percent dynamite to each hole. Then after you got your coal loose it would be what we call a "fresh cut of coal." We'd start [digging] with a number-four shovel. The motorman would bring us [an empty] coal car. [Later he] would come back with a mule or with a motor. A lot of places used mules to pull the coal from the face; some of the places used electric motors. They'd pull this coal back to the main hallways out of the mines. Then the tram motor would pick [the loaded cars] up and take them back to the tipple and dump them over into the railroad cars. Then they'd come and bring more empties.

In between each car of coal that you load there was a break period because they had to take the loaded car out and bring the empty one back for you. Naturally, you'd rest during that time unless you'd want to take your pick and dig some more loose coal. I never was much of a fellow to take a break on any kind of a job. I was always anxious to get the job over with and come outside to take my break. It's no place to loaf in, a coal mine.

Talmadge Allen, of Hueysville, Kentucky, lived in coal camps reluctantly. He began working in the mines at Garrett, in Floyd County, Kentucky, in 1926, when he was fifteen, because his father became disabled and there were six other children to support. He continued mining for forty-one years and retired with only one good thing to say about camp towns: on the farm a man had virtually no spare time; in the coal camps he could call his time his own after completing an eight- to fifteen-hour work shift.

[The farm has] always been my way of life, I've never been satisfied anywhere else. [Living] in the coal camps was a case of "have to." After we was first married I'd made my last payment on our furniture and the house burnt down [with] everything in it. I was still working at the mines and I had to rent a coal company house.

These processing plants were usually close to where the miners lived. There was dust in the air all the time and if it wasn't dust it was smoke from these old garbage piles that was burning. People had to contend with the scent of it and it's an awful sickening scent. It's sulphur. Just chokes you up. The coal dust, it was impossible to keep out of the houses. You'd see little children running around just about as black as their parents coming in from work. [You'd see] mothers and daughters out on Monday morning scrubbing their clothes with a washing board. When they'd hang them out on the lines if it was windy they was getting the coal dust right back on the clothes again. It was something you lived with day and night. [A woman] had it [rougher] than a man. The man, when he was at his job he was away from home. The woman had it to contend with day and night. Marriages [were stronger then] because the man and the wife worked together. He crawled around in the mud and water in the coal mines to make a little something to feed his family and his wife had a job trying to keep their clothes clean and keep their house clean, but you never heard no griping about it.

People that lived on a farm [were] in a different environment [in a coal camp] and it's pretty hard to adapt yourself to that way of living. Anyone who is brought up on a farm never gets away from that feeling of "I want to be back [where] I could have more freedom." You have more privacy on a farm and don't have so many things that you can't do. But above all, it's cleanness. I don't mean to say that people *want* to live like a hog in a hog pen: they had to live with the surroundings they had and a lot [were] awful bad. There wasn't any work done on the houses except what the family done. They never had no bathrooms. I've seen some nice homes in these coal camps but there were some awful bad shacks. The people felt, "It don't belong to me no way, I'll just let her go."

The man that had been used to living on a farm in his own home [with] his own way of life had to adapt hisself, which he resented. He resented [being] told where he had to trade or [that] he couldn't do this or that.

Each individual has to determine within his own self what is necessary for the time being. He can learn to be content even though he's throwed into an environment like that. He'll do the best he can, he'll not let it overcome him, he'll overcome it. He'll always be wanting a better way of life. He never loses sight of that good side—back when I had liberty on the farm, I could have my garden where I thought it would produce, I could put out anything I wanted to. Lots of times in the coal camps if the company allotted that miner a little garden spot [it was] halfway to the top of a hill.

A story about a man and his wife and his children used to be circulated around the coal mines. One Sunday morning the daddy spanked one of the children for something that they had done wrong and the child went crying to its mother, "Momma, that man that comes here every Sunday morning spanked me." There was a lot of truth to that because the children was always in bed when the daddy went to work and they was usually in bed when he got in that night. We was paid at the rate of $1.60 a day but we didn't know when quitting time was. If it took twelve hours, or if it took fourteen, we stayed there.

When you live on a farm [and] went in from your day's work you also had your chores at the house that you had to perform. [You had] to take care of your milk cow, your hogs, your poultry, and if it was summertime you had your garden to work out. If you was living in the coal camp you didn't have anything like that. You [could] sit around at the house, go out visiting, whittling, or telling tales.

I'd been used to work all my life. I was brought up to have a job at home when I was a small child. I was taught that it better be done when nighttime come; there wasn't no excuse. That child that was brought up in a coal camp didn't know anything about a farm: it didn't know how to take care of a milk cow; how to go out and feed a hog, or anything about gardening. That child that was brought up on the farm was taught, "If we don't work, we'll have nothing to eat."

In the coal camps it seemed as though they wasn't as close to one another as children that was brought up on the farm. Families that was brought up in the coal camps was moving from one camp to another. They never stayed long enough in one place to really get acquainted with people and to care for one another as they did on the farm. If a company got rid of a man, that family had to move, there wasn't no fooling around about it, so their dwelling was uncertain. If a man working on the farm lost his job at the mines he still had a roof over his head. It might not have been too good, but it was home.

You were confronted with different races, different languages, any time you went into a coal camp and that was [another] difference between life on the farms. Colored people had one part of the coal camps that they occupied and the white people left them alone. The only time there was any trouble with colored people was when they started making their own brew, too. They'd drink in their part of town, they didn't bother nobody else. When the white man got too much and he went up there to dominate them under the influence of brew, well, that's when trouble started. They was going to protect their home the same as a white man is going to protect his.

There's plenty of people that couldn't [make the adjustment] and for a lot of them [coal camps] killed the determination [for] a better life. They had to be subject to it for so long it killed the desire for a better way of living.

We was determined to get out on our own and we did. I got hurt in the coal mines in 1936 and I took what compensation money I drawed and bought [a] little farm. When I went back to work in the mines we went to building a little three-room house and we paid for that by the month. [When] we moved in we had to borrow doors until we could get the money to buy doors.

People worked like slaves and had to be content with just any way to live. [Their] surroundings, a lot of them was bad, just as bad as they could be. Conditions got worser and worser until it was nearly unbearable. There had to come a change.

Things began to change after the United Mine Workers was established at Garrett. The coal camps and the houses, they began to shine. You saw a better way of life begin to start. In Harlan County before it was organized, [miners were] completely dominated by the company's thugs. The men were made slaves. After it organized they accumulated a desire to have a better way of living. They could have a say in how and what kind of life they were going to have in a coal camp.

I've been a coal miner all my life and I know the living and working conditions around a mine as good as any man and we've gone a long way. People don't know what hard times is unless they knowed back in the beginning in the coalfield. Men have lost their lives producing this coal and the majority of the old miners, their health is gone, the same as my own. It's a way of life that we want to forget about now, we don't want to hold any grudge. I hope that people don't look down on the coal miners. Because he is disabled now, he can't be thrown out to the mercy of the world. Back in my younger days I've knowed of old horses that worked all summer and were [turned] out to die when wintertime comes. I've seen them so poor you can just about hang your hat on their hipbones. The majority of the people didn't do that, they [realized] that old animal had worked all summer to help make their crop and they [saved] food for that horse because he was a necessity of life. And so is the laboring man.

6

A PEOPLE'S RESPONSE

During the latter years of the nineteenth century the directions were given and the lead characters chosen for a drama that would radically change the way of life in Central Appalachia. Act One unfolded in the first two decades of the twentieth century when camp towns were built, the coal industry boomed, and people from Hungary to Hell for Certain flocked to the coalfields. Mountain people's reactions to living in the camp towns varied tremendously. Melvin Profitt found it easier and far more pleasant than subsisting on tenant farms; Marvin Gullett was ambivalent; and Talmadge Allen longed for a return to farm life.

Whatever the response, there is no denying that the burgeoning coal industry had irrevocably altered an entire region. Minerals replaced topsoil as the standard-bearer of the economy. Secluded farms and scattered settlements were supplanted by coal towns that developed overnight around tipples much as corn had once circled farmhouses. The population that a few years before had been composed primarily of white mountaineers suddenly became a microcosm of the nation's melting pot.

The twenties was a decade of hard times that came on the heels of wartime prosperity. During World War I money was so easy in some towns that miners occasionally wore silk shirts under their

243

overalls. In the early 1920's there were signs that the first tide of prosperity the region had ever known was turning, but the euphoria lingered and few took note of economic omens. The amount of coal being produced began to outstrip the nation's need for bituminous fuel. Competition within the coal industry increased as the number of companies proliferated. Oil was gaining popularity as an industrial fuel. Competition among laborers was fierce and men were replaced who were too old or weak to produce the tonnage their bosses demanded. Miners heeded the threats and worked faster. Safety precautions were sometimes abandoned in deference to speed. As the coal orders dropped, officials looked for ways to economize. Saving on the cost of rudimentary safety measures was part of some fiscal programs; as a result the number of injuries and deaths increased noticeably.

Mountain people placed a high priority on maintaining good relations with their supervisors, and because of this their initial response to hard times was one of loyalty. Mining officials often responded by extending credit at the commissary and by dividing employment among loyal workers. As the Depression worsened, patience wore thin on both sides, prompting employers and laborers to become adversaries in some places. Later the estrangement would culminate in battles for union recognition.

The second act in the drama, dealing with the effect of the coal industry on Central Appalachia, brought tensions and struggles between conflicting allegiances and ideals. There were the private tensions which rent marriages and disrupted communities as well as the more widespread tensions generated by a seesawing economy. In less than a generation the amount of money a family had to spend increased from a few dollars a year on the farm, to fifty cents or a dollar a day in the coalfields. During the boom years of World War I, when nothing seemed to satisfy the nation's need for fuel, miners' wages occasionally escalated to the unheard-of sum of ten dollars a day, though of course prices in the company store rose proportionately. When the war ended wages began the up and down spirals which characterized the pre-union coal in-

dustry. During the Depression, which began in the coal lands in the mid-twenties, wages plummeted and unemployment skyrocketed. When it was over, three quarters of the people living in eastern Kentucky alone were eligible for some form of public aid.

During the Depression the people of Central Appalachia once again faced a shortage of cash, but this time those traditional supports which had cushioned their hardships in earlier times— reliance on barter and bounteous gardens—were gone. Generations of tradition had made mountaineers a self-sufficient people but the very nature of the coal industry fostered dependency upon the company. The arrival of blacks and foreigners led to racial problems and prejudices which had heretofore been nonexistent. Even among white settlers of the area, social distinctions arose with the influx of wealthy outsiders and the development of coal camps. Most important, the very nature of the community changed as small towns arose.

Along with an alien way of life, an unpredictable economy, and the hard times of Depression came the old natural adversaries that, in changed circumstances, assumed new proportions. On May 30, 1927, just as the full impact of the Depression was becoming clear, eastern Kentucky and southwestern Virginia were struck with a flood that was unprecedented in Appalachian annals. Marvin Gullett, who earlier discussed life in the coal towns, described it:

Balls of lightning rolled on the ground. So much rain fell that it busted the tar-paper roof over our house all to pieces. It was mountain-to-mountain, that river was. Cars and houses and everything in the world was washing away. It washed the topsoil right down to the bare rock. The land wouldn't grow hardly nothing but broom sage after that. That flood set people back more than anybody realized.

When the waters subsided one hundred people were dead. Thousands of homes, bridges, and power plants were destroyed. Miles of railroad tracks were ripped out of the earth. And the crops that had been planted as a shield against the Depression were gone.

The new combination of challenges demanded a new response and it was not long in coming. Sporadic attempts to organize unions in the 1920's had lacked cohesiveness and had had little effect. All that changed, however, when the Depression reached its peak and the Roosevelt administration supported union efforts. What began as an ill-fated trickle in the 1920's became a flood of union activity in the 1930's. Soon United Mine Workers of America and John L. Lewis were the names of hope in the Central Appalachian coalfields.

Unionization was a direct response by mountain people to forces that affected their workaday lives, but its effect on social problems was limited. Mountaineers usually worked harmoniously with blacks and foreigners in the coal mines but outside, in the camp towns, segregation was the rule. Blacks and whites clung to dissimilar folkways, they seldom mixed socially, and each remained wary of the other. Clashes were inevitable. The Ku Klux Klan was revived in some places, not as a vigilante against people who let their corn stalks grow too tall as in "Devil" John Wright's day, but against blacks.

Another response by mountain people to the control wielded by outsiders on their daily lives was a movement toward the church, especially the Old Regular Baptist Church, as the last bastion and protector of traditional values. One of the basic tenets of the Old Regulars is that no man, be he pauper or coal baron, shall control the church. Outsiders were sometimes welcomed into the fold on an individual basis, but the church stayed clearly in the hands of mountain people and there appeared to be an unspoken agreement that it would remain that way.

When the companies closed, miners had few alternatives. They could remain in the camp town, provided they had enough money to pay rent; share a homestead with kinfolks; squat in a deserted cabin, barn, or chicken coop; or they could become hoboes. Some people did leave the region in search of work in urban centers and *thereby began on a very small scale the out-migration that would become a movement after World War II. Many foreigners still had relatives in large cities. According to Harry Caudill, three quarters of eastern Kentucky's foreign-born population left during the Depression and never returned.*

For those people who remained in the coal camps, earning money became a challenge similar to the one mountain people had faced in an earlier time. Some people trapped and hunted for ginseng; some who were luckier became government employees. Others, such as Flora Rife, a respected citizen of Weeksbury, Kentucky, today, and Henry Scalf, a retired teacher and historian who talked earlier about home life, were more creative in their efforts to earn money and if their methods skirted the law, so be it. Times were desperate.

Flora Rife was reared on a farm and remembers there was seldom any money in the house, but she says, "You didn't have to have money in those days because you made everything from soap to chairs." The Depression years were different, however, because the basis of the economy had switched from barter to cash and the good topsoil was gone, so Flora and her husband did what had to be done.

"Coal miners was hit harder than anybody. They had no gardens, [so] they'd go up on a little steep hillside and rake them off a little garden and tend it, but they didn't have no way of putting up and taking care of stuff like the farmers did. Farmers [like us] was hit hard about tax money and things like that, but they wasn't hit too hard about food. We had enough to eat, but we had four children and another one on the road, and we didn't have no way of making ends meet for money and doctor's bills, so my husband put up a moonshine still and made whiskey. Now that was a shame, but we had to do it to make a living.

We sold whiskey by the gallon to the bootleggers and the bootleggers sold it out by the bottle. It went from a dollar and a half to three dollars a gallon, but, really, it's [all] one kind. I remember one time this man come and he wanted ten gallons of whiskey. I set up three cans on the table and I told him, "This [is] a dollar and a half a gallon, this is two dollars a gallon, and this is three dollars and a half a gallon. Now, you pick what you want."

He tasted the cheap first, the two dollars next, and then he tasted the three dollar and a half and said, "I'm going to take it all in the best." It was all the same whiskey, but he bought ten gallons of the three-dollar-and-a-half whiskey.

After we started selling whiskey, we had a machine drawer full

Flora Rife

of money and scrip all the time. People would buy whiskey when they wouldn't buy food.

We never was raided because every time [the] revenuers would come all the neighbors done the same thing we done. They all had big dinner bells hanging out in their yards. The first neighbor that seen a revenue man would ring the bell. The next neighbor would hear that bell a-ringing [and ring her bell]. The houses [were] a quarter of a mile to a mile apart and since the revenuers had to walk or ride horseback that give all the neighbors time to get their whiskey in the clear before the revenuers got to their house.

I remember this one particular time when we got the ring. I had the whiskey in the kitchen tempering it down; had, I guess, twenty or thirty half-gallon jars sitting there. I didn't know what I was going to do with them. I happened to [remember] the tomato patch [was] fresh hoed out the day before, so I took these half gallons of whiskey out and laid them down right beside the tomato plants, took the hoe and raked the dirt up over them. The revenuers come and they seen me out in the garden working. They didn't even stop; they passed on and went to the next house.

[Another] morning my husband had just brought some [whiskey] in the house, set it down, and told me to bottle it up. Just as I got started there come a knock on the door. I opened the door and there stood this man dressed up in a big brown suit. I thought sure I was going to die with a heart attack, thinking he'd come in and find us with all that whiskey. He said, "Lady, have I scared you?"

I said, "No, you've not scared me. What did you want?"

He said, "I want to know: could I hunt quail up here on your land?"

I said, "Law, yes! Hunt all the quail you want to." It just tickled me to death because he didn't get in that whiskey. Of course, it was a hunting suit [he was wearing], but at that time I didn't know it.

We made whiskey during the Hoover Depression, about in '28 and '29. Then Roosevelt was elected President and he was a Democrat. Since that got the Republicans out we all knowed we [were] going to have better times and good works. We made whiskey till the mines started hiring again; then my husband got him a job and we quit and never made no more whiskey.

Henry (Buck) Scalf began teaching school in 1921 under the old trustee system which Cora Frazier described in the first chapter. Trustees were unpaid elected officials who had the privilege of selecting local teachers. Often teaching positions were the most lucrative jobs available in mountain communities and people would go to great lengths to win the jobs. About the only requirements were endorsement by the trustee and passing a certification exam, which is where Buck, and other enterprising people, came in.

The questions were prepared at Frankfort, and don't you think they weren't tough. It took about two days to take that exam under the direction of a superintendent and nearly everybody would do nearly anthing in this world to get to teach school. Cheat, they'd really cheat.

The best way to do it was steal the questions if you could. The way we did it here in Floyd County, we'd go over in Martin County* and bribe the assistant superintendent [to] get us a set of the questions. We'd come back to Prestonsburg and write the answers out so when we went in to be examined, say on agriculture, we'd know what the questions was going to be and we had the answers in our pockets. Now another way to do it [was] change numbers [with a legitimate applicant]. If [I] had number eighty-eight and he had number sixty-eight, after [taking] it [I'd] just switch numbers on [my] paper. I'd fail, see, and he'd make a passing grade because he'd have my number and I had his. They usually gave me a hundred dollars to get so-and-so through the

* Martin County, Kentucky, adjoins Floyd County.

teacher's examination, and don't you think [a] hundred dollars wasn't a lot of money in the midst of the Depression.

[In 1932] we had a tough school election in Pike Floyd Hollow mining camp. My candidate for trustee was elected [but] we had to have an assistant teacher. A certain doctor came along and said, "I want my sister to teach that school. How much you suppose I'm going to have to pay the trustee?"

I said, "That's going to have to be a deal between you and the trustee. You might get it for about a hundred, or a hundred and fifty dollars." He gave [the trustee] a hundred and some dollars to hire his sister, the doctor did. You see, it was a desperate time during the Depression.

The county attorney in Pike County got a hold of it and summoned me before the grand jury and I told. The trustee was my good friend, the doctor was my good friend, but I couldn't barefacedly lie about that bribery. You could see my ethics were improving. The sheriff came down to arrest this trustee. I had to borrow the doctor's car and drive him into Lawrence County, Kentucky. Of course he got away and the case was never tried, but I'd [have sent] him to the penitentiary. My evidence would have done it.

[Another time] we wanted to get a girl through an examination who was niece of the county judge who was a straight man, Judge Edward Hill. We wanted Judge Hill to put pressure on the county superintendent to let us cheat. He didn't want to do it. [On the] morning of the examination Judge Hill met the county superintendent on the street and he said, "Mr. Stevens, I've been requested to talk to you." He made the proposition to him, to let him let these certain people get certificates.

The county superintendent said, "Judge, what would you do if you was in my place?"

The judge said, "By God, I wouldn't do it, but I told them I'd ask you."

The county superintendent said, "I'm not going to do it, either." So we didn't have much luck that time.

One time [in about 1928] we got too brave and the state superintendent got a hold of what had gone on and he held up every one of our certificates. [He] called about a dozen of us down [to] Frankfort. We went down to see the Superintendent of Public Instruction and they introduced me as Henry Stratton. The Superintendent of Public Instruction said, "I want to tell you what I think about Floyd County: I think that man, Henry Scalf, that's been getting all these certificates for people ought to be in the penitentiary." He didn't know, of course, that he was talking right to me, Henry Scalf. That kind of shook me.

I began to think as the years went on it was wrong. One thing, we got to the point where we could get certificates for people who just wasn't good third-graders.

What made the state legislature do away with the trustee system?

Over [on] Prater Creek they had two or three of the old-line families supporting different candidates for trustee. By the time the election came up there was so much antagonism and so much hatred engendered by the election just some little incident was needed to set off an explosion. [One side was] running one or two votes ahead and it was getting down to just a few minutes [before] closing time. Somebody asked Green Conn, the clerk of the election and timekeeper, "How much longer we got?"

He said, "One minute." They had an argument. He hit a woman and he got so angry that he slapped her. When he slapped this woman, guns went to popping. The room was crowded with people. They went through the windows [and] doors getting out of that building. Five men were killed there and about that many wounded. At the next meeting of the legislature [in 1936] they changed the law and let the board members do the hiring of the teachers. Best thing that ever happened.

The death of a breadwinner was one of the worst tragedies that could befall a family during the Depression and it happened in Charles Clark's family. His father, John Clark, had profitable jobs

with several coal companies but his death in 1927 spawned a de-
cade of lean years for his wife and children.

When the Depression was over young Charles worked in the
coal mines for several years, but soon became disenchanted with
the working conditions and wary of the dangers. In 1938 he left
the mines and accepted a position as a school principal. He
served as superintendent of Floyd County, Kentucky, schools for
twenty-six years and lived in Prestonsburg, which is one of the
places where his father worked. Charles talks about his father's
work, racial tensions, and the growing fatalism among miners.

John Clark was employed by a series of coal companies as a
"town marshal" or "company officer." Town marshals settled local
brawls, transported payroll money from incoming trains to the
home office, roused miners who overslept, and maintained a tenor
of law and order in the camp town. In effect, they were responsi-
ble for many of the duties that the old self-appointed law men,
such as John Wright, performed, but they did them under the of-
ficial auspices of the coal companies.

"The law was really in the hand of the town marshal and was
rather wild in those days," said Charles Clark. "In fact, my fa-
ther, in following his vocation from the time he was eighteen until
the time that he died, was forced through the use of pistols to kill
three men."

There was some early racial difficulty in Garrett. A company
officer [named] Tom Blackburn went up to the colored hollow
one Saturday night to quell a disturbance. He was from Prestonsburg and he was killed that night and he was very highly respected, the old man Tom Blackburn was. The whole town decided that was the last act for the colored, so they got on every
side of the hollow with high-powered rifles and just riddled the
houses. The next morning there wasn't a colored person in Garrett. Some of them left food cooking on stoves. Where those colored people went, I don't know. That happened in '23 or '24.

Right Beaver was a very violent place all during the twenties and thirties. I was principal of Garrett High School for fourteen years beginning in 1946 and a bus driver who had been raised up there [once] sat in my office and wrote the names down of thirty-nine people who had been killed violently between Wayland and Bosco* [from] 19 and 19 [to] perhaps 19 and 36. I am sure we missed at least 50 percent of them.

There were seven or eight thriving mining towns [here at the time], and I'd say that what happened on Right Beaver happened in West Virginia, Pike County, and Perry County. The mining element [had] plenty of money, throwing it in all directions, drinking a lot, love of guns and willingness to pull the trigger.

Were people's attitudes toward life and death affected by the nature of deep mining at that time?

I wouldn't be surprised if that wasn't a very great factor. I've done some deep mining myself [and] you get to the point where you accept this danger. I spent two years operating a truck mine during the later days of World War II. It was difficult to get your employees to set safety timbers that they knew would save their lives. In fact, after me lecturing these men several times and threatening to fire them, one of them said to me, "Ah, Charles, you know this damn slate wouldn't fall on a good Democrat." They just accepted it philosophically and I suspect that must have been a factor in their attitude toward life generally: pretending that the danger didn't really exist, accepting it. I am confident that that fatalistic tendency of Appalachian dwellers is more rampant in the mining area. I think [it is] just like their attitude was toward drinking or spending their money: easy come, easy go. I'm sure that was the direct result of a mining experience.

I suppose one of the things that influenced my character and personality perhaps more than anything else was being a son of a

* Bosco, Kentucky, is now officially called Hueysville.

officer who was constantly being condemned, even in my presence. Sons and daughters of peace officers in those days either had to become immune to extreme explosive criticism of their father or react very much like their father would: by shooting and raising Cain. My attitude, I think, was one of "build up an immunity." My younger [brother's reaction] was directly opposite of my reaction. He was explosive and when they asked him if he was the son of "Bad" John Clark his answer would be, "Hell, yes!" My reaction was one of slight embarrassment, not that I thought less of my dad, but my younger brother reveled in it.

To give you an illustration about what my reaction was to the question, "Are you 'Bad' John Clark's son?" I was shining shoes in the old Prestonsburg C & O depot and a big tall man came in with riding boots on extremely muddy. I [heard] someone call him John Hall and being alert to what people was saying I immediately concluded that he was "Bad" John Hall from Wheelwright. He hired me to shine his boots. I had one shined, when he asked me who I was and I told him I was John Clark's son. He grinned [and said], "Oh, *Bad* John Clark's son!" I just eased the shined boot off my box and turned and left him with one boot shined and the other just as muddy as it could be, and I never said a word to anybody. That was my reaction to his asking if I were "Bad" John Clark's son. It didn't please me at all.

My father did much of his work in the Wayland, Garrett, Lackey area. In fact, even after we moved to Prestonsburg, Circuit Court Judge Williams, knowing that my father had a Right Beaver background, would on special occasions when he had complaints send my father up there as a special officer. [One time] apparently Judge Williams had received several letters from the good citizens of Bosco stating that each time the passenger train went up or down there was a certain character that was selling moonshine and whiskey almost wholesale and he sent my father up to find out who this bootlegger was. My father went up on the train which got to Bosco about eleven in the morning with the expectation of snooping around Bosco to find out who the man was selling the moonshine on the C & O station platform. He had been there for a couple of hours loafing around on the platform when a middle-aged man came up to talk to him. My dad didn't recognize him [but] it developed the man, [whose] name was "Cabbage Head" Hughes, recognized my father, all right. [Dad] asked this man if he knew where he could buy a quart of moonshine. My dad gave him five dollars and "Cabbage Head" disappeared for a little while and he came back to the station with a shoe box in his hands and he said, "Now, I didn't find

Charles Clark

the whiskey but I did take time to buy me a pair of shoes. You hold this box and I'll go up the creek and find you the quart." After a long, long wait and still no man with the whiskey, the train pulled in. My father couldn't wait any longer, so he got on the train with the shoe box under his arm. In telling my mom about it after he got back to Prestonsburg, he said he noticed after having been on the train for a little while that it was a heavy shoe box, the heaviest pair of shoes he ever saw in his life. He finally opened the shoe box and there was the quart.

That actually happened because when my father came in from Right Beaver he was laughing [and] still had the quart. He made the comment then that a man that was smart [enough] to outsmart an officer, he, John Clark, would never arrest him again if he sold him a barrelful.

We lived [in Wayland] for quite a few years but my father then left Wayland and the family went to another mining town, Moss Bottom, just north of Pikeville. [I've] wondered if some of the shooting scrapes he got into there might not have contributed to [leaving Wayland]. These early town marshals almost invariably had to do some shooting and they seemed to be roaming souls. If things got kind of hot in one town, they moved to other towns. In fact, when I was about twelve or thirteen I had been in six different schools so I really didn't know what grade I belonged in.

About a year before my dad died he got into a shooting scrape here in Prestonsburg I remember very vividly. He was running a little restaurant near where the main C & O bridge was and he'd had some difficulty with a man here in town. He and some of his cronies were sitting in the restaurant and this man rode up on this horse and called my dad to the door. He was obviously drunk and decided that he had a grudge against John Clark and he was going to shoot him up, apparently. My dad talked as firmly as he knew how to him. The man wheeled on his horse and left. In about forty-five minutes he came back. He called my dad to the door again and they shot about the same time at each other. The first shot my dad fired from [his] .45 automatic went through the man's leg and killed the horse. The horse fell on this man's right leg, but this was a cool cucumber. He lay right there behind that horse and emptied the rest of the shots out of that pistol, just raising up over the horse and firing, then sinking back behind the horse. There must have been four or five pistols emptied. My older brother was in the restaurant, and he got a pistol and shot several shots. My dad had a complete arsenal of pistols and several of my dad's cronies—I won't mention their names—got one and they were all firing. When the man who had been riding the horse shot one pistol empty he raised up as if to surrender and walked right toward the restaurant, dragging one leg behind him. His second pistol that had hit the street as he and the horse fell came out of the holster. When he got to that pistol, he grabbed that pistol up and emptied it and then he wasn't more than ten or fifteen feet from the restaurant. After he shot the second pistol, he gave up.

This was in the summertime. My father was sort of on the outs with the mayor and the town council at that time and they notified him officially that he had to get that horse out of the street, especially, I assume, since he was the fellow that killed it. He hired a man to come and haul that dead horse down under the bridge into a sand bank next to the river. My job all that summer was to burn that horse. Of course, as long as I burned him you could smell the flesh burning, but you couldn't smell the stink of the dead flesh. The minute that I ran out of driftwood you could smell the dead flesh and complaints were coming from all over town. My younger brother and I gathered driftwood, I suppose, all the way from the Virginia line to the head of Beaver Creek to burn that horse.

One of the killings that my dad was involved in happened at Garrett on Right Beaver [while] the family lived at Prestonsburg. The circuit judge had sent my father to Garrett along with another deputy sheriff to serve some papers and they were staying with old Aunt Susan Hughes who operated a store in Garrett. Aunt Susan was telling my father about a young man who had been on a crazy drunk for two or three days and had shot his wife through the hand. The wife had fled the home and was hiding to stay away from her husband. While Aunt Susan was telling my dad about this, this young man walked down the hill looking for his wife.

The young man was coming down the hill toward the railroad, still with a pistol in his hand, and my father and this officer decided they were going to take him without having to kill him. Since he was walking toward a boxcar one of them was going to run pretty fast and come in front of him as he walked down behind the boxcar and the other one was going to come behind him. They [were] both going to speak to him at the same time, arrest him, take the pistols off of him, and maybe bring him to Prestonsburg and sober him up. My dad was the one who was walking in front, facing him. The timing was off and he stepped up with his pistol in his hand, directly in front of the young fellow, and told him he was under arrest. The young fellow raised the pistol as if to fire and my dad shot one shot and hit him in the middle of the neck.

I remember this very vividly because he said to my mom, as the young man fell he looked up at my dad and said with big, bloody bubbles coming out of his mouth, "Why did you do this to me? I never saw you in my life." The young man died about four or five hours after that, and to show you how concerned my father was and how that worried him, he got a letter about three weeks after that from this boy's father telling him that he wanted the boy's pistol. Well, the other officer who was with my father had taken the pistol, put it in his pocket. My dad was so interested in trying to find the gun that belonged to that boy because his father wanted it, that he made several trips to West Virginia to try to find that pistol to give back to the old man.

It wasn't more than a year and a half after that until my dad got to the point where he just had to resort to drink, and I don't believe the man ever drew a sober breath . . . until his death in 1927.

The Clark Depression predated the Big Depression because my mom was left with six youngens with no means of support. She was completely dominated by my father and you would expect when he died for her to have just folded completely, but [she was] the strongest woman that I have ever known in my life. Even in the worst days of the Depression she refused to accept government commodities. My mom was willing to work as a cook, paid by federal funds, but she would never let us eat at the soup kitchen.

After my father died my mom moved the six children to Stephens Branch, which is twenty-five miles from Prestonsburg, and having no money she got permission to move into a boarding-house. Bailey, Ferguson and Stephens Elkhorn coal companies were operating on that hollow. I remember something that made an indelible impression on my mind. An old man who had been one of the co-owners of the mines where we lived spent a lot of time trying to collect rent in those days. I remember a ruckus that he had with my mom because she had managed to buy a little scrubby calf and raised her to a milk cow and this old man, being destitute too, would go to the milk gap each afternoon with a quart tole can as the women were milking. He would insist on taking a quart of milk for house rent and pasture rent from everybody. My mom, her attitude was, "I can either feed six children or that old rascal." After several explosions he never bothered her.

Since there was an acute shortage of meat products every male on Stephens Branch in those days made "Hoover boxes." It's a rabbit trap, a box maybe twenty-four inches long and maybe eight inches in depth and eight inches wide, with a lid. You put a stick under it to hold the lid up and you put a piece of apple or something in the back of the thing. To get in, the rabbit had to knock the piece of wood down and by the time he got the apple the door had fallen down on him and he couldn't get out. When you killed a rabbit, after you ate the body you tried to tan the hide and sell it. There was a lot of trapping. Possum hides, I suppose they didn't sell for more than fifteen or twenty cents apiece, but my god! fifteen or twenty cents was really something in those days.

We raised a garden; Mom managed some way or other to sell eggs; we even dug May apple roots and scoured the hills for ginseng; gathered walnuts and hickory nuts and sold them; and she usually managed to have a hog. When the Depression really got into full swing and all of the mines closed, people who owned property in the areas surrounding the mines, and who had livestock and acreage where they could raise corn and other produce, were much better off than [people] in the mining camps were.

I'm sure that we were affected greatly by the Depression. Thinking back on it, and this may sound kind of nutty, but I wonder if it didn't give us some strengths of character that an affluent age couldn't possibly give us. You had to share in a family and my family was very close. We all had some little something to do—either getting coal and kindling in for fuel to cook and keep the house warm, or getting coal and kindling into the neighbor's house for some small fee. Now in this age of affluence, it appears that we have lost our perspective about the honor of honest toil.

Marvin Gullett, who talked about life in the coal camps, discussed the attitudes that lay behind the racial tensions that Charles Clark mentioned.

I was raised up to be prejudiced. We was Scotch-Irish and we was always standoffish because we wanted to be isolated. [We] thought anything that was foreign was against [our] way of life somehow. Around the mining camps there were many colored people segregated [in] what they called the "Nigger camp." I never even associated with these colored people; to me they was just as foreign as could be. We was taught from early times that because they had caused the great Civil War over slavery a Nigger was unworthy to be free, he wasn't even worth [associating] with because he'd been sold into slavery. My father was very prejudiced against colored people. I've had many arguments with my father: "Why did you hate the colored people so bad? You like to hear them sing, you like to talk with them, you work with them, what is wrong with them?" He'd say, "I don't like colored people because they have been slaves and they work as cheap labor. Whatever the boss puts on them they take it and they won't open their mouth."

They would have drinking parties in the colored camps, take dope, and sometimes one of them would go crazy and start shooting. The deputy sheriff would have to go over there and subdue the colored people, make them stay on their property. Most of the time, though, the colored man was kept down, he was very humble back then. He was a good worker and pretty sure of his job but he couldn't mingle too much, he couldn't go to a white man's home at all.

I can remember an old man [who] lived to be nearly a hundred years old named George Bates that my boss brought over from Brushy Mountain Prison in Tennessee and he made a good worker. One time he brought some moonshine whiskey and the deputy sheriff come and abused him and he said, "If I was back home I'd kill that sheriff but here I have to take it. I've killed seven men in my time but they're even worse up here than they are down in the deep South."

I remember seeing a lynching when I was just a kid. That was unforgettable. I forget what year it was, I believe it was along about '33 or '34. There was a colored man [who] lived in the camp and his wife had been going with a white man. The white man was such dark red skin that he looked like a colored person. [The woman's husband] thought this was a colored fellow [who] had been going with his wife and he come up to this white man and slapped him over the head with an iron bar and killed him. It was a mistake but he had to pay the penalty. All the mining pop-

ulation got together and took him out and hung him to a tree and
shot him full of bullets. If it had been a white man he wouldn't
have been lynched, he'd been taken to jail and he'd had a trial.

Even to this day this prejudice is carried on a whole lot but as
time goes on people have to change their lives. I long to see the
day when the colored man has the chance to be like any other
man, not to be treated like dirt.

*When the coal companies that survived the Depression re-
opened in the mid and late 1930's, there was a gulf between
miners and coal operators that even hints of renewed prosperity
would not close. While officials sought the maximum return on
every dollar spent (many even required employees who owned
their own homes to pay rent on company houses), miners lobbied
for increasingly bigger shares of the profits. For a while management could afford to ignore the workingman's pleas because labor
was cheap and more abundant than ever. Job security was pre-
carious and industrious workers were often rewarded with notes
alongside their pay checks advising them to "SPEND MORE AT THE
COMPANY STORE." As the tunnels under mountains grew deeper,
men had to walk, or crawl, farther and farther underground to
reach their working places. Requests to ride to the face in empty
coal cars were usually denied by management because of the potential hazards, or because it would "inconvenience" the company.*

*Coal officials of course had their own problems. As the indus-
trial need for fuel began to rise, the number of coal companies
seeking to fill the orders again swelled. Spurred by the old get-
rich-quick philosophy, some new firms lured men away from their
employers by offering wages of four dollars a day or more. When
experienced miners accepted the bait, their former employers were
under new pressures. Officials compensated by economizing.
Some tampered with scales that weighed the miners' coal trucks,
while others ignored safety precautions. Everyone raised prices at
the company store.*

In the face of these new clashes between management and

labor, miners began considering the merits of unions. The move toward unionization in Appalachian coalfields was initiated by some of the same organizers whose efforts were thwarted in the early twenties; by John L. Lewis, who was elected president of the United Mine Workers of America in 1920; and by an increasing number of laborers who noted the gains union members were making in other industries. The underlying appeal of the union was that it represented a means through which miners could exert some control on the coal companies, rather than being interminably controlled by them. The primary issue was of course money, but there were many other matters that needed settling as well.

Gabe Newsome of Dorton, Kentucky, began mining before the advent of the union in the eastern Kentucky coalfields. He talks about what coal mining was like without the union, as well as about some of the difficulties which arose when the union began to organize.

I started mining about 1927 at Dorton, Kentucky, [for] the Wright Elkhorn Coal Company loading coal [with] my two brothers. They took me in between them because I never had mined. I was only seventeen years old and the first day I ever worked, I loaded seven cars following the machine. Me and my brothers loaded coal there for thirty-three cents a ton.

The cost of living was cheap at that time but still you couldn't hardly live. [My brothers would] go to the scrip office and they'd say, "Can't get no scrip today." Working six days a week, the wages was so low they just figured you out with a pencil, I reckon. People lived awful hard at that time.

When I left Dorton, I went into West Virginia and loaded coal over there a while. I couldn't even make my board over there. I worked about a month and was getting in debt to this lady. I just told her, "[Would] you druther I'd just try to work on and see if it'll pick up or you druther I'd go home?" She said, "Well, I'd druther you didn't get in debt too deep but you suit yourself." So I pulled out and thumbed my way home.

Gabe Newsome

In 1929 I got a job at Consolidation Coal Company at Jenkins. I loaded coal there a while; sometimes you'd lay there two hours and never get a car. Sometimes you wouldn't get over two or three cars a day. I left there and went over to Fleming. They put us to laying tracks on a eight-hour clean-up shift. You had to stay there and lay every track, if it took fourteen hours, but you only got paid for eight. We was working for [thirty-three cents a ton] again. Sometimes, we'd work twelve and fourteen hours to get that all laid up. You had it to do or you didn't have no job. They just absolutely told you [if] you couldn't get it, that the other man could. When you was loading coal, they say, "If you can't clean the cut, take your tools; the other man can."

I come back to Dorton then in '32 or '33 and I got a job loading coal for thirty-three cents a ton. We'd load coal of a day, come in and eat our supper, and go back and haul water that night for two dollars a shift. We'd come back in that morning from the night shift and lay down behind the stove and sleep while [my girl] got our breakfast and packed our bucket and we'd go back again.

I took a notion to get married and went to the scrip window, and asked them for five dollars cash advance to get married on. They said, "Nah, we can't do that unless your brother stands good for it." He was on a machine, making just a little bigger money, you see. And me working six days and three or four nights a week. I got my five dollars and sent on and got my license, and got married on Saturday. I went out to work that morning, [got married] that evening, and hauled water that night. It was pretty rough.

You had to pay house rent if you got a job and the house a-sitting there empty. Even if you wasn't married and didn't want a house, you lived in your own home. The company owned the houses and if you got a job, they made you pay house rent, just taking that much away from you. I remember "Tennessee Slim," we called him, a boss over there, said, "Gabe, you got to pay house rent." I'll not repeat what I said to him but I said [if] that's what it takes all right then. If you had your own farm [within] a mile of it, you had to pay house rent or you don't get a job.

I used to work in a company store when I wasn't in the mines. I remember one time where I worked for Creed Fleming; I'd help mark up shoes. This shoe [was], say, $4.75. He'd say, "Now, you make that five dollars and if [your customer asks] for a pair of socks, throw it in; he's paying for the socks anyhow." If you asked for a pair of socks they'd throw it in and you'd think they was giving them to you. If you didn't ask for them you was paying for them and didn't get them. They'd get it one way—if they couldn't beat you out of it, they'd figure you out of it.

[The owner of each mine] carried his own compensation. Like Butler Wright, he carried his own compensation. This man got killed around there and they sent my brother out to stay with this widow woman and her brother. Butler sent word to try to get me to marry her [so he wouldn't have to pay] her compensation and I wouldn't do it. Offered me three hundred dollars to marry her. I said, "Why it'd cost me more than that to get rid of her." That's the truth, buddy.

They all just throws you around like driving a mule. That's all there was to it. They said up [at] Jenkins one time, "You be careful with them horses and mules; we apt to get one of them killed and we have to buy them." Just as good as said not [to] pay attention to the men. My grandpa said one time that the boss told the men right in the mines, "Boys, keep that mule out of that electric wire there. Them things cost money; they're not just hired like men." They just didn't care, buddy.

In 1933, the union come around and boy, we had a time, but we got it organized. They had to slip around first and get us started; then Butler went to trying to fire everybody. They fit* everybody when we was organizing it. I seen one constable come up there and this union man knocked the yellow dog down and this fellow walked over and took him by the arm and said, "You're under arrest." His brother walked over and said, "If you want to stay all together, you'd better walk on out of here and leave that boy alone." He just turned him loose and went on.

What was a yellow dog?

That's just a man that was going against the union. We'd bark at them, "Goat, goat."

* Fought.

And brother, we faced guns and everything else. I remember one night they threatened to blow up Union Hall. We had two machine guns. They was this old big Nigger operating one and my brother told them I'd been in training camp, with a machine gun. So they sent me out to him. I remember he said, "White folks, anything happen, just lay on the ground; I'll take care of you."

I went to Leslie County one time [and saw] Tom Rainey and his gang. Old Tom right up there, buddy; he called the judge everything on earth and told them we was gonna organize. He was a union leader, you see. I bet they was five thousand people there. We had to walk a little over a mile from where we parked.

[After we organized, we] had a contract telling right in there just what you had to do and how much to pay for each job and all that stuff. You had to hold your hand up and take an obligation, they called it. The first raise we got was forty-six and a half cents a ton, from thirty-three [cents]. You signed a card and back then you paid seventy-five cents a month starting off, now you pay four, five, or six dollars. If I ain't lost it, I've got my first union card. You had the union's protection for your job and everything. So it wasn't very long till the bosses knowed they wasn't all the boss; that we had officials that was boss, just let us do so much and let them do so much. You take a union card; it's better than any insurance you can buy. Union ain't what it used to be, but if it wasn't for the union we'd be hurting.

The union is the best thing in the world as long as they'll carry it out [right]. The trouble [is], if you ain't careful, they mistreat you after they've held up their hand and swore they wouldn't. It's not as strong as it used to be about things like that. Now most them will take your job or anything else and pay no attention to their oaths. They'll be sneaking around to the company if you ain't careful.

I remember once I was running a mine for Fletcher and Slim Johnson. They got slack up at Jenkins, so they came down here and shut us down. More little mines they could shut down, more they could sell. Come and shut us down and never thought that my family eats the same as his family. They come around where I worked at the tipple and asked me to sign against my boss for the union, and I was getting more than union pay. I wouldn't do it. I had my [old] union card when they come around, five hundred of them, and I was there by myself and they motioned me to shut her down and I just shut her down. I went out there and said, "Was you men over in Leslie County when they put in the courthouse 'Tom Rainey and his Gang not welcome'?"

"No, we didn't go around no such a place."

I said, "No, you'd be more of a union man if you went. I was right there and I can show you the picture of it." I'm a union man, but if I'd signed for the union, I would have just signed myself out of a job. And I always said that I would provide for my family, if I had to work for a quarter a day. So I signed against the union for the first time in my life.

If it hadn't been for the union, we'd just have been slaves right on; that's all there are to it.

The initial steps of gaining miners' sworn allegiance to the United Mine Workers were taken surreptitiously. When company officials were mindful of what was happening they ordered the town marshals to intercept union meetings and to arrest supporters on trumped-up charges if need be. Often organizers were fired arbitrarily and sympathizers were cajoled or threatened. As the union movement gained momentum thugs were imported to intimidate—murder if necessary—the organizers.

As time went on many of the mines in eastern Kentucky and southwestern Virginia were organized, some more peacefully than others. Some officials, particularly those who operated small companies, saw in unionism the potential for stable wages and increased prices and this overshadowed their personal antagonisms. Others, such as the powerful members of the coal operators' asso-

ciation in Harlan County, Kentucky, bitterly resented any en-croachment by the union and were prepared to fight for years. In the end, victory by the United Mine Workers in Harlan County was tainted with an epithet—"Bloody Harlan"—in which no one could take pride.

Gobel Sloan was there in "Bloody Harlan" when Evarts, a town owned by Black Mountain Coal Company, was organized by the union and today his memories of the battle remain vivid. Gobel was born in 1904 on Caney Creek, near Pippa Passes, Kentucky, and left home when he was sixteen to become a coal miner because his father was "poor, dirt poor." Living conditions in the coal camps never bothered Gobel nearly as much as conditions in the mines, which he found to be deplorable. As conditions worsened his faith in the union grew. Today Gobel, who is Verna Mae Slone's brother-in-law, lives in Haysi, Virginia. Haysi is near Splashdam, one of the mines where he worked as a young man. Gobel discussed the issues that were involved in the campaign for unionization, about the battles, and about the bittersweet aftermath.

[In] 19 and 30 I was working at Splashdam and I recollect an old colored man, Tom Holland they called him, he was as good a man as you ever saw. I mentioned something about the union. "Lord!" he says, "Mr. Sloan, don't never name the union here. They'll fire you."

I was awful bad to swear and I ripped out two or three big oaths. I said, "Well, they'd just have to fire me. I'd sign it today."

I looked and here come Kelly Beavers, the general mine foreman. He said, "Bud, if you ever sign the union a-working for me, you'll get fired when I find out. I'd fire you today but you're too good a coal loader." See, I was loading more coal than ary a man they had down there; they called that "carrying the weigh sheet."

I said, "Mister, you fire me and I'd go somewheres else. When it comes around, I'll sign it."

Gobel Sloan   (Photograph by Lyn Adams)

"Ah," he says, "you wouldn't aggravate me that much."

It wasn't no time till I quit, but at the first of '36 they organized. The man that owned the mines, old man Bill Lethem, when he heard they organized he just headed over dead.

In September of '36 I told [Kelly Beavers] I was coming back. "Well," he says, "I'll tell you one thing: you'll come back out a union man." He [supported] the union after he got it.

In '33 [union supporters] tried to organize Harlan County. They had to work it easy, not let [company officials] know they's in there, if they did they would have got beat up. They'd know which [miner] to get a hold of [to] get union talk started. Sometimes [someone would tell] on them and they had to get out of there, and get out of there in a hurry, or they'd been killed. It was tough going, I'll tell you that, there for a while. There was lots of men killed. Thugs was hired by Harlan County coal companies to keep us from organizing. They was give orders to kill and there was plenty of [union supporters] killed in Harlan County. [Thugs would] catch one or two union men, maybe ten or fifteen of them, give them a good whipping, beat them to death.

After we got union, it went the other way. They knowed if they come in the bunks* of the union men they'd shoot them down and be done with them. [We] had the law on [our] side after we got the contracts. We are swore to stand by one another and not let our brother be hurt.

Why would a person become a thug?

For the money. They didn't care, just so they could get the money without having to work for it.

About '36 or '37 we just took a notion that we wanted a union [at Evarts] where everybody would be treated equally. We went in to win, we didn't go in there to lose. Me and Danny Willis, the president of our local at Splashdam, and Ed Francisco, went over to Jenkins and got that union local to go with us.† The president of the union at Jenkins called to Wayland and Garrett and got them locals to come. We called West Virginia and got that union over there. About ten unions all went together. There were over four thousand men right there in Evarts. It was wrapped up with men. [Earlier] scabs in Harlan County [had] made a bunch of union men push a bus out of there. When we went, we went prepared to not push and they found it out mighty quick. We wasn't scared. I don't guess we was feeling any pain, we had plenty to drink. We had a big truck with canvases over it and two big machine guns pointed right straight at any of the thugs that come along and we intended to use them. [We had] five or six hundred men, women, and children, why you know we wasn't aiming to set there and let them mow us down. Before [the thugs] knowed what had happened we held a meeting. All these men from Harlan County that wanted a union poured in there.

I couldn't tell you all who made the speeches. A miner's wife had the same privilege to speak as the miner did. [They'd] tell

* A "bunk" is a section within a coal camp.
† The Splashdam, Virginia, mines were about one hundred miles from Harlan, Kentucky. Jenkins, Kentucky, is about sixty miles from Harlan.

how hard they was living, difference it would make if their husband was getting enough. I heard them get up and tell about having to pack their husband's buckets with cold taters—just taters. John L. Lewis was there. That man, he'd go anywhere. He told them it would be better for the miners and for the company, too, and their union guaranteed that they would get more for their coal.

There was a lot of unions before the miners ever organized and John L. Lewis got in with these union presidents and got the sale. He went plumb into Cuba and talked Cuba into buying coal from union companies and [to] drop the ones that wasn't. John L. Lewis was one of the sharpest this country ever had. He left one time. Everybody thought he'd just took what money the union had and left. Oh, they was up for killing him. He was gone about three months, but when he come back there was a big raise on [the price of] coal, a big raise on shift work. I went from $4.55 a shift—I was running a cutting machine—to $7.20 a shift.

The meeting [at Evarts] lasted about three hours, [then we took a vote], and sent three of our local presidents down to the owners of this company. They told them, "We've got the majority of the men and if you don't recognize the contract you ain't going to work tomorrow."

They said, "You couldn't have."

They just took the vote and laid it down. We had over three hundred majority. They recognized the contract right there and signed it the next morning.

When they recognized the union then everybody signed a union card and went on in and worked. Everybody went in lively, they knowed they was going to get justice and [who] wasn't singing or whistling, was cussing or acting the fool. Back when it was un-union, the very minute the boss turned his back on you, somebody would be setting down. We had more privileges, we knowed what we could do and get by with and wouldn't be jumped on. If the boss got rough on you all we had to do was say, "Now look here, Bud, you getting out of line. If you don't straighten up, we're going to the outside." That meant *his* job, not ours. Any time you or I violated that contract, they could fire me. Any time a boss broke it, they had to fire him. He was un-union.

[In the contract the company agreed to pay] fifty-five cents an hour and time and a half for all time over eight hours. You got your bathhouse dues paid. We was having to pay two dollars a month for me to bath when I come out of there, they had to pay for that, they had to furnish the bathhouse, furnish the water, and a man to clean it up. He was a union man. They had to run a man-trip [to] haul the men from the starting place to their working place and they had to have certain cars to haul them in; they couldn't just pile them up in any kind of an old car.

[The union would] take a notion to organize a place and I [would get] me a job [there] and I had cards to organize this mine. [The boss] wouldn't know [I was an organizer]; if he knowed it he wouldn't give me a job. I'd get to talking [to a miner] about how much more money we'd be making if we was a union.

I'd just say, "Now, you sign this card. Nobody will ever know it." He'd sign it and I'd put it back in my pocket. [At one mine I] had every one of these men except old man Isom Vairs. I says, "Isom, how would you like to be a union?"

"Lord, fine!"

"What about signing this card?"

"No, I'm afraid George will fire me if I did." Every time you'd speak to [Isom] he was just one of the greatest union [men] in the world, but when it went down to place his name, he went and told George Wright.

How fast were you fired?

Next day. If I would have got that one I would have took [all the signed cards] over to District 28 and the first thing you know a man representing the union would have walked in there and told Mr. Wright, "I've got the signers now. Majority of your men. You're going to recognize this union; if you ain't we're going to picket you." If I'd just not said nothing to Isom Vairs I could have got it. But I wanted it solid, I wanted every one of them.

After that happened they all backed out, they wouldn't stand up to what they signed. They'd know this was their job and they didn't want to be out of work. If they'd just said, "We signed it, we're going to walk out," and then come out, why that mine would have shut down till [Wright] recognized the union. I wanted that last man and messed it all up.

What were some of the other rights union supporters wanted in the thirties?

They was wanting more pay. We was loading coal for twenty-two cents a ton. The cars down at Splashdam, you couldn't get over a ton on them to save your life, I don't care how big you loaded them. They had blocks fixing the scale. We was loading two ton of coal and getting [paid] for one. If we could make two dollars a day we was lucky. We couldn't do a thing in the world about that till after we got organized. When we got a union we hired a checkweighman, and buddy, [he'd] walk down, take him a bar and pull them blocks out. We went to getting a ton and a half and two ton on our cars then.

When they slipped and put them back, the president of our local told us, "Don't kick, I'll get a man in here." Well, he calls a mine inspector and a FBI man. Here they come. The company didn't know who they was, nor nothing about it. [The mine inspector] run the cars up on [the scale] and walked down under it, took the blocks off, pushed the car back on it, and that car [now] weighed 3,800 pounds and it had weighed 2,100. He says, "We know to the day when they was put under there. Now you pay these men for their coal; average their tonnage up." They never put the blocks under it [again].

We got our right to protect ourselves. If you thought a place was dangerous you didn't have to go in it till it was made safe. [Splashdam] was one of the hottest mines that ever was blown with gas. You [could] hear the gas just like bees. I crawled in there [one time], laid down flat on my belly, [put] a carbide light up in it and let it blow out. Fire burned right over my back, scorched my eyebrows off. It's a wonder we hadn't all been killed. One time it blowed up and killed ten men. It blowed railroad cars out of that driftmouth plumb across that river down here. Well, they didn't care nothing about it, they didn't care no more for a man than I do for that old bench sitting out there. [If a man] got killed, they just hired another one. After we got a union, if that place wasn't safe, we didn't go in it. We [had] a fire boss check every place in that mine to find out whether there's any gas. If there was gas he'd come out and report it and before you went to work men [curtained] that off and put air around the face of that place. When that gas got out of there, why you'd go on and go to work.

Back when there was no union if you worked twenty year for that man you had no more seniority than [a man who had] just been hired. After we got the union we got seniority. If a job come open the oldest man got it if he could do it. Then the next job come open, the oldest man on that section, if he could do the job, got it.

Back when [there] was no union, why you wouldn't know one morning to another whether you had a job or not. If they took a notion to get shut of you, they just [hired] a man in your place and he'd go in. There wasn't nothing we could do about it.

I was working at Splashdam and I drawed seven dollars and something one pay day and I got a little slip in with my pay: "Trade a little more at the company store or we'll have to cut you off." [They wanted] to fire me, put in another man who would trade all in the company store. I traded all I needed but they wanted me to trade [more] so they wouldn't have to be out no money. They'd sell you a plow point for fifty cents when you could go down to the hardware and buy it for a quarter. Their stuff was just about as high again as the other store. They wasn't giving the working man justice.

After we got the union, if we was off over two days, they had a perfect right to fire us unless we was sick. When you went back you'd take a doctor's slip. He'd give you the slip without any trouble. He was a union doctor; we paid him so much a month. Before we got the union, if you laid off one day, and if they took a notion to fire you, they just fired you and there wasn't nothing you could do about it. When we first got the union we got a hospital card. We had to pay a dollar a month for a doctor, but if we got sick and had to go to the hospital, the hospital bill was paid. The miners' pension started in '50. Black lung [benefits] started in 19 and 69. Back when we was no union if a man got knocked out he was just knocked out, he didn't draw anything. If you got disabled to work you didn't draw anything, you're just on the mercy of other people. If a man got killed, his wife got fourteen hundred dollars back when there wasn't no union. [Today] if a man gets killed, his wife gets fourteen thousand [and] she draws his Social Security as long as she stays his widow. Now, is there any difference in a union, or not?

In the 1930's when union wars were being fought, company officials had their own problems and some, such as Boyd Frederick (B.F.) Reed, were inclined to look to the UMW for help. B.F. is a native of Shamokin, Pennsylvania, who moved to Floyd County, Kentucky, in 1927 and purchased a small mine that was in financial trouble. The Turner-Elkhorn Mining Company suffered further setbacks during the Depression and the early thirties brought little relief. B.F. discussed his reasons for being receptive to union organization and countered what Gobel Sloan said were some of the workingman's grievances. He lives in Drift, Kentucky, and as president of Turner-Elkhorn he continues to be involved with union negotiations.

The first sign of a union in Floyd County came in 1933 shortly after Congress passed the National Recovery Act. The coal industry in eastern Kentucky was almost nonexistent. The Depression had just about wiped out many of the operations [and] wages had sunk very low. We were looking for a way out. One operator by himself could do nothing because of the very severe competition in prices. We were concerned about what would happen to us through unionization, but we hoped it would bring a stabilizing influence to the price of coal and wages and we accepted it from that standpoint.

In some other areas of Kentucky, particularly in Harlan County, there was quite a lot of conflict, [but] when the union

B. F. Reed

came to Turner-Elkhorn there were no problems. We accepted it and went on from there. We were advised that the union organizers would be here on a certain day and we instructed all our personnel to encourage the men to sign the union application. If there had not been a very severe depression that prompted the operator to look for some relief and to accept what Congress proposed, I doubt seriously whether the union would have gotten a foothold. At that time many of the operations in Pennsylvania, Ohio, and part of West Virginia were union; the "captive" mines—that is, mines that were owned and operated by steel companies—were not union and the union did not have a broad base.

All the operators in the area joined the Big Sandy Elkhorn Coal Operators Association and negotiations with the union were carried on through that organization. I was present at the first meeting of the association, and so was Harry LaViers,* and I don't remember anybody else now living that was at that meeting. The leaders in the negotiations were the large operators in this area: Elkhorn Coal Corporation [and] Consolidation Coal Company. Association members filed a list of the rates of pay that they were using at that time and then at a meeting we adopted a standard rate of wages. We negotiated with the union on those rates. My recollection is that before the union came in the wage for a skilled man was four dollars a day, but many people didn't pay four dollars a day. They may [have] put it on paper but they operated through the company store and the man saw very little money.

After [the initial contract was signed] the association would meet and discuss various things. We would appoint a committee and they would meet with the committee of the miners and after so much negotiation would agree on a new contract. When you were negotiating a new wage contract and you were having a hard time staying in the coal business at the old rate of wages,

* Harry LaViers discussed John Mayo and development of the coal industry on pages 138–151.

you resisted increases because you were never sure that you could get your customer to accept that increase and if he didn't you were out of business. Generally the new contracts were arrived at without too much trouble.

In those early years there was very little else that became difficult, at least for us. In later years other problems developed. When mechanization came along the piecework method of payment sort of went out the window and you paid everybody by the day. That was a radical departure because many men worked in the mines who were physically handicapped and they couldn't do a good day's work. As long as they were paid by the ton they simply made less money than the fellow that was more able to work. When you paid by the day you no longer employed handicapped people because they weren't able to produce like the normal person. During the thirties and forties everything was hand-loading; the man paid for his explosives and he paid for his tools.

During contract negotiations in the thirties did miners ask the companies to provide the explosives and tools?

At that time, no. That was never an issue.

Was safety an issue?

Only the operator thought about safety. I don't recall any instance in the years prior to the late fifties that safety ever became an issue in a wage contract. About 1937 the Big Sandy Elkhorn Coal Operators Association employed a full-time safety director and his job was to visit all the mines and do what he could to improve safety. We had a Department of Mines in Kentucky, which was not well organized, [that] made inspections and required certain safety measures and the operator complied with those rules. In later years the state department became much more aggressive and I would say that the change began to be felt in 1948.

Fatal accidents [occurred] where an experienced miner took risks that he should not have taken, but he had taken them many times and he became unconcerned. I'm sure many people lost their lives for that reason. Naturally, the reaction of anybody is frustration [when a miner is killed] and sympathy for the man's family and regret that the thing happened, and I don't find anyone having any other feelings. I don't think you could ever say [accidents were] all the man's fault or all the company's fault.

Up until 1969 the medical profession told us that [breathing] coal dust is not harmful. In 1969 there was a meeting in Pittsburgh and the doctor there said, "We have come to the conclusion that it does endanger a man's life, and affect his lungs, and should be a compensable matter." Of course, in 1962 in Kentucky [Governor] Bert Combs had the Workmen's Compensation law amended to make pneumoconiosis a compensable disease. At that time there was a lot of disagreement [about Combs's decision], but history has shown that he did the right thing. There is no question that coal dust is injurious.

In the days of hand-loading coal did company officials value mules and ponies more than they did men?

When they tell you the mule is worth more than the man that was just somebody's way of saying something funny. I don't think anybody ever really believed that. Some mine foreman may have made a statement like that but he did it in pure jest, he didn't mean it.

The miner today is a smart fellow, reasonably well educated, alert, ambitious, and a pretty good guy all the way around. He was a little different in the hand-loading days. The story then was that you need a strong back and a weak mind to work in the mines. To some degree that was true. The miner was a rougher fellow, less educated, and he lived differently.

Relations in relatively small mines such as we operated where there were less than a hundred employees were good because the management knew personally just about everybody that worked at the mines. That was especially true in the early days before we had good roads because the miners lived in the area where the mine was operated. Once they came to the office I knew every one of them by name. One time we had an idle day because we didn't have any orders. I was in the office working and one by one employees came in and we sat there talking about various things. One fellow pulled out a gun and talked about his .38 and that prompted a full discussion. There were seven people in the office and they all laid their guns on the table. I said, "What in the world are you fellows doing carrying guns around here?"

"Oh," this one fellow said, "I never go anywhere without my gun."

The other fellow said, "The same with me. I always have a gun."

I said, "You don't take them in the mines?"

"Oh yes, I take my gun in the mines all the time."

That's the first that I knew mountain people really relied on guns and that was hard for me to understand until something developed at our own mines. We had a power plant to make the electricity that was fired by a boiler and early one evening, but after dark, my brother noticed the power plant wasn't running right and said to me, "Would you mind going down there, waking that fellow up?" I walked down to the powerhouse and sure enough there he was asleep. When I spoke he made one jump across the passageway to a chair. His gun was on that chair and his first instinct was to reach that gun. He looked up, saw who it was, and said, "My God! Don't scare me like that, I could shoot you." I realized then people were scared that the other fellow was going to shoot. It wasn't that they were bad people themselves, they knew that everybody had a gun and they were afraid [others] were going to shoot. When they found out that I didn't carry a gun nobody ever bothered me. Today the people don't carry their guns in the mines. The fact is very few people carry a gun at all.

As the owner of a coal company, what was your attitude toward John L. Lewis?

Looking back I think he was a good leader, a very good leader. We cuss him, and fuss about him, and we tried to hate him but he was the best labor leader in any union I know of. He was very determined and when it came to a wage contract he made a demand and he stuck with it. His language was usually pretty rough and he didn't say good things about the coal operators, he sort of made your hair stand up, but after all this settled down, I [realized] he was just doing his job.

One advantage John Lewis had was he was elected by acclamation and nobody ever questioned his rule, and he generally used good judgment in picking people around him. Weakness wasn't one of his faults. He was a good man, had a good family, and you couldn't buy him off. I'm sure [people] tried [to buy him] every way in the world, but it didn't get far enough to even score a ripple. They found that the best way to get along with him was [to] sit down and talk with him, talk open and aboveboard. He had the respect of people in the coal industry, both the big and the small, and they respected him because he did his job and he didn't confuse it with personal gain. I think [this] is the difference between a good labor leader and a poor one. The fellow you can buy off, whether he is a labor leader or anything else, isn't much count. Today [union leaders] are elected by the rank and file. Too many people vote not from the conviction of what is good or bad, they vote to get an advantage somewhere or another. That's true in our labor unions as well [as] in our public elections and I see problems ahead.

When John Lewis was head of the United Mine Workers his philosophy was that the union should interfere as little as possible with management. That was one of the principal points in his wage agreements. Maybe I am prejudiced but in recent years they haven't followed that principle, they have interfered more and more in management to a point where [the union] no longer operates for the benefit of the miner. They did it sincerely in an effort to eliminate what they considered abuses and to accomplish equality, to get away from the boss having favorites. The objective was good, but it brings about other inequities that may be worse than the inequities they attempt to eliminate.

Today management is educated to the point where they could

do just as good a job, and a man can get just as good treatment, without the union as he does with the union, but whether it would stay that way or not I don't know. Any supervisor that is worth his salt is going to treat his people all alike; he's not going [to] pick one fellow and give him all the gravy and push the other fellow down. The supervisor [of] any count is not interested in favoritism, he is interested in the quality of work that a man does and when he has a new job to fill he'll pick the man he believes is best equipped to fill that job. Under the union contract this privilege is taken away from him. He is required to take the fellow with the oldest seniority, even though he is not equipped to handle that job. The theory is, "Train him." Our experience is that you can't.

All of the things that they do to interfere with management must be added to the cost of coal. Things like seniority, job posting, and job training become very expensive under certain conditions and the public must pay that price.

Associated with, though apart from, the other ways in which mountain people were responding to the changes that had been heaped upon them was their relation to the Old Regular Baptist Church. For many mountain people, their religion became the sole repository for and protector of an indigenous culture that was being assaulted from all sides. The words of Sam Johnson, who was born in 1892, illustrate the vital importance of religion to the daily lives of many mountain men and women. Sam said, "All I want to talk about is the Lord," but he did a lot more than just talk; he lived by His side day in and out, often praying the whole night through. Sam was not a sinful man, although he did smoke a pipe and take aspirin now and then; he prayed because he believed deeply, just as his parents had believed, and their parents before them.

Before his death in April 1975, Sam lived at the head of Alum Cave Branch near Garner, Kentucky, with his wife, Rhoda Jane, and their daughter, Lauda. The absence of electricity, piped-in water, and an automobile necessitated a humble lifestyle that was made rich by peaceful surroundings and Sam's apparently boundless love for the Lord. Their home was a twenty-five-minute walk from the road and forty-five minutes from Casey's IGA Food Store in Leburn, and until shortly before his death Sam did all the shopping. Sometimes the spirit of the Lord filled him with such joy, he ran to the hard-road.

In the summer of 1973 Sam recalled:

I've been going [to church] regular now ever since 1908. That's when I started out to do right and the Devil hindered me. I knew I was a bad man, I wanted the Lord to forgive me. I couldn't give up the world, I loved the world too much. You have to love God with all your heart, with all your soul, and with all your strength, and with all your mind, and you can't love nothing of the world. I had a hard time getting right, it wasn't a easy job with me. It was years in the place of days. When God opened up my understanding I seed what kind of man I was. I thought shore I's bound fer tarment and couldn't shun it. My sins was before me as mountains. I didn't *do* so much, but I wanted to, you see, [so] I's guilty. I couldn't pray, I just moaned and groaned. Carried a burden fer a long time. Didn't want to eat and I didn't want to sleep, and I didn't feel like I'd be fit to be with nobody. That's the way I felt about it. Some [sinners] get through in a hurry, but I didn't. A man has to suffer fer everything [he does] wrong. He's got to suffer fer it all before he can enter into the Kingdom of God.

I drunk a little liquor and picked the banjer. I've played the fiddle and cursed. I didn't get out and steal, never did steal nothing. We're commanded not to drink no strong drinks, you know: "Thou shalt not drink no liquor," that's in the sixth chapter of Numbers, I believe is where it's at in the Bible. It's Old Bible. One thing I do know, I never had nary bit of desire to drink no strong drinks since I felt the Lord forgive me. I'll take an Anacin every now and then, but I wouldn't take some of them pills that'd make a man drunk.

The Lord is my doctor now. I like to suffer fer my mistakes. When I make a mistake and say something I ought not to say, I don't care how much punishment I get. If I don't suffer fer Christ I ain't been raised with Him.

I don't pay no attention to the elections and don't vote. I quit voting right smart bit ago. Too much evil around the voting place. God tells me to shun all kinds of evil and to keep myself unspotted from the world. I do smoke a pipe. I coughed one time for twenty years—just coughing all the time—and I went to smoking and it helped me. Some people thinks it's wrong to use

Sam Johnson

'baccer, but I never did see that it was wrong, but it is a bad habit. A man's got a family to raise, it'd be better fer him to do without his 'baccer than let his children do without something to eat. I wish I hadn't used it, but the doctors told them to make me use it and I got well.

Nineteen-thirty-four was when I felt the Lord forgive me and then I went to praying for the other people and I pray right on, day and night. I don't sleep much, I'm talking to the Lord all through the night. That old Satan's got plenty of power, he's going to get everyone he can. People's got to strive to enter into the Kingdom of God before they can get thar. When God forgives ye, you're no longer the keeper of yourself. You'll not fall from grace when you get salvation. After a man is borned again he cannot sin for the seed of Christ remains in ye.

If people would live right and have faith they wouldn't have to run to the doctor so much and they wouldn't shorten their days. If you afflict a widder, or an orphan child, any way and they cry, the Lord will wax hot and send a sword and kill ye. You can shorten your days, or you can do right and God will lengthen them. God lengthened one man's days fifteen years and I believe mine's been lengthened.

Every man that God wants to preach, He calls him and that man will qualify for the job. If ye didn't know a letter in the world, [or] in the Book, and God blesses ye to preach, you'd preach plime blank what he wants ye to. You'd preach the gospel. A preacher gets in the stand and he don't make up what to preach, he don't think about what to preach. You have to get shut of this natural mind before you can preach, and then just open your mouth and h'it will come to ye.

I'm just a sometimes preacher [now]. I started the thirteenth day of August 1935 preaching. I was assistant moderator and moderator about eighteen year down at Ivory Point Church and got so bad off I had to resign. H'it was [1973] May since I preached any I've been so bad off, but I ain't quit, I don't reckon. It's a great big job, moderator of the church. He does the church work and preaches. He asks them all whuther they're in "love and fellership" with one another and if anything is wrong. They generally answer, "Love and fellership" all the time [whether] they is or not.

There's so many of them confesses their hope in the Regular Baptist that ain't a Regular Baptist. If I see a man out committing sin willfully, I know he ain't right. No guessing. My Bible tells me he ain't right. They have to be borned again to be a Regular Baptist. When you're borned again you belong to the true church, whether you're dunked in the creek or not. If anybody joins the church that's not fit for the church he ain't added in, he just adds himself. When God adds a man in the church he's going to stay, he's going to live right. He'll walk pleasing with the Lord every hour, every minute, and every second through the day. He can be hindered a little—he don't live perfect—but he'll make it. Your conscience'll tell you just exactly how you ought to live and if ye don't, and ye won't repent, then you'll have to go down to the lake that burns of fire and brimstone.

I ain't no goody-goody feller, but I want to please the Lord every second through the day. Wherever a man's heart is, there's his treasure also.

Reverence for the Old Regular Baptist Church remains deep and many people continue to share Sam Johnson's faith in it, but as with everything else the church is changing. Lawrence Baldridge explains that most of the changes are as ideological and subtle as saying, "This is our church," rather than, "This is the only church." Other changes, such as the loosening of dogmatic strictures, will follow in time, but more than likely they will come from within the church, not from outside.

Lawrence is a native of Hueysville, Kentucky, and was reared by parents who were strong believers in the Old Regular Baptist Church. When he left home to attend college in Pippa Passes Lawrence parted from the Old Regulars and allied with the Missionary Baptist Church.

After completing undergraduate studies, Lawrence entered Southern Baptist Theological Seminary in Louisville, which was another divergence from the Old Regulars, who do not stress formal pastoral training. Since then he has become pastor of the Missionary Baptist Church in Pippa Passes. Lawrence discussed the Old Regular Baptist Church from the point of view of someone who has left the structure but remains close to the ideology. In doing so, he offers an insight into the inner religious struggles of many Appalachians, especially those who have migrated from the region.

My experiences as a child in the Old Regular Baptist Church were warm experiences of good people being together in their religious expression, in which they were totally uninhibited in their faith in God and love for their fellow man. The worship services were at least two or three times longer than they are today, and at that time you would have two or three more preachers than today. Now people are more concerned about getting through about twelve or one o'clock and that represents an invasion from outside: back then they were concerned about getting through whenever they got through. Also, I think they were more emotionally joyful at that time than they are now: there was more of what they called the "power of the spirit" present. I believed that the Old Regular Baptist was the *only* church because we had been taught that. I thought that everybody else was going to Hell except the Old Regular Baptists. Then as I opened up to the facts of life [I realized] this just wasn't so.

When I was eighteen years of age I was at Alice Lloyd College and I was presented with the possibility of expressing my faith in Jesus Christ personally as my Lord and Savior. I believed that He is Lord of all. I accepted that both intellectually and emotionally and also by faith. Later, I found to a large degree the traditional church was incompatible with my kind of freedom of expression. For example, I was told that you are not supposed to go to dances; no matter if those dances were chaperoned, and no matter how good they are, they are sinful. I was told that you are not supposed to go to movies because movies are sinful. Of course I was going to movies at that time, I didn't see sin in it. I never felt it was a sin to play musical instruments. I'd heard the inconsistencies of preachers that preach against the radio. In fact, I remember hearing one man preach over the radio against television! I never felt it was a sin to play sports and I was told it was; some of the people who told me that have changed themselves after they had sons or grandsons who played on the basketball team. I felt that as a young person I wasn't being offered any freedom in the traditional church. As far as the faith I had, we were very compatible, [but] in the ultimate analysis I had to have freedom to think, and freedom to be, and the [traditional] church did not offer that freedom in the sense that I understood it.

When I talk about the "traditional church" I want to make clear that I am talking about the church that I love very dearly, and about my own background of which I am not ashamed at all. But at that time the traditional church preached against almost everything, and for only one thing, and, to their credit, that was Christ. There is a whole bunch of people in this community who are members of the traditional church who feel these church demands are ridiculous, but they give them up because there is a higher value involved, and that's the value of peace in the family. They are independent in some ways, but familism always has been, and always will be, a stronger value.

I felt also that Sunday School was a good thing [but the traditional church does not sanction Sunday School]. Most of the preachers in the traditional church had little or no education. How can you teach unless you can read the Bible? They haven't had many teachers who could teach the Bible; now they have a whole number who can, so they will change.

The traditional church has never emphasized the need for young people to know or understand the Bible. They feel the "age of accountability" is later in life. That doesn't mean that young people don't go to their church; they do. Here in our church we have almost all young people. We can't build the church on the older people because they are too traditional, they won't accept our church. In urban America about 40 or 50 percent [of the] people are [church] members; here it is probably closer to 10 or 20 percent. Membership here is smaller because [of] that absolute standard of black and white. I don't think you can expect to have people involved in churches unless the church does offer some kind of religious freedom to them. [Few] people are church members, but religion is part of life because the closer you are to the land, the closer you are to religion. When you are close to life and death you are religious, because life is a very religious subject and death is a very religious subject. Old Regular Baptists, and us too, could get many members if we tried to get members on the same basis that some other churches get members, but we feel that people who have [not] been born again should not be church members. Baptists have always stood for a regenerate church membership.

I made my decision not to join the Old Regulars without feeling that there would be any particular pressure on me from society, and there wasn't a whole lot because I was living in an area where the family structure had started to break up to some degree. The strongest sanctions came from my own immediate family. They were quite understandably disappointed and they let me know it. Also, there was a lot of pressure on them from the standpoint that they had a son that was no longer an Old Regular Baptist. They've long since accepted my decision, however.

Had I become a member of the Old Regular Baptists, or a preacher in the Old Regular Baptist Church, there would have been much more compensation for me individually than there is now. Their compensation is not monetary; [it] is in terms of social approval, social applause, political power. Had I become an Old Regular Baptist preacher I could have a lot more people to preach to and a lot more funerals to preach, and so forth. The status of the Old Regular Baptist [preacher] is extremely high because he represents the values of this immediate society. It is very difficult to come from the traditional church into another church. Tremendous pressure is put on [such a person] because the family orientation is so strong. You are breaking a code of ethics and values and that is the family code; you are dishonoring the family. In a sense it is like a Jewish individual becoming a member of a Gentile church. [Here] I represent what might cause a break-up in the social values structure. In a sense, [some people] can say I'm here to set a father against his son and a mother against her daughter.

In Hindman* I would probably be more like the people in that I'd have more middle-class identification and be judged by achieved, and not by acquired, status. If we went to Maytown [or] Martin, or Hazard† it is the same. When you start going to your more rural areas it is different because there you have more traditionalism and more familism. To some degree I suppose I am a threat to community and family solidarity. I represent that aspect of change that their children are going through in the cities.

The church has been in control of the people and therefore it hasn't changed as much as some other institutions [but it is changing]. At one time they said, "This is the only church," but [now] it's "our" church and there is a distinct and subtle difference here. The outside is invading every domain of mountain life including the sanctuary which has been considered the most private domain of men. The reason [they] say it's "our" church is because it embodies mountain values: the traditional church embodies traditional values. They now seem to realize that other expressions of the Christian faith are valid [and] this is a new thing in the Appalachian region, because at one time it was an absolutely closed door. The next change as I see it in this immediate area will be from, "This is our church," to "These are our churches."

The thing that is alike in all Baptist churches is a tendency

---

* Hindman, the seat of Knott County, is seven miles from Pippa Passes.
† These are larger towns located within thirty miles of Pippa Passes.

toward a lay leadership. The church is always in the hands of the people; it is very seldom in the hands of any paid leadership, and it is never in the hands of a hierarchy. This accounts for the strength of Baptists in Central Appalachia. The second thing is the idea of freedom in the congregational type of church polity. Church polity is very important because that says every individual member has a right to vote. It is a demonstrative religion that appeals primarily to emotion and the heart. The service is very informal. People shout a lot and the preacher preaches with a lot of emotion and rhythm. The people are usually members of the same family, or extended families, and in most communities it is a family affair. It is also very worshipful because they are absolutely sincere and they believe with all their hearts in what they are doing.

The pattern of the traditional church is informality. They know exactly when the whole congregation stands, when to be seated, when the opening prayer is going to come. It is almost liturgical in that sense, yet it is informal. What keeps it that way is that the traditional church has more preachers who are uneducated. Their delivery is totally extemporaneous and always involves folk things, something that is person-centered, related to the family.

I think the Old Regular Baptists have given a whole value structure to the mountains which has been good. When you start talking about social values, you [are] talking in terms of right and wrong, good and bad, what's desirable and what is undesirable. They have had a very good effect on society in terms of crime being lower here than in other areas, although it's increasing now which shows that the values are breaking down. The church in this area has tremendous value, because the church is an institution that is—to some degree—strong enough to resist the outside pressures of change, and is not willing to change just because the outside says to change. It does keep the values that are deemed important by society and gives people strength to deal with the outside. On the other hand, it can become provincial and an island in the midst of a world.

Colonialism exists in Appalachia mainly because the people have been fooled by the shrewdness of the outside interests [that] own everything. I think to some degree the traditional church reinforces that because it does preach only about heaven and it leaves earth out too many times. This laissez-faire attitude of religion in Appalachia toward social problems has reinforced the outside ownership of coal and resources. I don't want to imply that the traditional church has been alone in this because the fact is that the outside church has been just as guilty here as the traditional church. Too many times the membership of the outside church has been made up of those people who have been colonialists and [of] the people who have exploited. There is a feeling of an invasion of privacy by the press, the media, the VISTA workers, by the whole influence of governmental aid in the region. The whole area's become more open to urban society [and] seeing different values creates a change possibility. The church will never resist outside influences entirely; it will always change as an institution, but it will change more at its own pace than at a forced pace.

The traditional church doesn't take any interest in social issues largely because it doesn't know what social issues are. It has traditionally had an uninformed membership, and if you don't know what social issues are you can't organize to fight them. I get involved in the issues myself [and] I often talk about them from the pulpit, but I always discipline myself. I'm not called to preach issues, I'm called to preach the gospel and bring issues in as they relate to the gospel. I have a message and I preach that message. I preach the Good News, not good views. But I certainly do relate my Christianity to life and to all aspects of life.

Even though they don't have a formal structure of teaching, there is more of a God-consciousness in this society than almost any society in America. Almost everyone here believes in God. The reason for this is you're close to nature, alone with the stars, the mountains, and with the streams. Young people here feel a strong sense of religion, a much stronger sense than the more sophisticated urban young person who is almost totally divorced from reality in the sense that he is an urbanic. When you have concrete buildings and concrete streets, and all your food out of cans, how can you have a strong sense of your identity with nature? If you can't identify yourself with the creation, you can't possibly identify yourself with the Creator. Here we do.

7

THE CRUEL CHOICE

As the nation prepared for another war in the early 1940's, Central Appalachia thrived. The latest bust-to-boom cycle, which was started before the national Depression in 1929, was complete and the coalfields flourished again. During the war production increased nearly 500 percent in some places and wages took a similar, though seldom matching, leap. Between 1939 and 1945 the average weekly earnings for a bituminous coal miner had risen from $23.83 to $56.84. The jump was caused primarily by the increased number of hours miners worked each week and also by changes in the pay rates that had been negotiated by the union. Automation was accelerated to meet the nation's need for fuel, which once again seemed insatiable, and to fill the vacuum created by the exodus of thousands of patriotic mountain people who went off to war.

By the time the young people returned home, the boom times were fading and another national recession was coming. The realities of automation were never more apparent. Prior to the war Central Appalachia's bituminous coal industry's peak years had been in 1918 and 1926 when about 527 million tons of coal were produced annually by nearly 542,000 workers. In 1944 the region's yield reached 620 million tons, an increase of nearly 10

297

percent, but only 65 percent of the 1926 work force was needed to produce that amount of coal. The silver linings of wartime prosperity were quickly shattered as young people came home to find work and found unemployment instead.

The returning soldiers, as well as many of their older kinfolks, who sought work in the late 1940's had few alternatives. They could remain at home to face welfare and unemployment, or employment at levels barely above subsistence, or they could leave and find work in industries that customarily flourish after, rather than during, wars. The choice was never easy but the young did have several advantages over their elders: industry was anxious to hire veterans; their GI Bill of Rights was a useful reward for military service; and fighting a war had removed fear of the unknown. Between 1950 and 1960 30 percent of Appalachia's young people chose migration and left the region.

Initially, there were some rewards for the people who remained at home. Buoyed by the boom years, many company managers were optimistic about renewed prosperity, but as sales declined and competition with oil and gas industries increased they retrenched. One of their economies was selling their thirty- and forty-year-old camp town houses to employees and veterans whose wartime savings accounts were still flush. The price tags for the deteriorating homes were usually modest and they seemed like a good investment. However, as time went on mines closed and the homes became one more albatross for their owners.

In the few mines that remained viable, mechanization made deeper and deeper inroads during the 1950's and the introduction of the continuous miner wiped out still more jobs. The continuous miner, a huge piece of equipment that contains dozens of steel teeth capable of gnashing and ingesting an entire face of coal in seconds, eliminated the need for blasting, undercutting, and hand-shoveling. Use of this machine has become so widespread that today it is simply called "the miner."

As jobs became scarcer and more technical in nature, mountain people who had shunned out-migration gravitated toward welfare *programs. Originally, "welfare" was to be a temporary post-Depression, self-help measure, but by 1950 the number of public-aid programs had proliferated and become entrenched in the nation's economy. An individual's decision to seek state or federal aid was not made easily, because welfare and migration were contrary to Central Appalachian mores.*

The post-war years were a time for decision-making in the mountains and the decisions were never easy. Migration was not a simple solution because the ties to home were generations deep and the urban centers of Michigan, Ohio, Florida, and Pennsylvania were almost as alien to the mountaineer as Hazard had been to the foreign immigrants a few decades before. Although mountain émigrés frequently followed similar patterns by settling in the "Little Appalachias" that border urban centers, no two people responded alike, as Barbara Caudill, Pearl Cornett, Orla Pace, and Will Pennington explain so well.

Of course, not everyone in the mountains had to leave or resort to welfare during the fifties. There were still some jobs to be had and some mountaineers inherited their forebears' penchant for creating new ways to earn a living.

The migration of people from the hills of Central Appalachia to the urban centers of the North and South following World War II was prompted by the mechanization of the coal mines more than anything else. Mechanization was itself an outgrowth of the Depression years that received a hearty welcome from the officials of large coal companies because, in the long run, machines were more efficient than human beings and less expensive to sustain.

The phenomenon of mechanization is of course not unique to an industrial society, but it is ironic that in the United States its origins are found in the coalfields of Central Appalachia, one of the nation's least industrial regions. Mountain people are not "yesterday's people" but "tomorrow's people." They have had to face the impact of automation on the job market well before much of the rest of the country. The failure of local, state, and federal authorities to devise creative ways of providing employment for those people who were thrown out of jobs because of automation has been one of the major failures of this century in the mountains.

Milburn (Big Bud) Jackson and Elroy Dowdy are coal miners whose lives were greatly affected by mechanization. Their comments about the way in which they, as old miners, responded to a machine age in the hills leave little doubt why so many young people fled the hills or resorted to welfare.

Milburn Jackson lives in Cranes Nest, Virginia, and described camaraderie among miners and discussed a personal philosophy that allows him daily to confront the mines and their machinery with some equanimity.

I don't believe that a person who works in the coal mines is any more endangered than my wife sitting there on the porch. The whole house could fall in on her. I would say that a person is about as safe in a coal mine as [he is working] in a garage checking automobiles because there is a lot more men working in the coal mines than there would be in any garage. There are a lot of people who get killed in garages and there are a lot of people who get killed in the mines.

I never worry about slate falls, which happen every day, but one thing that I would be worried about is insufficient air. I know what smothering [is like], buddy, for I've had asthma ever since I was about four years old. I believe I would rather a rock mash me up and kill me instantly than to cut air off of me and make me smother. I would wake up a lot of times in the morning fighting and slinging my arms because I'm smothering. A person that has never smothered don't know what a feeling that is. There is a health hazard in the coal mines: you ain't got sufficient air and that causes lung trouble, you get rock dust. That's why I hope and pray nary one of my kids will go into the mines [but] they probably will.

In certain ways I think [the new machinery] is a great improvement; on the other hand, it has cut a lot of poor laboring men out

Milburn (Big Bud) Jackson

of work. In the [mechanized] mines you have to work as the machine tells you. Every day that you go in there, you're in danger, you have got to stay one step ahead of [the machine]. In West Virginia forty or fifty people were killed. Some people say, "It will never happen to us over here." It could happen here just as it could happen in West Virginia. If that rock has a certain time to fall, it's got no special person. I don't believe that a person has got a time to be called. I do believe if you'll take safety precautions and watch yourself you can prevent that. A lot of people say you can't keep death from slipping up on you, but you *can* shorten your days. If a person will watch hisself and see that he is safe he will never die in the coal mines. You've got to re-spect [the mine] and not be afraid of it. Fear in a coal mine is one of the biggest dangers. If you get scared in a coal mine [while] driving cars and look up, you'll kill yourself or kill somebody else.

I've always wanted to work in the mines and I'll be in the mines for the rest of my life. Whenever I was a boy growing up I wanted to go in the mines more than anything. That's all I lived for; that's all a person could [live for] back then.

In other words, once coal dust gets in your blood you can't get it out?

That's right. I believe that with all my heart. I can't stand that hot sun. When I come in from work I don't set foot in the garden until that sun has gone down on the other side of the mountain. It burns me up. I sweat in the house. If you change jobs you'll sweat. If I change from one side of the machine to the other, I'll sweat and burn up. If I get back on that other side of the machine, I don't sweat.

One time I was working in the mines and a [boss] hired a col-ored person to work with me and I had knowed the colored boy all of my life. It wasn't long after that until I got me a different job with more money. [In] about three or four weeks [the boss] come back up and said, "Jackson, if you will come back to work for me I'll fire every damn Nigger on the job."

He thought I quit because he had hired that colored feller, but I would just as soon work with a colored feller as anybody. I said, "Lordy have mercy, that's the furthest thing from my mind. I would just as soon work with him as with my twin brother as far as that's concerned," which I would because I was in there to make a living, not to take partiality on no man. I said, "I ain't coming back because I am working for more money." If a colored person is a friend to you, he's a friend to you. Our neighbors right around us here is a lot worse than a colored person as far as the friendly part. There's some of them that won't even speak to you. If you speak to them, they'll drop their damn lip down to their ankles and walk off.

I've had some dreams, some awful dreams, about coal mines and I've told my wife that I would give anything not to go to work. I've dreamed that nothing would happen to me, but I would be digging my buddies out from under a rock fall. You talk about something that would really hurt, that would.

Do you ever stay home from work after a dream like that?

No, I never have; I'll tell you the reason why. If I was there maybe I could help him if it did happen. When I got that finger cut off that about drove me crazy. That's the worse I was ever hurt in the coal mines. I got that finger cut off the twenty-sixth day of January [1963]. The third day of February those guys got killed [in the mine where I was working] and I was off with my finger. I went to the doctor that day and here come Jimmy, my brother, and told me about the fall. I didn't know whether [Little] Bud was killed or not. He's my twin brother. I couldn't get no information nowhere. I was walking the floors. I took off and went to the mines. I don't guess there was a prouder person ever walked up in front of a mines [than I was] when I saw Bud standing there. I would have give a hundred dollars to have been in there when it happened to find out what was going on. I couldn't have stopped it but I would have knowed what was happening.

Elroy Dowdy's attitude toward the machines that dominate the coal industry lacks any resemblance to Milburn Jackson's equanimity, and with good reason. Mechanization was the bane of the career he tried to develop and he continutes to ponder its significance at his home near Doran, Virginia.

[When I worked for] the big coal company [and] it came down to where we was working one, two, and three days a week you couldn't make ends meet and had too many expenses to continue under them conditions. Naturally, I changed [jobs]. I changed from this union mine to what they call a "scab" mine because they were working four, five, and sometimes six days a week [while] I wasn't working but one, two, and three days a week in the union mine. Anybody can see the point: one has to make a living; they are going to stay where the money is. Anything that I have ever done I have always tried to build up to where I could get the most money out of it. That is common sense because if you are going to work you should get the most for it.

I believe in protecting yourself, too. You take a coal miner, why nine out of ten has got a family and he is all that they have got to look to. Many of them are six feet under and if they had

Elroy Dowdy

just stopped and set up a safety post [or] not run in front of a motor, [they wouldn't be dead]. But they take these chances.

It is coming to a point that if you can't handle modern equipment you ain't going to be able to work in the coal mines. The companies would rather hire a young man and train him and put him on that equipment knowing that he has got a longer period of time to work. When a man comes around forty to forty-five years old it is a pretty good problem for him to change [jobs]. Seniority rights in the coal mines has got most of the older men cut out.

I have applications in at all these places, but I am experienced with old equipment and I have not had no experience with new equipment. I went and talked to a superintendent at Jewell Valley [about] why the old miners couldn't get a job. He said he would be more than glad to give me a job but, "This is our problem: when a machine helper, or a joy helper, quits, seniority rights [demand] that the next man in line moves up, and nine times out of ten it is a motorman and if a man can't run a motor we can't hire him." I have never been familiar with motor equipment, that's the reason I ain't in the big mines.*

Hand-loading coal was the safest way to load it. Any time you put machinery in the mines you are endangering yourself. We know that the new type equipment is a lot more dangerous [and] faster than the old. The old type equipment was pulled with ropes. The new type of equipment is hydraulic. Everything on them is hydraulic and there is a whole lot of difference in them. It takes time to train men for equipment like that. Here's the point: the olders had to be able to pass a physical examination, which I believe I could do, but there are a lot of them that have

---

* The interview with Elroy Dowdy took place in 1967, pre-dating by six or seven years most of the interviews in *Our Appalachia*. In 1969 Elroy was successful in getting another job with a mining company. However, in 1974 he again became the victim of mechanization; this time more tragically so than the first. Elroy was aboard one man-trip car—a low tram that hauls miners through a coal seam to their working place—when the brakes on another man-trip vehicle failed, causing it to crash into his car. Elroy's back was seriously injured in the accident and he has not been able to work in the mines since then.

something wrong [and] they will turn them down. That's the end for a miner.

I believe these new companies want young men. I made a survey and went around and watched their crews. You find one man out of thirty in the thirty-five- to forty-year-old [age range]. The rest of them is under that [and] that's the way they are going to keep it. Another thing, you take a young miner and put him in the mines, he can handle that new type of equipment but the old miners have got the advantage [of understanding] mining more thoroughly than they do. There are problems in a mine such as high coal or ribs falling off, things the older miner understands and watches out for which a young miner won't know. Self-experience in the mines takes time, and it takes time to make a miner.

It just takes one rock to kill you. One time they hired a new mining boss. He comes into the mine where I was loading. The shot foreman comes along and he tamps it up to shoot the coal. This [boss] goes back behind me and [removes a timber] between me and the next pillar row. At the time I didn't know what was going on [until] I heard somebody holler, "You had better get out because it is going to fall in."

I said, "It ain't going to fall." I throwed on a dozen more shovels of coal and the timber broke all around me. I started running on my knees about thirty or forty feet [to] where my bucket and shirt [were]. I reached my bucket and started to reach after my shirt and a rock split out over my head. I started running. I run out from under that rock and it poured in like pouring [water] out of a bucket. That's the closest I ever come [to] getting killed. It was just over a silly thing that a man would do. If he hadn't cut that little stump out it would have never happened.

Everybody knows [the mines] was booming in Virginia and West Virginia during war times. People think they would go on making big money, but that's not so. I have worked in these big mines and I was making around three hundred dollars every two weeks. When that went down I had to go to a smaller job like I do now [and] I ran anywhere from eighty to ninety dollars a week. If they have breakdowns, sometimes it's forty or fifty dollars. Lots of times a poor man can't meet his bills and that piles pressure on everybody. Where there ain't no industry, there ain't no future.

Around here a miner is considered the breadbasket. If a miner don't make money our merchants don't sell nothing. It takes so much to live, I don't care what you do, whether it is a miner, or a factory worker, or farmer. If that income is not there somebody suffers. Generally, it is the laboring man that suffers, and his family. It pinches me lots of times to pay my grocery bill, much less pay anybody what I owe them. When I was making three hundred dollars every two weeks I could keep my bills paid and didn't owe nobody too much. Back then I was making enough money to meet my bills but now I ain't. This is what hurts the poor class of people.

More people left this part of the country in the last twelve years on account of work than any state I know of unless it would be West Virginia, the sister state. The biggest portion of them are in Ohio, Maryland, and places like that. They went because they wanted to get out of the coal mines.

Barbara Mosely Caudill was born in an isolated Breathitt County, Kentucky, hollow in 1928 and her childhood resembled that of her grandparents far more than it did her peers who lived in the coal camps. She didn't ride in an automobile until she was thirteen and she had to quit school after the eighth grade because her father was fearful of allowing her to leave home to attend high school. This background and Barbara's reverence for mountain life profoundly influenced her approach to migration.

When she was sixteen Barbara married Less Caudill. After the war she and Less lived for a while in Indianapolis and Cleveland, but they soon got "a hungerin' for home" and returned to Ulvah, Kentucky, to live with his parents. For a dozen years Less worked at whatever jobs he could get, but when he exhausted eastern

Kentucky's employment opportunities the factories of Indianapolis seemed to be the only answer. For reasons she will explain, Barbara never moved up North and Less has commuted between Indianapolis and Ulvah for nine years. At home Barbara looks after their four school-age children and makes cornshuck dolls to supplement Less's income. Both are counting the years and days until he can retire.

When the war was over we went to Indianapolis and stayed two months, and then we went to Cleveland, Ohio, and spent

Barbara Caudill

two months but we wasn't satisfied. It just wasn't home up there. We enjoyed being here in the hills [where] it was so much more peaceable [and] people were much kinder to us. [Less] wasn't qualified for anything except loading coal on his knees [and when] he got those ruptured cartilages in his knees he couldn't work in the mines anymore. He tried to find other work around here: he tried for a mail route; he went to vocational school and took auto mechanics, [but] they only offered him fifty dollars a week at the only place in Whitesburg that wanted somebody. He worked on Operation Mainstream—that was for unemployed fathers that was too old to work at real hard labor jobs like loading coal, or too disabled to work in the mines—until the election came along and they told him who to vote for. He told them nobody would tell him how to vote. He didn't get any more work after that.

When my husband left [for Indianapolis] Billy Joe was twelve years old, Matthew was five, our baby, one. I didn't know what I was facing without him at home or I wouldn't have let him have went without me and the children because it's been so hard on me. I've had to be father, mother, the one to pay the bills, the one to buy the coal and see that it was hauled to the house, and I've had to be the one to get up in the mornings to build the fires. I've had to be everything and that is more responsibility than any one person can live and bear up under. I've not done a perfect job, nobody could, but I've sure done the best I could do.

We contemplated on moving [to Indianapolis] so many times because [Less] and I wanted to be together and we wanted him to be with the children, but the children didn't want to leave their schools, their friends, and home. Every time we'd start to leave home Robert Dale would get a chisel and hammer and go around every rock on the hearth [writing] "Home Sweet Home." They loved this place better than anything.

Billy Joe always said he wanted to go to college and by the time we got enough money so that we could afford to move, he was ready to go to college. It was that fall that we paid the rent on one of those condominium apartments [in Indianapolis].

When my daughter called and told me that building was ready and we could start moving I froze. I tell you, I almost had a heart attack. Less was home on vacation. He said, "You don't want to move out there and I don't either. Don't worry, we'll keep them here." We would rather suffer than suffer the children. I couldn't have a bit more moved off and left Bill there in college. He said if I moved he couldn't go because I had to be there to support him. He couldn't stay over there—he thought—without getting to come home every weekend.

I was so worried about my children moving to the city because they wouldn't know how to make a go of it. You know how country people take advantage of what they call the "city slickers"; they play every trick in the book on them if they get a chance. Country children [in] the city get the same treatment. When we go out there to visit I would hear every day of children being destroyed, being drowned, run over by cars, fall out of cars and get killed. I heard of children being on dope. One dose of it calls for another and they go from bad to worse. A lot of them wind up in prison and a lot of them wind up dead. I didn't know how to move into the city and keep all that away from my children. Back here I know what to prepare them for and how to cope with it, but out there I wouldn't. I thought that I would lose my last breath if I got in the city and my child went around the corner [and] I knew there was a chance that I'd never see it again. It's a fear because I didn't understand the city and I couldn't understand it because I've never lived in it long enough. I was afraid of the people because they know how to live there and I don't. To plant me in a crowded area, I don't know how I could cope with it. I can sit here at the house and make dolls and I can hear the traffic and I can hear the bulldozers, but the voices I hear are birds singing, or the chickens cackling, and I'm not afraid of them.

I had an uncle that was a hillbilly from one end to the other and he went to Austin, Indiana, during World War II and he worked long enough to save up five hundred dollars. [He] started home, got to the bus station in Cincinnati, and somebody picked that poor guy's pocket and there went his savings. It's people that you can't trust that I'm afraid of. It's not the honest people, [but] you can't tell an honest person from a crook when you see them. People like me and my children are vulnerable to things like that because we wouldn't understand what they would be meaning until they'd already have us in trouble. I know how to make it here and I didn't know whether I would know how to make it in the city.

I'm afraid of the city and I've often wondered if I was right being like that. My husband feels the same way. He has been there almost eight years and the only route he knows is how to get to work, to my daughter's, and how to [go] fishing. When he has to go downtown to get something he gets my nephew to go with him because he says he doesn't know exactly how to get there.

Has Less made friends with many people in Indianapolis other than with those who came from down home?

No, he don't get along with them. I guess he's just too much of a hillbilly and always will be. He's a person that is kind of hard to get along with. You have to love and respect him to get along with him. He's outspoken and he won't go out of his way to make friends like me. I would walk a mile to get to meet a nice person but Less won't. I don't know why he's got that kind of an outlook, but you'd just have to know him to understand it, and you'd have to love him an awful lot to put up with it. My children say he's grouchy, and he is, but he just faces facts and speaks them as they are. He don't beat around the bush and he won't go out of his way to keep from stepping on somebody's toes. When he lost that job because he wouldn't vote for the county judge a lot of people would [have told the boss] they would vote for the one they wanted them to vote for, but not Less. If he couldn't get anything honest he didn't want it and I've become the same way.

I filed an income tax return on what I made before I even made enough because I was afraid that I would get in trouble with the government. I was always thinking up new things to earn money to help the family. I took in washing when I didn't even have a machine. I cut hair. I made dolls. Last year I made over four thousand dollars. That was the most I've ever made and I know I won't be able to make that again because Hill 'n Hollow crafts at Whitesburg can't buy as many dolls from me as they could last year. Their contributors stopped donating money [and] the craft members have to make it on their own now. My mother always taught me one thing, it comes from the Bible: You can't do wrong and get by with it; somehow, somewhere it will catch up with you. I've always believed that and I have had things to happen, just little small things, to prove that it is true and this is why I report my income. That would be the most terrible thing in the world to have the IRS get after me.

[Recently] I applied to this Eastern Kentucky Housing Development to try to get us a house built because we've had to live in these three little rooms close to thirty years. The government officials had the gall to tell me if there was a divorce pending between me and my husband that I could get a house built. I said, "If it takes breaking up my home, I don't want it." There's not a castle on earth full of silver and gold that I would trade for the love that my family has got for one another and the experiences we've shared together here in these little rooms. The ties that bind our family together, nothing will ever break.

If I get my house fixed it will be because I get it honest and if I can't get it fixed honest I'll live in it thirty years [more]. I'd rather live in it the way it is than to get one board put on it dishonest. A certain [person] told me, "If I was you I'd get a divorce and get the house built and then you could remarry." I said, "If I have to do that I do not want it." I've got to be honest because I'm the one I see when I look in the mirror, not them. If I have to live in this house that I'm ashamed of the rest of my days to be honest, I'll do it. My husband's the same way.

Almost from the start Pearl Cornett's response to migration was destined to differ from Barbara's. He was reared in Town

Mountain, Kentucky, near Hazard, and left home in 1928 at thirteen to attend Cincinnati's Woodward High School. After graduation he returned to Kentucky for several years, became a schoolteacher, and married Eloise Brown. During World War II they moved to Pittsburgh, where Pearl, who had received a medical discharge from the army, felt he could serve his country by working in a defense plant. After the war they returned to Town Mountain to rear their children, but times were lean. "Looking back," said Pearl, "it seemed that if you didn't teach or you weren't a coal miner there was nothing left but to leave." In 1951 Eloise and Pearl Cornett rented their home and moved to a Cleveland, Ohio, suburb.

While some mountain people have abhorred life in a big city and yearned for the day when they could return home, Pearl and Eloise enjoyed Cleveland and immersed themselves in its civic and Bahá'í Church activities. However, as retirement neared, their thoughts turned toward home and in 1973 they returned to Town Mountain, where they lived until Pearl's death in 1976.

The reason we left Kentucky, we thought that there wasn't [enough] income coming to the family to educate our children and do the things we felt parents should be able to do. This was back in the early fifties; teachers' salaries were low and the biggest industry in these mountains was coal. Many of the coal camps were closing and men were leaving the mines and going to northern cities to get work. At that time my salary was about $225 a month. This was for ten months of the year. I was principal at Dunham High School in Letcher County, Kentucky, [which] was all black.

Then you heard a great talk about integrating the schools in Kentucky. [As a black] I feared integration in that they might integrate the students and not the teachers, and I thought black teachers would be cast aside and white teachers would be retained. Now in Kentucky I can definitely say that this was an ungrounded fear because they did use the black teachers.

[My mother] didn't like the idea of me leaving. None of my people, the older ones, felt that I should go. I didn't tell them I thought that I would be unemployed if the schools were integrated. My real reasons, I just didn't reveal to anyone. My wife and I, we just felt that we'd have a better chance to make a go of it and this, I guess, meant income, because we didn't feel that we were making the money we should make. I taught with many women who was married to coal miners and the coal miners that did have work made good money. So, socially there was a difference: they had income from their husbands and their own income, and when you take $225 against what they had, why it just sort of gives you a feeling of insecurity among the people that I worked with. Those were some of the reasons that I left.

I was born and reared right here near Town Mountain. My mother was a highly motivated person. Although she had very

(Photograph by Lyn Adams)

Pearl Cornett

little education she expected a great deal out of her children. She
expected education to solve all of our problems. Even our father
who had about a second-grade education, his idea was, "Educate
my children." That's all they talked about in the home. There
were eight of us and we lived in a common ordinary home here
in the mountains, but it seems like they always dreamed that if
they could just educate their children that would be fulfillment
for all the insecurities, and all the things they longed for in their
lives. Even after our dad died when I was thirteen, [Mother]
never let us get to the point where we felt that we couldn't do
what had to be done. Her idea was: you don't feel sorry for yourself, you just get out and work for what you want. She had many
character-building mottos. Any time I said, "I can't" do something, she'd say:

> I can't is a coward,
> A poor, pale, puny imp.
> No meal in his bag
> And he walks with a limp.

She would just make you see what "I can't" was.

She sang a great deal in her work. Sometimes I'd kid her:
"Mama, do you ever get tired of singing?" She'd say, "Alas for
those who do not sing and die and carry all their music with
them." She was a wonderful, wonderful person that would in-
spire you without you really knowing what she was doing.

[When I finished the eighth grade] rumors were that a high
school [for blacks] was going to start and my aunt taught the
ninth grade one year to give us a start so we wouldn't have to go
away from home. The next year they did start a county school for
blacks in Vicco, that's thirteen miles away, and a city school for
whites here in Hazard. It had to be done on a segregated basis
because of [the] Day law. Some man by the name of Day around
19 and 8 had a law written into the Kentucky constitution about
educating blacks and whites in the same building. Anyone who
taught mixed classes would be fined a hundred dollars a day, and

any student who sat in mixed classes would be fined fifty dollars a day. That was the Day law. So we had to catch a taxi at our own expense and pay our way to Vicco to get to the county school. I went to school there [for the tenth grade] and then for the second year [of high school I went to Cincinnati].

I found out after I got there that I was nothing like ready to be a junior in high school [so I repeated the tenth grade in Cincinnati]. I think that was one of the best things that [could have] happened, [because] I did get a good education from one of the very best high schools in the country. There I was very backwards, although I had always thought at home here that I was very bright and wide awake. I'd never been out of these hills before and [was suddenly] turned loose in a large five-story school building, a block long each way, where classes changed on bells. I remember having my schedule so messed up I'd always end up with the same two classes in the afternoon because I was using my lunch period for a class period. The first evening when school was out I kept going all the way around this building looking for a way out. There was no exits on the basement floor to the street; you had to come up a flight of steps to get out. I don't know how many times I circled trying to get out of the building.

I was just about the most homesick person that you'd want to see. I remember I went to a movie one night and Kentucky was the setting. You could hear the whippoorwill just as plain; Will Rogers was setting there rocking; and Stepin Fetchit was playing "The sun shines bright in my old Kentucky home." I couldn't hold it back, I just boohooed. I wanted to get home so badly. After I stayed there enough to get oriented I begin to enjoy it. I would come home every summer and I'd really look forward to going back and would be afraid that for some reason I wouldn't get to go back to finish high school.

[I graduated from Woodward in '35 and] this was those hard years, Depression years, so there wasn't much work to get. I came back home and this was when I realized that I'd have to go on to college. I went to Kentucky State College in Frankfort in '35, finished college there, and then came back home to start teaching for $89.10 a month. [By] '47 I was [teaching], driving a school bus [and] I coached football for about $200 a month. After I made principal I got $225 a month.

I [had] a friend that I'd gone to college with that lived in Ohio, who was urging me, "Come to Cleveland, come to Cleveland. You can make it big." I left this principal's job. My superintendent hated to see me go. He said, "This is the way you fellows do: you run away when things are booming outside and then when things get tough you'll be back looking for jobs."

We stayed in [Cleveland's] inner city for less than a year [and] I told Eloise, "Honey, we've got to find us a place outside of Cleveland, or we've got to go back home, one, because this is no place to bring up children." Having studied some of these social problems that [cities] have, I guess that made me more familiar with what I'd see going on. I know there's many people that live in the ghettos who have outstanding families and I think there are many, many losers who have lost their families that live in ghettos and I just didn't want to have to take that chance. If we had had to live in the inner city I guess I would have been back home quicker because the inner city is definitely a poor place to bring up kids.

We bought thirty-five acres of land [in] a small rural suburb of Cleveland [that had] good farm land, all level and tillable. I don't know how we were lucky enough to [buy] that because many blacks had been looking for a place like that. I guess that whole spirit that I was telling you about my mother had something to do with it: whatever you want you just go after. Wanting a place out, I just begin to look. When I'd see a place advertised I'd go out and check on it. I know a lot of black people would have somebody else call and they'd start getting the runaround early. We found this place, the owner was wanting to get away from Cleveland in the worst sort of way. I bought it with a friend of mine that worked at the same plant I worked at. We had a two-family house on this farm, with up and down, so he and I went in together and bought it.

I guess we'd been there three or four months and been making the payments [when our] real estate dealer come out one day. He said, "Boys, I haven't been telling you fellows this, but they've been raising a lot of Cain about you. They are wanting to get you out of the community in the worst kind of way. Some of the influential people out here have forced the Westside Federal to foreclose, but don't worry, I've been doing some work."

There was a Negro group that was taking over a savings and loan charter. He knew the ones in charge and he told them about us. This fellow that was head of Supreme Savings and Loan came out and looked at our place. We were working, sweating away, when he came. He liked what he saw. He said, "Boys, don't worry about your farm, I'm going to buy this mortgage." We never had any more trouble after that. The first few Sundays we was out there the cars would come by just bumper to bumper, filled with whites staring, looking at us, to see what's going on. That was the movement, I guess, to get us out.

The kids enjoyed everything they had there. They had good standing in the school, in the community, in the church. We worked with people and served on committees; just really lived a real involved life.

I worked for General Motors, mostly, as an arc welder. A big corporation like that is very impersonal. *Who* is General Motors? You never heard of him. It's some foreman standing over you that's trying to push out of you all the production he can for somebody that's going to get a big vacation out of it, or a big bonus. You do have the feeling that you're sweating for somebody else's glory. The attitude towards work a lot of times on these jobs is to do as little as possible. In your small towns you'd have people who're more interested in giving a fair day's work for a fair day's pay. In the city a lot of times they like workers from the Appalachian region for the fact that they'd put in a fuller day than the average city worker. They'd been used to hard work: mining, farming, or whatever. In the city fellows were used to an easier pace and you'd come up with some hard work, he just sort of shirked it and shunned it.

At one time I guess we had this feeling that we would not come back, but I could never completely cut the ties with the mountains because my people were here. When we both began to feel this way we just decided to come home and we haven't regretted it.

Looking back, how would you compare the quality of life in Cleveland and Hazard?

This doesn't have near as much to offer socially and culturally that a place like Cleveland has [where] there are all kinds of stage plays, ice follies, and athletics going on. All year long there is something to attend or something to go to that's really exciting and worthwhile. There's no comparison along those lines. You might say, "Why would you leave a place like that to come back?" and many people don't. In my case, those things just don't hold the fascination for me that they held at one time. Having seen it, why it's not hard to walk away from. It all depends upon what you're looking for. If it's peace and quiet you probably want to get away from the crowds and the pushing. Anything you went to, there was a large crowd.

Maybe the things that I really set value on were things of childhood, the things my mother said, her simple ways of looking at life and some of her mottos, things that seemed to apply more in a city like this than they would in a place like Cleveland. I guess if I'd been born and reared in a place like Cleveland I'd probably never come to a place like Hazard to live, but having been born and reared here it was pretty easy to come back to.

In a small town everybody knows you, everybody speaks. [I'll] be in the garden working and I'll see a hand [wave], sometimes a white hand, sometimes a black, it doesn't matter. Same thing if I go down to the bank, I can stop and chat with the teller quite a while. This means a lot. I'll go to a Little League baseball game, well, you're sitting up there with the mayor and he knows you. When you go to a Little League baseball game in Cleveland I'd know a few of the parents, but I wouldn't know any mayors. There's not the rush and the dog-eat-dog atmosphere in a small town that you have in the city. Seems like everybody takes things seriously. It's just the old traditional way that they go about religion, even. Of course, I don't get along with that so much. The church in Cleveland was far more active, the outreach was much greater than it is here. When you think about ministers from Yale Divinity School compared to some of the ministers we have here, there's quite a difference. All in all, I think a small town compensates in other ways for some of the things that you give up in a city like Cleveland. Many of [our friends in Cleveland] couldn't understand why we wanted to come back. They thought, "Oh, you're glad to be in a place like this and not in the mountains of Kentucky," but they didn't realize how I felt about it.

Men, women, and children each faced a different set of problems when they migrated to the cities much as their kinfolks had years before when they moved to the coal camps. While men contended with assembly lines and production quotas, women either sought jobs for themselves or remained at home to rear the children in a new environment. As Harriette Arnow portrayed so powerfully in The Dollmaker, *a novel about migration, it was often the children who fared the best or suffered the most. While their ties to the hills were not yet as deep as their parents', they had to endure the barbarisms that only other children can proffer.*

Orla Pace was born in 1961, and migrated from Kentucky's Laurel County to Cincinnati under sad and unusual circumstances in 1975. Although her words reveal a fondness for the mountains and a reluctance to accept certain city ways, Orla declares, "I will stay up here as long as I live." Harold Dean, her brother-in-law, who is a Cincinnati bus driver, explains the apparent contradiction. "Look at what she has up here: we have a nice house, a telephone which she enjoys, a living-room suite, and a car. There is much more to do up here. Also the television reception is much better than it is in Laurel County."

Three months after she moved to Cincinnati, Orla recalled:

I guess you'd say I lived up in kind of a holler. Name of the holler was Hogskin. It was an awful name but I liked the place.

I got two brothers and two sisters. Sandra's the oldest and I think she's twenty-seven. Etta just had a birthday and she's twenty-four. Charlie's nineteen. Bradley is fifteen. My dad, he died March the ninth and Mommy died July the seventeenth, 1975. Since Etta and Sandra was married everybody has a choice which one we'd go to: come up here [to] Etta's, or stay down in Kentucky [with] Sandra. From what I hear, if Sandra and Etta hadn't been able [to take care of us] they would've put us in a home. I was with Sandra a lot and I hardly ever seen Etta, so I come up here. [When I left home] everybody said, "She won't like it, she'll be wanting to come back to Kentucky to her old friends." Well, I like it. I miss my old friends but I'll make new ones.

Schools are better than down in Kentucky. They're a little rough but you get used to it. The first day I was kind of scared; I thought it was different and I couldn't do the work. Down at Laurel Creek you didn't have to call a teacher "mister." Whenever I wanted something I'd go, "Munsford," and holler at him. Down home there's eight subjects that you had to take, ain't no excuse, you *had* to take them. If you didn't get your homework done, you'd stand up there and get about ten licks. They hurt, too, though I only got about three of them. If you missed so many [answers] you got swats [with] a big old stick with holes in it. It's different up here.

Down in Kentucky my girlfriends said I talked like a city slicker, but up here they call me a hillbilly. Every time they see me, "There's that little hillbilly. Look at her." I don't like people to call me "hillbilly." Other day I was coming back from the store and this boy that lives up above us [called me] "sowbelly." He goes, "What'd you have for supper last night, sowbelly and dressing?" When you're a hillbilly you don't have the things they have to eat up here. In the hall boys and girls, they look at you so funny. They're mean. Mommy always said people who are mean, don't fool around with them.

Down home, girls just skin up a tree or do anything [boys do], but up here they won't. There are no trees to skin up, probably. Up here you can't have a dog unless it's licensed. Down at home you can have a dog any time you want to. Your property, you just do as you please down there.

[In church] I don't know their songs. Down in Kentucky I could've got up and sung them all myself because I knew the songs, but up here it's different. [During] most of the [service] we sing, but up here they preach.

Another thing, they ain't got no bars down there. If you get caught drinking you go to jail.

Up here they sit up all night and sleep all day, but down in

Orla Pace

Kentucky you go to bed with the chickens and get up with the rooster.

[In 1954] at thirteen, Willie (Will) Pennington took one look at the concrete jungle that was called Cincinnati and fled home to live with an aunt in Laurel County, Kentucky. His reaction was understandable because the changes he would have been called upon to make in the city were awesome indeed. In 1956 when Will finally mustered the courage to settle permanently in Cincinnati he was adding another link to the chain of kinfolks who had migrated there.

My mama's sister and her husband came up about '35. When they left, they left with nothing [and] caught a bus to the city. When they came back he was driving his own car, he had a nice suit on, and he had *money.* Surely the other people were envious of him to an extent. They'd say, "If he can do it, I can do it." I don't think [possessions and money had] really mattered to the people until they got exposed to [them]. When one of their own was the one who had it, and especially when that one says, "It's nice to have a dollar in your pocket instead of having nothing in your pocket" [people's attitudes began to change]. Before you wasn't exposed to it, nobody had it, and I don't think it crossed their mind too much. You'd see people in town who did have things, but "Them are other folks," and they were different from us. Now, "This is one of our folks."

Today Will is a teacher and administrator at Cincinnati's Porter Junior High School and lives in a modern split-level home just north of town in Sharonville. He and his Kentucky-born wife, Ethel, are satisfied with how their lives have evolved in Ohio and they have no plans for returning to eastern Kentucky where the options are fewer and the future appears dimmer. No doubt Will's attitudes toward home were shaped by earlier experiences.

I was born in 1942 at Hooker, Kentucky, in a log cabin and [lived there] until I was in the third grade and we moved to Laurel County. You'd rent a farm and tend tobacco on halves, which meant that you got half of whatever you grew. The problem was you're dealing with six tenths of an acre of tobacco and only talking about a cash value of a thousand dollars. Your share might be five hundred dollars; that's your cash money you can count on coming in.

[When we moved from Hooker to Laurel County, Dad] felt he could do better if he could get on a farm that had more tendable land. Money was the issue, really. Where we lived only had ten acres that you could tend with mules; the rest was just hillsides, poor land. People [had] planted and planted on it, there was no fertilizer, and [they] wore it out. That policy of farming brought about the fact that they had to turn to some other source of income later on [and] I think it might have led to one of the reasons for accepting welfare.

[When] we settled in Laurel County we rented a farm from a jailer. We were contracted to provide all the potatoes for the jail. That did give us another cash crop other than tobacco, but the problem is that you have good years and bad years with potatoes. Some years you have an abundant crop; other years they don't turn out very good at all. It gets so tough going to raise your family, especially if you're trying to farm, that [many men] back in the late forties and early fifties [began to despair and think] the thing to do was to come to the city and get a job.

[After] three or four years we still didn't have very much. Through his travels [Dad had] seen other people had a lot more than we had. He said, "Why can't I go somewhere else and acquire a job that would make more money?" [He was supposed] to come to the city, which he did, to find a job and after he got himself established come back down and get us. That never did [happen] the way it was intended. What happens, you take the mountain man [and] he comes to a big city. Well, there's a lot of vices in the city. [The same vices] might be down there but they won't be as out in the open and they don't have as much stigma tied to them if you get involved in them. We—my mom, my sister, and brother—stayed down there and I went to school at Bush until I was in the fifth grade and when the split came my mom couldn't make it. He wasn't providing support and she was working in tobacco making three dollars a day and sending three kids to school.

My mama, she didn't like the city at all, but she knew she had to work somewhere to put her kids through school and have a place to live. When she came [to Cincinnati] she stayed with the same aunt [that came in 1935] till she got a job. To show you how spendthrifty she was, she made thirty-five dollars a week; that was about twenty dollars more than she was making down home. She managed to save about a thousand dollars in a year and a half. She wanted the money in case she didn't have a job. See, back down home you'd be working in somebody's tobacco this week, but you might not be working nowhere next week.

The biggest migration of my people was in the late forties and early fifties. [First] one person goes and another person went and [finally] six out of eight on my mother's side [and] thirteen out of fifteen on my dad's side [moved to Cincinnati]. They wanted to do better from what they were down there [and] it was getting to be such a task to survive. [The government] cut down on tobacco allotments on some of the farms and a lot of my relatives were renters so you only got a part of what you were growing anyway. Then if you had a bad year, you didn't have that income.

When [my mom] came up I didn't like the schools, I didn't like all the trouble I's getting into, so I went back [home]. If you're used to living in the country and roaming the woods like I did, then you come up here and roam this concrete jungle, it's a totally different story. After a period of time I wanted to be with my mom, so I came up in the sixth grade and I had a lot of trouble adjusting. I went back to Bush in the seventh grade; then I came back up here again and I went to Cutter [Junior High

School]. I had a lot of problems at Cutter because they cap* in the inner city. They'd cap on your father, they cap on your brother, they cap on your shoes, they cap on your hair. I didn't mind all that till they'd cap on my mom. They'd say things like, "Your mom wears boots," [and I'd say], "You're not going to talk about my mom because she's the one who stuck with me." They'd start capping on me and I'd punch one of them. They'd do it again and bam! we'd wind up in the [principal's] office.

They had their days with me, there's no doubt about it. One thing that really sets you off is your personal appearance and the way you talk. Kids up here, they've got hair that comes down to the ear lobes and the duck tail bit, whereas I had a flattop and the type of Levi's I wore were not the type they wore in the city at all. Mine were loose-leg and the ones they wore were peg-leg pants. So I had to make an adjustment and that was an expense on the part of your mom. She wanted us to be accepted in the schools, so she did without a lot of stuff to get us a pair of shoes, to get us a pair of pants, to get us the shirt.

I still have that problem with the language barrier. In the country instead of saying "tomato" you'd say "mater." Instead of saying "yellow" you'd say "yellar," "usens" instead of "we." We say, "Let's go over yonder and see that movie"; they say, "Do you mean you want to go 'over there'?" I used to refuse to read out loud in class or to get up and give an oral report. [Now] my philosophy is that we've got to communicate. One person says the proper way to communicate is to say "potato," instead of "tater." If I'm talking with you and we understand each other, it doesn't matter to me what language we're using if we communicate.

You had to run with a gang if you lived up here. You couldn't live on McMicken Street and be a loner because every group of guys that ran the streets would pick on you. [If] they [knew] you belonged to this gang they wouldn't mess with you because they

---

* "Cap" means to make fun of.

didn't want to mess with the gang. Any time you come out on the streets you had your own turf. You could run in this certain area and you didn't have to worry, but if you went into another gang's territory you could rest assured if they encountered you, you are going to get your head worked. Another thing, you didn't mess with another gang's women. God, if you did there'd been a mass waiting on you when you come out of school. [Gang members] didn't want to get suspended, so they'd wait till you got away from the school ground and then they'd have their [fights].

When I went to Cutter in the eighth grade the gang would have members standing at the flight of stairs and [they] had a shakedown racket: "How much money you got, man?" You had to fork it over or get your behind whipped after school. You [could] go to the principal, yes, he'll take care of that one but he don't take care of the group and it's the group that was going to get you. I got tired of fighting that battle so I thought the best thing to do is join them. The guys that I teamed up with were guys that came from down home. Even though I'm from the country they don't just welcome you in. You had to prove to them that you're worthy of their gang, that you wasn't no coward, or you didn't squeal.

I could do a physical thing at that time as good or better than any of the other kids could do and that was play basketball. When I went to Bush High School we started basketball in September and played all the way to April. In a city you play basketball about three months out of the year, so I was much more highly advanced than they were and they knew it. When they'd choose up sides you know who was picked first, so I got to know them. If I didn't have that skill it would have been a much harder road. I had these faults—I talked funny, I dressed funny, and I didn't look exactly like they looked—but I could do something they couldn't do [and] things just started to jell. [By the time] I went to Taft High School I didn't have any problems because I [had] developed the personality to deal with the kind of problems that you encounter in the city.

Looking back from where I'm at now, Dad and Mom splitting [was] probably one of the better things that happened. [If they hadn't split], no doubt I'd been a farmer. [I'm] not saying there's anything wrong with farming, I just don't think there's much future as a small farmer. I've got things now that I'm sure I could have never afforded if I'd been living on a farm. My brother graduated from college and he's the office manager for Eagle Picture. [To] look at us today you'd never think [we] came from such a background.

[My mom] doesn't live in Cincinnati proper [anymore]. She lives in Florence* where she [has] more open territory around her. [When] you live in the country you've got freedom: freedom to go, freedom to do. The air you breathe, the noise, the pace that you live in, all of that changes [in the city]. My grandfather comes up here and he'll stay a week and that's it; he wants to be back down there even though he's living by himself and he's seventy-five years old. He just doesn't like the city. He told me:

> The city is like an anthill. You ever watch an anthill? The ants are constantly coming out of their little hole, back and forth, packing this, packing that. That's what the city reminds me of. You watch the expressway, here comes all the ants, the cars. [They] go in this building, they stay there all day and they go right back down the hill again. Most of your life is just running back and forth, punching in, punching out. Going home, read the paper, sit there and watch TV, going to sleep. That's your life and on the weekend you'll try to cram something into it.

Did your parents ever consider going on welfare as an alternative to leaving eastern Kentucky?

No. There is no way, even today, that they'll accept welfare in any form or fashion. As a matter of fact, it burns her up to go to

* Florence, Kentucky, is twelve miles south of Cincinnati.

the food market and they ask whether it's going to be cash or food stamps. When we lived on Walnut Street [in Cincinnati] there was a fellow who was as able-bodied as my mom was but he lived on welfare. He used to laugh [at her and say], "You're a fool for working. Why don't you go on welfare?" She would have made more on welfare than she would working for thirty-five dollars a week, but she wouldn't do it. She said, "What I get is going to be from me and not from somebody else." When we lived back [home] I don't remember anybody that I come in contact with that was on welfare. They shared things within the group, [but] they didn't accept things from somebody outside.

What happened to change that?

Many things. The fact that the price of things went up so drastically, the fact that the tobacco crop just doesn't provide the money they need to offset expenses. A lot of those hillsides have been planted so many years without any type of fertilizer on them they're no longer in a condition to grow anything. Another reason some people went on welfare is that they constantly [felt] like [they were] beating their head against the wall; they tried to make ends meet and couldn't.

What happened was when one person [went on welfare], he lived through the criticism and then another person joined him, and another person joined. The status of being on it—"That's a terrible thing to be on welfare"—started to drop out of the picture.

Back when we lived down there you had pride in what you were doing because everybody else was doing about the same thing, especially people that was in the same poverty level that we were in. Maybe you'd have a cow, or a bull, or a boar hog and you knew he'd be the best around and that was [reason for] a lot of pride. When you start giving people stuff they lose pride. Now, there's people down there that will not work because they're afraid they'll jeopardize their food-stamp program. That person lives in an old run-down place and it *is* run down, clean-wise.

Back before people lived in some run-down places, like we lived in a log cabin and it wasn't the best-looking thing on the outside, but you go inside and it's clean. The clothing we wore was clean. This individual today, the kids go around little dirty fellows, they're not taken care of properly at all. There's no pride in keeping yourself looking respectable or keeping your kids clean, and I think that's sad.

We have kids right here* that can receive a free breakfast, they can receive a free lunch. If your mom and dad cannot afford your shoes and clothing, we can buy that for them. When you set that up in the eyes of the kid, what reason does he have to go out and get a job? When the Happy Pappy program first started, to receive help they had to go out and do something for it, that's the reason he had some pride. They cleaned off the roads, they cleaned out the streams, [and] they received cash money that they could do whatever they wanted to with. Don't ask me why that program ended. It's a lot better than the program they got now where they just *give* it to you.

For many mountain persons migration was never a realistic alternative to the bleak job market in Central Appalachia because they were unable to work. Some suffered physical disorders that were frequently linked to careers in the coal mines; others, including Bessie Gayheart, had dependent children and felt their place was at home. People who have never faced hunger and long-term unemployment often callously view public assistance as the easy way out, but those who depend upon welfare tell a different story. They say it is not easy; that while it does indeed put food on the table the not-so-subtle ways of welfare soon lead to embarrassment and loss of dignity.

In the United States there are many different forms of public assistance programs ranging from the socially acceptable federal aid to financially troubled corporations and tax write-offs for

* At Cincinnati's Porter Junior High School.

mortgage payers, to the much maligned Aid to Families with Dependent Children. It is the latter that Marvin Gullett and Bessie Gayheart address themselves to.

Marvin Gullett, who discussed coal towns and racial tensions in Chapters 5 and 7, planned on having either a farming or mining career but those hopes were dashed by an illness that eventually led to a life on welfare.

The young generation can't imagine what a hard time people had through the thirties. It happened to hit me right at the time I needed to go on to [the sixth grade]. I'd come home and I'd start clearing up land, help Dad farm and put stuff in. Dad didn't want to be on the relief rolls [so] he got a job in the mines. He had to work all the time and he got such little wages, eleven cents a ton; everything depended on me. I was the oldest boy and the others was too lazy or not big enough to work. I worked on WPA when I was thirteen years old, pick and shovel. I had to do that or else starve. That was too much to put on me at an early age.

Finally [in 1940], a year before I married, I did have a nervous breakdown. Come to find out I had heart trouble and I had bad nerves, too. Up to that time, though, I worked at several jobs. I [did] a lot of hard work, carried loads on my back that would kill a horse at one time. Of course, that strained my heart and made it worse. During the war they weren't particular about letting disabled men work. I worked at Blue Diamond mine a little while and [then] I went out to Michigan and tried farming. I sold my home and moved to Michigan because my folks had moved out there. While I was out there I had [another] nervous breakdown [in 1947]. When I got back I still had my money in Hazard Bank [so] I bought a big piece of bottom land at the mouth of First Creek. I farmed it but I couldn't make a living. It's not that I wouldn't work—I never was afraid of work in my life—[but] I had this nervous breakdown on account of living through the Depression days. [Also], I'd hurt my back in [a rock] fall and something happened to my spine. From then on I was always disabled. [In] 1948 the company doctor told me, "Your heart is the worst heart I ever examined; it stops and starts again. You will never be able to work at hard, manual labor. The only thing you can do is get this Aid for Dependent Children." It took nerve and courage to [accept] it. I didn't like to, but I had to. When you ain't got no other alternative then you want to do the best you can. What else can you do? You [can] try to rob or steal. What will happen to you? You wind up in the federal pen somewhere, which is good enough for you if you are foolish to do that. I didn't try to steal or get anything dishonest. I didn't feel there was any slur on it because that's what it was for. See, I wasn't a feller trying to cheat, or somebody [wanting] to get something for nothing.

The most I ever had was $185 a month, [which was] when I had nine children at home so you had to be a pretty good manager to send them to school, provide enough to eat, and keep a roof over their head. Unless you [have] raised a family—and raised them right, give them what they need—you ain't got no idea what it takes to raise eight or nine kids. It [was] pretty hard at times. We didn't suffer for food because I got food in regardless of whether I got anything else, but there is other expenses. You have to go in debt for new furniture [or a] washing machine. [Social workers] used to think it was awful if you bought a television, [even] if it was an old used one. If you done that your check was stopped. If you went out and bought a head of stock that might supplement your check through the winter, they were against that; that would get you cut off. They got it fixed in a way that you couldn't help yourself hardly. You had to spend that check each month and [were] not allowed to lay up any of it. [They] encouraged some people not to have anything instead of telling them to [plan] ahead and put in a good garden plot.

I always have been independent and I never did beg to them. I'd demand they give me what I know is due me by law. I'd [state] my case and [when] they cut me out I appealed it to the state board in Frankfort and they ruled I [should] get it back. I got a letter here from A. B. Happy Chandler. When he learned [in 1957] about what they was doing, he gave me a quick hearing and I got back on. I had to go through a lot of hardship while I was waiting and that made it hard on the kids. After I was put back on they had to treat me a little better. I'd go up there and they'd call me in quicker. Here lately they began showing that they can just treat me any way [because] I'm getting old and my kids [are] getting out of school and getting married off, but I have to live just the same as if I didn't have any kids.

Sometimes you don't get waited on one day and have to go back another day; that costs me money. They'd say, "Come back next week," and I'd have to pay double fare. They didn't care, you are just another number to them. They act pretty independent; bureaucrats are always that way. Somebody that has got a little office job [has] to use their authority to make you feel little, make you feel bad. They try to act like it comes out of their own pockets [when] they are hired to hand it out.

There have been some abuses [with food stamps], I admit that. Some people take the food stamps and trade it to money and get whiskey. The merchants is crooked enough [so] somebody [can] get the money back on the food stamps. Of course, all we ever got with it was food. There is a lot of people that might cheat, but I'll tell you one thing: 80 percent of them spends the money honest and gets what they need with it. Some stores don't want to let you have credit if you trade with stamps, seems like they are a little more independent with [food-stamp customers]. They'd rather have the greenback than just a piece of paper. I believe [some] feel like you are beholden to them and you got to toe the line. Most of the time [though, merchants] are glad to get the stamps because it is the same as money.

I [have often] fumed at the bureaucracy which was set up to help [the poor] in this country. To think that they'd try to make out like you was a vagrant with a hand stuck out [when there was] a law passed by Congress to help the poor people, I can't understand it. The same idea has been propagandized to set these wealthy people against the poverty people. A large segment of the American people has got the wrong impression about [welfare]. They think that it is all just a cheat, a fraud. Ninety percent of [the welfare] people are due it.

In time the whole American people [will] have to go on relief if the recession don't end. Then these people that is so proud, what are they going to say when they have to take it? The way the world continues you could be begging some day. If you come to that you will be glad to take whatever somebody gives you and you [will] say, "I've got no other alternative." I guarantee if you live long enough you will have to do that.

Bessie Gayheart was born on Kelly Fork near Cordia, Kentucky, and today lives close to her homeplace. She is an active volunteer with the Citizens for Social and Economic Justice, a group organized to relate to issues facing low-income mountain residents. The group's most recent accomplishment in which Bessie participated was starting a food cooperative near Hindman, Kentucky.

I'm Bessie Fields Smith Gayheart. I was born in 1931 and I went to the eighth grade. Education was pretty hard to get in those days, so I never did make it to college or high school. I guess I got more education in my older days than I got in school from finding out what complications there is in life and what people have to go through to survive.

When I first went on welfare I would have been more than glad to have gone out and gotten a job. I could [have gone] to Hazard and got a job for a dollar and a quarter a hour, eight hours a day, but by the time I bought gas I wouldn't have had enough to [buy] a loaf of bread. My first thought [when I had to go on welfare] was that it was something I didn't want to accept. It was a thought that almost put me in tears. We have lived in Indiana and I had worked very hard. I was used to feeling free to go

Bessie Gayheart

out and spend what I had earned for the things my family needed; I felt good with life and what we was doing. When I got my first welfare check I felt embarrassed. I didn't have the courage to go out and cash a check like I would my own pay check. I could go out and sign my pay check, smile while I was doing it. When I got my first welfare check, I felt embarrassed, but I had to depend on it.

When I first got food stamps I felt embarrassed about going into a store and having to watch what you was laying on the counter. You would have to have two piles, one for the food and [one for] the soap powders and detergents that you paid cash for. This is embarrassing. Our kids can't dress like the other children and they [have] not been able to compete with buying books, which is not give to you. They're ignored in their sitting quarters. They're not dealt with like ordinary students [because] they're a "welfare recipient."

I had quite a few probems when we first signed up on welfare. My husband become sick and he went into the hospital. He had a drinking problem, so I guess they considered this not being very sick [because] it took quite a lot of time to get [necessary] medical evidence which is very hard to come by if you don't have money to pay doctors' bills and to pay for the reports. You just don't go out and pick them up by saying that you need them.

There is just so many inconveniences that discourage you. If they send you a paper and you fill it out [you have] to walk to the post office or drive. If you don't have a car you've got to hire someone to take you. If you've got a car, it's a problem because you don't have the money to buy the gas. I have had appointments to be there [at] nine-thirty, and it would be three-thirty before I'd get out. Maybe one worker would [see] one [person] in forty-five minutes or an hour and the rest of them [were] at coffee breaks. [They make] you feel that [you're] not worth anything, that the world would be better off without you.

Most of the workers in Knott County is pretty nice, but there is some of them that acts just exactly like that check that you're going to get is going to be pulled right out of their own pocket and give to you. I have had them to ask me some pretty personal questions: "What do you spend your money for?" "Do you drink, Bessie?" If they ask me something like that now I tell them that it's none of their business.

When me and my husband got divorced they asked was my ex-husband living in the house? It would go right down to the point of almost asking if you slept with your ex-husband last night. They had me pressured one time to the point where I was just about ready to give up on everything, but I began to realize that my kids had to live and since I couldn't get a job and support them I had [to endure it].

When I was divorced there was lots of women just like me that was afraid to remarry because of the position that it would put their family in. You're never sure that a man can get a job here. You're never sure that he can come up with enough to feed a family. I was afraid to marry, afraid of what might happen to the children. [Eventually] I was married, was cut off, and then I called a lawyer and talked to him. My sister had remarried just a little bit after I did and I told him about her. We filed a joint suit against the welfare department in Pikeville. It was about three or four months [before] I got a letter telling me that I had won the suit and I should go back to the welfare department.

I have had lots of experiences that has taught me to stand up and say what I feel. [I saw] that our coal industry rules our political people. Our political people rule our welfare department. Our school boards rule our schools, and they're political people tied in with the coal companies. I believe [our] political system is rottener than hell. When a candidate runs for something he is running for a servant of the people, but how many people do they serve when they get in there? They serve the industry, money, power, and theirselves. I can't say I have any feelings for them whatsoever, because if I had the opportunity, I'd put my foot in their face and I'd shove it.

I kept my mouth shut for long enough that it began to bother me and I finally decided that I would take part in some of these meetings that people were attending about strip mining. They were all talking about what [strip mining] had done to them and it seemed like the people was lingering on the thing that had happened to them. I said, "We have all talked about what has happened to us, but I have never heard anyone talk about what we're going to do about it." I asked them if they would [be] willing to come out with me tomorrow and stop overweight coal trucks. The roads were tore up, especially Old Fifteen down toward Homeplace Hospital, and it was a concern to me if a person had a heart attack that they might not have gotten them to the hospital in time.

We went out and we stopped coal trucks the next day. I stuck with this thing of fighting strip mining for quite some time. I was on welfare and I would get notices that I'd have to come in and re-sign up more often than other people was doing. At first I didn't pay too much attention to it, I would just obey the notice. [When] we went to really putting the pressure on the strip-mining operations I got a notice in the mail that a field worker was going to be at my house the next day. He talked to me for quite a while:

"Mrs. Smith, don't you believe that you're spending too much time away from home, that you're neglecting your children?"

"No, I don't."

"Really now, if you didn't attend so many of those meetings, don't you believe that your kids would be happier?"

"I'm not sure they would. I do the best for them that I can. I feed them, I clean them, I send them to school and I give them as much as a person on welfare can give a child. I never leave them alone. I think you have sat behind that desk too long and don't know what's going on around you; otherwise you would be doing the same thing I'm doing: looking out for the future of your children [rather] than just the dollar that you're making to take home to them."

About a week [later] I got a notice from the welfare department that I was discontinued from welfare, that I hadn't filled out the forms which had been sent to me. In fact, I had received two sets of forms in less than eight weeks—you're only [supposed] to receive one every six months—and I had filled both of them out and mailed them in. That was pretty close to check time [and] when I said I would call a lawyer they let me speak to the supervisor and I said, "It's not my fault that I didn't get my check." Eventually I got the check.

I don't think I would ever opened my mouth on any issue if it hasn't been for having to go on welfare. I've seen good people broke down into nothings; people that have worked hard all their lives becoming alcoholics because they had to beg somebody for help. The begging comes when we have government policies handed out in little doses, just enough to wet their tongue, not enough to quench their thirst. We need a welfare system that will keep our people well enough to let them enjoy life instead of punish life and live it lonely. Give them an opportunity, don't break their spirit and their pride, and you'd have a working nation. If you've got a good man, turn him loose, don't bring him down to the lowest standing and put him on his knees begging to people. When you start begging you start hurting. Then you become nobody, then you become walked on.

All the monies that are going into our welfare system today should be handled something like this: there should be work for the men that is able, there should be assistance for men that's not able, assistance for children that can't help themselves. This assistance should be in the form of what it is now but with different attitudes. Our federal programs [that have men] move brush off the road or sweep the courthouse is not helping the situation of the people at all. This is robbing the people of a thing that is most precious to them and that's pride. If you strip people of pride you might as well shoot them because they ain't worth a damn. The programs are good for one thing: to keep you [alive] from day to day, but not building a thing for the future.

They want to keep us where they can control us and say, "We have done this for you, what are you going to do for us?" They ask me what they've done for me, I'll tell them they ain't done a damn thing for me. What I've had done for me I've done myself and I feel that way even though I draw welfare. I wouldn't be drawing it if I hadn't fought for it.

8

"WE'RE NOT PLAYING CATCH UP"

Since the 1950's the wave of migration away from Central Appalachia has ebbed and some people who left are coming home. Nonetheless, high-school graduates and dropouts are still faced with a difficult choice. Ready-made employment opportunities are few, and the presence of black lung and other disabling diseases among older mountaineers is a reminder of the tragic legacy that the mining industry has left its former employees.

The spirit of independence and initiative is alive and well in Central Appalachia, however, and many young people are choosing to remain in the mountains. For some, such as Lewis Burke, who lives in the head of Skull Hollow, the personal challenge of deep mining overshadows the dangers, and they seek work in traditional modes. Others, like Benny Bailey of Hindman, Kentucky, are creating jobs where none existed. Here, as in other parts of the nation, the future rests with people such as these and what they are saying is important.

Many young mountaineers feel they have the potential for devising new directions because their region is largely unfettered with the trappings of modernism. The absence of large-scale development is both a blessing and a bane; perhaps it can be used to advantage by noting the pitfalls of "progress" elsewhere and by

343

designing new solutions that encompass the unique needs and aspirations of mountain people in the 1970's.

The most immediate problem is, as it has always been, employment. Migration and welfare are unacceptable solutions to the scarcity of job opportunities in the mountains. It is unfortunate that nearly all the institutions which have thus far worked to "develop" the region have dealt with the unemployment problem only indirectly. For example, while the coal industry seeks to expedite the development of the region's mineral riches by strip mining, it succeeds in drastically reducing the number of laborers needed to mine coal. Developers of the tourist industry in western North Carolina are also limiting the opportunity for self-sufficiency by building ski slopes and summer homes where farms used to be. The planners of the Appalachian Regional Commission concentrate on building an infrastructure, while a generation of people is raised without decent jobs.

The people who talk about the future of Appalachia recognize that employment, education, race relations, and health care pose certain problems in mountain life and they know there are no easy answers. Nor is there a consensus among them about how the problems should be approached: Benny Bailey suggests one course of action, while Simeon Fields recommends quite another. Nonetheless, each has the will to remain in the region and the desire to seek new solutions to old problems. Surely this is a good first step. Much of the historical difficulty that mountain people have had in coping collectively with the problems of an industrial society has centered on the failure of their leaders to invest their money, raise their children, and take their risks in their home counties, once they achieved economic security themselves.

The exodus from the mountains affected racial and ethnic minorities most heavily and the proportion of blacks in Central Appalachia is lower now than in the period prior to World War II. Nonetheless, as in other parts of the nation, racial integration has been the source of perplexing social problems for blacks and whites alike. Blacks have never constituted more than a very small percentage of the mountain population and they have tended—certainly not always by choice—to live in predominantly black sections of communities such as Lynch, Kentucky, and Blacksburg, Virginia.

Robert Lampkins' attitude toward the status of racial equality in the mountains has been forged from his experiences. For years Robert, who lives in Blacksburg, Virginia, has wanted to become an independent heavy-equipment operator. He prepared himself for that goal by traveling to Florida to study heavy-equipment operation and by earning praise from his employers, but self-sufficiency has eluded him. The main problem is his inability to borrow the large sums of money he needs to buy his own heavy equipment; the covert problem is a feeling that whites, especially white financiers, resent and fear independent blacks.

Today Robert makes beer-can flip-tops for Reynolds Aluminum Company in Bristol, Virginia, and while he has not given up hope of reaching his goal, he is redirecting his thoughts and is focusing them on black Appalachian youths.

Before I went into the service there were several things I wanted to do, but the people—I'm speaking primarily of white people— [would say], "There is nothing for you." I could work for these people on the farm, but as a young black man I was wanting to do something for myself, something I could be proud of. At the age of seventeen I cried to my mother to sign my enlistment papers and after a period of days she signed.

When I got back to the United States [from Korea] I reported to Camp Pickett, Virginia. I stayed there fourteen months, made staff sergeant [and] was assigned by the federal government [to be responsible for] a little more than three million dollars' worth of equipment and [the] men [who handled it]. It made me feel good to know that I can be trusted with equipment and human lives.

After spending time in the military services I came home and decided to go back to high school. I only had an eighth-grade education, so I started putting two and two together. Two and two in the military service is four if you apply yourself, but in civilian life two and two is nothing if you don't have somebody pulling for you. I came back to high school, went into the tenth grade, [and] came out with better than a B average. Then I entered the eleventh grade and found this young lady that I liked very much and we got married.

I went over and talked to the cafeteria manager at Emory & Henry College and told him that I just got married and I had to have a job. He gave me a job: thirty dollars a week [with] long

Robert Lampkins

hours cooking, cleaning, painting, you name it. I worked there for a little over eight years. I worked up from dishwasher to second cook at fifty-five dollars a week. [By] now I have a wife and I have a son; I can't make it at fifty-five dollars. The man that sells you groceries, lights, water, and utilities doesn't care whether you make a dollar or whether you make a hundred dollars. I picked up an application at Olin Chemicals [in] Saltville, Virginia, which required that every employee have a high-school education. I know that I do not have a high-school education, but I did not stop. A few years back Olin and the United States government had opened what is known as a hydrazine plant, which was controlled by the government. [I took] my army discharge and application direct to the hydrazine plant. I caught the colonel in charge coming out the gate and I [said], "Sir, what does a man have to do to get a job?"

He said, "Fella, what is your name?"

"Robert M. Lampkins."

"What was your rank in service?"

"Sergeant."

He says, "Sergeant Lampkins, you take this application to the personnel office at Olin Chemicals and tell them I sent you." From that day to the day I got a job at Olin it took exactly eighteen months. In the meantime, I'm still working at Emory & Henry College. I had a milk run [and I decided to use] the thirty dollars a month I was getting from delivering milk to build a house.

That's when everything began to start looking up for me. The farmers that I had once worked for traveled this road. [When they saw me building a house], they'd run over in the ditch; they would turn around in their cars and look as if to say, "What is that boy *doing?*" That "boy," that these farmers speak of, happened to be a Negro that has the desire to do and will say no to nothing. I have learned from my three years in the military service that you got to fight and fight hard. When I speak in terms of "fight," I don't mean to put up *your fist* and start swinging; I mean picking up a pick and shovel and getting down to the nitty-gritty. Don't tell people what you can do: show them.

Finally, my job came through at Olin Chemicals. Robert Hill, Senior, from Glade Spring, Virginia, and I both started work at Olin's, April the twenty-third, 19 and 63. We worked hard in [the] chlorine gas [division] and the men accepted us. I was assigned to a section on B floor; Robert Hill was assigned to a section on A floor. They would not let two blacks stay together.

Well, Robert Hill is very intelligent, and I don't consider myself a dumb man, so [when] we were assigned to a section we watched for fifteen minutes to see exactly what they were doing. This is something that the white man doesn't know; that a Negro that really wants to do can be working side by side with you and also watching what's going on around him. The second day we was at work they did not know whether we had been there five years or two days. Robert Hill and myself worked hard. Every time they asked for overtime hours, we accepted because we needed the money even though the work was hazardous and dangerous.

One year passed; things are really looking good. Pay was now ninety-five dollars a week—never made as much money in my life. Robert Hill and myself [were selected] out of a hundred and thirty-five employees to be lead man who is in charge of three other men. [Then] the company wants to make me a utility man, a man who is capable of doing a combination of things. For seven and one half years we worked top jobs. We was learning from the first day that we walked into this plant till the day they closed the door. When an [opening] came for permanent employees, who were they looking for? Robert Hill and Robert Lampkins. They had confidence in us. It hurt me when the plant phased out because my next step would have been top operator [and I would have been] responsible for millions and millions of dollars' worth of equipment and human lives.

[When the plant closed, I wondered]: why can't I get this type of work on my own?

What I really enjoy being around is heavy equipment. I bor-

rowed some money from the local bank and I bought a little tractor outfit. I drove it in at night because I [knew] if I didn't the
white man would condemn me before I even got the switch
turned off. I was right. The next day I had a telephone call: "Boy,
what do you want for that tractor you got sitting out in your
yard?" I knowed what was taking place; if I had any weakness or
coward in me I would have sold it. I had something that I was not
supposed to have in the white man's eyesight; that is something
to compete with him. You, as a black man, are fine as long as you
stay down where you belong, but when you get in a position
where you are on the level with him as far as a home and material
things are concerned, you are in for it. I speak this to the truth
and I'll lay my hand on the Bible and swear this is the truth.

[There's] a lot of tricks that this man has been using in years
past, but his tricks are going to run out in the future, because the
black man [in] this day and time is working hard with machinery,
going to school, and learning books. We're using these books to
get the knowledge that we have so lacked in the past and we'll
learn the little tricks that this man is using to keep us down.

I was still wanting to take my trade [as a] heavy-equipment operator [and had] completed a sixty-lesson course [in Florida] from
March to September. The object of this was to get something that
I [could] do myself. Working for the other man is all I have been
doing all my life; I have to take whatever he wants to hand me. It
is time for me to make a move and I'm doing just that.

The day I graduated from Universal Heavy Construction
School, the school stated that if I was ever back in Miami,
Florida, seeking work, that I had a job, not as an operator, but as
an instructor from the school. They wrote me a letter to give to
any contractor in this country when I am ready to seek work.
When I came back [to Virginia] from school I took a copy of my
letter to a well-known lawyer in the area [who had] a lot to do
with the local banks. I said, "I'm ready to seek help from the local
government and from the federal government on buying some
machinery. Are you ready to give me a chance?"

He said, "I don't know whether you're ready for this or not. I will recommend that you go and work with [someone] and let him pay you what he thinks you are worth."

I said, "This is what I'm trying to get away from. You and all the other people who are in control don't want a black man to get ahead because if you let him get ahead then you won't have nothing to look down on."

I approached the Small Business Administration from Richmond, Virginia, [and said] I was wanting to borrow money to buy a back hoe, a front-end loader, a trailer to haul the back hoe and the front-end loader, and a dump truck. I talked with this man for four hours or longer and he stated that I could not get a small business loan due to the fact that I do not know exactly what I want to do!

The white man has made all the rules and regulations, he knows every trick in the book. What a black man is going to have to do is this: start at the bottom again and [work] back up, buying only what you can. For a Negro to go out and, say, borrow $90,000 from the SBA [is unheard of]. That's impossible. The rules they has set up is for a wealthy man, and if he cannot pay $350 [on his loan] per day, per year, then there's no hope.

What [am I] doing? I'm plowing, disking gardens, mowing hay. If it can be done with machinery, I will try and do it and make good money. I put my whole heart into this plowing and they say, "Where have you been all these many years? You could have been getting all of our work." How can I get your work when you don't give me a chance at it?

I set my own prices according to the people; I don't have no set price for everybody. If I see a poor family that can't afford to have their garden plowed and disked, I will plow and disk it free, but somewhere along the way someone is going to pay me for it. My attitude is, I'm going to help my people that I grew up with. You'd be surprised how many dollars I have saved this community by being able to wire their house, fix their broken water pipes, paint, and do this and that. I enjoy it because not everyone has money to pay professional people.

I haven't give up on [wanting] to be an independent building contractor but there is one other thing that is more important than fulfilling my personal dream: to see my children get an education that will prevent them from having to scuffle, work sixteen and eighteen hours a day like I have for survival. In the past it has always been said, "Keep the Negro out of the classroom and put him in the fields." Black people [in] this day and time are not accepting what the white man wants to put on him. Ninety-nine and two thirds percent of the white people in the United States of America know that the black man and woman can cook and clean and this is what I am teaching my children to get away from: "A Negro is fine as long as he is in the kitchen preparing a meal or on the floor cleaning."

You can see from all respects that it's just not meant for a black man to be equal in this United States at this day and time. In years to come I can see it, but as for right now, I can't. It's strictly left up to the younger blacks and whites to be "One Nation under God," because the younger generation is getting away from tradition. As far as I'm concerned, you can take tradition and throw it out the window, lock it [up], and forget about it, because it's no benefit to anyone that is involved in it.

People are going to have to get off that old tradition [of being able to say], "I paid so-and-so seventy-five cents." That is no good. What can you go into the store and buy for seventy-five cents an hour? If people could get money into their pockets it would begin to solve the other problems, but that first step [is] the most difficult one to take. If I take my children out here to help in the tobacco, I pay them. That encourages them. My daughter will tell someone that her father paid her $2.50 an hour and she expects them to pay her the same. I'm [telling my children]: if you want what is out in the wide world, you are going to have to sweat a little. Nobody is going to give you anything, not even a drink of water, if you don't ask them for it. You don't find volunteers anymore because everybody is out for themselves. It's proven out to be dog eat dog.

Lewis Burke's decision to remain in Floyd County, Kentucky, was not made quickly. He left home in 1957 and migrated to Indiana and Ohio where he "walked the high steel" and earned an average of $16,000 a year. For a while the challenge of connecting steel girders while being suspended five or six hundred feet in the air was intoxicating to this man who quietly admits, "I like to play with my life," but after twelve years he returned home to the land in Skull Hollow that belonged to his great-great-grandfather.

Today Lewis works in the mines. He is a deep miner, not a strip miner, and the distinction between the two is of the utmost importance to him. He is aware of the dangers inherent in deep mining, aware that some day he may be another black-lung victim, but he believes stripping poses far greater threats. His feelings for the inviolate nature of the earth are so deep that he is prepared to "shoot" (a blasting term meaning to destruct with dynamite), should the coal company that owns the minerals beneath his soil attempt to strip. Lewis believes the future of Appalachia depends upon people like himself, people who have convictions and are willing to forsake big money and physical amenities in order to preserve something more important.

Not many men will walk the high steel. It is rough work, [but] coal mining is more dangerous. When you get in the mines you have been to hell and back. It's like having a big hammer over your head all day; any second a small piece [could] fall from the top and all at once the whole thing would set down [upon] the earth. The most dangerous thing in the mines right now is the explosives and dust. [Miners] throw powder and dynamite around like it is nothing. When the federal inspector comes in he will tell them to fix [unsafe conditions] and then he will leave. He will come back thirty days or ninety days later and say again, "Fix this problem." It's never fixed. Mining is really a hazardous job with no future. I look in this vicinity and I see guys that have been in the mines twenty-seven or thirty-seven years that can't get up out of a chair hardly, so stiff because they worked on their knees all their life.

Lewis Burke

I've played with my life; this has been a challenge to me. You don't justify it, it is something that you have to do. It was a hard environment to get used to. You have to wipe all fear out of your mind in the mines. You have never saw darkness until you see dark in the mines. I had been used to being in the air swinging around on steel, and here I am a mile and a half under a mountain. Every now and then you will ask, what is it doing outside? Raining? Or is the sun shining? When you [come] outside it feels like walking out of hell right into heaven. It takes devotion, it takes courage, it takes a special kind of man to be a good coal miner.

I have never done strip mining and I would not do strip mining [because] you are tearing up the land, you are taking away the hills, and when you [do] what is going to be left for the people who live here? Have you looked over Floyd County, and Knott, and Pike County, and Letcher County and seen the damage that strip mining is doing? What are we going to live on when the coal is all gone? What are they going to farm on? Where am I going to raise my garden? What's in the future for my kids?

Deep mines hurt, but it don't hurt like strip mining does. Strip mining destroys the beauty of these mountains and when you destroy that, you're finished. If you get in with a good deep-mine company they employ five, six, seven, or eight hundred [men]. A strip mine would employ only eight or nine men at the most [and each man] would get more [coal on] the average day because he can get to it real easy. All he has to do is take a dozer and cut the top of the mountain off. They take the mountain. They take all the trees. They take all the energy out of the hills. When they strip a mountain you can forget about it.

Why give your resources away when this is the only means of living that you have around here? They want to take away from the mountains, but they don't want to put nothing back. All they are going to leave you is just your body, your beat-up body.

Strip mining is my biggest worry right now. Island Creek owns this [land] under me and if they come here to strip mine there will be war, and I mean war, because I have no intentions of getting off of *my* land. We have our family cemetery here and if they come in and tore that up you know I'd fight. I would fight them with everything that I could get a hold of. If it took shooting, I would shoot. Me, just an individual little person, I don't have a chance against people as big as Island Creek or Peabody Coal Company in the courts. I would try to work out things with them, but it is hard to work with someone that is coming to take your land, and your home, and you don't have no place left to live. If they come in here and pushed my house over the hill, where do you want me to live? Are you going to relocate a country man in the city? Are you going to give him, say, fourteen thousand? Money can't replace the environment that you live in. You get used to a certain area and this is your heart, this is your mind. Money can't buy something that is in you.

I'd say 95 percent of the coal miners in this area, District 30, feel like I do about a lot of things, [but] they are afraid to open their mouths. I speak the way I feel in my heart but you will find in this area everything is hush-hush-hush until you get a guy like me and I don't hush-hush-hush. In this area, if you spoke out against certain people they would just starve you out; they wouldn't give you no work.

The future looks bad for me, if you really want to know the truth. If the mines all work out I [could] go back on the high steel [or] live off the land. If it got right down to it I could do without the car and TV because if I was living on a farm, why would I need them? I can take a mule, feed him, and plow him. I can raise my own hog and get bacon, sausage, pork chops, and grease. I can raise my own cow and get my milk and my butter. I could take my corn to the grinder and have it grinded and make my cornbread. The only thing I would have to rely on [stores for] would be nails, flour, salt, and clothes. I would also sell stuff [if] they [didn't] have so many government laws. Now if you start to peddle you have got to have a permit before you can cross the street. Everything has got to be USDA inspected.

In self-sufficient living you don't face as much danger as you do in modern city living [where] you always face the dangers of somebody hitting you in the car, or of somebody shooting you. All you have got to fear here is the animals and if you won't bother them they won't bother you. Modernism will bring trouble for this area; it will bring trouble for the coalfields. Any time you have got a population explosion like we have in southeastern Kentucky right now you have got trouble on your hands. You have no sewage facility up in this area at all; most of the people dump their sewage in the creek. This is very filthy. When they get through with [the streams] the coal companies rip off the hillsides. What is left?

[People who can't be self-sufficient] have two choices: to go on their government food-stamp program or the Happy Pappy gang. This is about the only way that a person could live in this area unless he's got a farm where he could raise his own food, and they are not leaving too much here to farm when you get right down to it. They are strip mining all the land. What are you going to farm? A rock? When you put a person on food stamps you put him down: you belittle him when he is not employed, or you state that he is a lazy person. The people in this area are not lazy; there is no alternative for them.

I'll tell you what I'd like to see for the people who live here and I'm talking about the depressed people: I would like to see a big factory come into this area where a person could go to work every day and make a standard living. I'd like to see the strip mining move out of this area because it's ruined the country.

A man comes to a point in his life where he can conquer or be conquered. Like me, when I left here with an eighth-grade education I went to the iron workers and I took a test that most high school guys didn't pass and I passed it because I had made up my mind that I was going to climb that steel. When I came [back] in this area I had made my mind up that I was going to coal mine. I rely on myself as an individual. [This] is what the trouble is in this country anymore: we're like a big bunch of gullible ducks. When the government throws the corn, we pick up the grain. The government is not a government of the people, it is a government that makes the people do what it wants them to do. When you do this you are taking a person's individual freedom. It is up to me as an individual. If you can make a mountain you ought to make it. If you can build a big home, you ought to build it, but don't step on the small person to do it. Don't belittle someone else to profit yourself. If there is a mountain to climb [and] you say, "I'm going to climb that mountain," you can do it. It is determination. A lot of people in this area have determination but nobody has never brought out the real them. You should speak out [about] what you think is right and what you think is wrong. A hush-hush mouth never gets nothing. If the people in this country ever learn to stand on their own two feet and tell people what they think, they will be a lot better off.

Not long ago members of the American Revolution Bicentennial Administration produced a film about three community projects which, they said, exemplified the Spirit of 1976. One of them is the East Kentucky Health Services Center, located in Knott County, Kentucky. While the center itself is unprepossessing and would perhaps be little noticed in a larger place, its significance to the county is incalculable.

In the late sixties there were only two physicians serving Knott County's 14,000 residents. There were no dentists, X-ray machines, or medical laboratories. Recent gradutes of the University of Kentucky and Ohio University—Dr. Grady Stumbo and Benny Bailey, respectively—recognized the need for more medical services and decided to do something about it. Money was the biggest obstacle, but they ruled out federal funds—the mainstay of most community medical programs nowadays—as a source because of the regulations that are invariably attached to government grants. According to Benny, federal guidelines are designed for cities and often list requirements, such as buying $15,000 ambulances "that won't get off the paved highway," which would be ludicrous, if not hazardous, in the hills of eastern Kentucky. The alternative to federal grants was soliciting the money from foundations and donors, an awesome challenge, especially since the fund-raisers hailed from Spewing Camp and Frogtown, Kentucky, and had no ties to the corporate board rooms of New York and Chicago.

Within eighteen months Benny Bailey and Grady Stumbo had raised $1.5 million and in January 1973, the non-profit East Kentucky Health Services Center was open. At that time there were four full-time staff members; by 1976 there were twenty-two.

Benny's philosophy about the center and the future of Appalachia is: "We're not playing catch up"—we welcome outside capital and know-how, but will not indiscriminately copy what has worked, or has not worked, in Pittsburgh, Louisville, and San Diego.

What I would like to see happen over the last part of the century is a model for living. It is possible here because people haven't got ingrained into a system and [become] defensive of that system. It is pretty hard to change the way the police department in Louisville operates; it is pretty hard to move into Rochester, Minnesota, and start a different type of health-care delivery than the Mayo Clinic. [In] Knott County, Kentucky, it is not so hard.

I resent the [idea] that we got to take the same road that the rest of the nation took in their development. I'm not sure that urban America and great technology are the kinds of things that people [should] be looking forward to in the year 1980. I'm not certain we would like to have a great big factory here that would kill people with the pollution. Also, I'm [not] sure we would want to build a great big university and [then have to] turn the National Guards loose on campus and kill two or three students. And I'm not so sure that the health-care system where people have to use the emergency room as a general clinic is the kind of health care we want to give our people. Instead of striving to make our school system look like New York City, and our health care look like California, maybe there are some things we don't want to catch up to. This nation has some things that we probably should copy, but there are also some good things in Appalachia that we don't want to destroy because somebody says, "Appalachia doesn't measure up to this standard, therefore you had better put on your shoes and try to catch up." If a person in Appalachia likes opera or ballet or some of the things that are valued by middle-class Americans, that's fine, there's nothing wrong with that. But I don't want to see them trying to like it just to satisfy somebody else. I'd rather listen to Flatt and Scruggs than to Beethoven and that don't mean I'm uncultured. That means I just got different taste. Has nothing to do with intelligence whatsoever.

What you are going to see is people in Appalachia who are able to stand on their own feet and think for themselves. The old rough mountaineers, who everybody has a real romantic picture [of], sitting on the porch rocking, but he can't read or write, is over. Our people are getting very well trained, able to think for themselves, and I think they will point the way to the new directions. The out-migration from eastern Kentucky is no greater than the out-migration from Pittsburgh, New York City, San Francisco, Los Angeles, Phoenix, or Dallas, [but] there is no industry to bring people back here to work. If you had an engineering degree or a Ph.D. in economics, what would you do in Knott County? The [counties are] going to have to develop an economic base. I don't want us [to] develop an economic base with a dozen factories and dehumanizing effects on people. There must be another way.

In spite of what a lot of people would say [the culture] of the people is certainly not a culture of history's people; it's a culture of today's people. The morals that people have is just as good, if not better, than anywhere else in the nation. There's all kinds of things that people can learn from the culture here in the mountains just from the humanistic standpoint. Some people may come in here and not find anything good. That is fine with me as long as they don't laugh about "them crazy hillbillies." Some things are just as important to us as things are to them. I am very willing to let them have caviar. God knows, I wouldn't eat it, but people who do like it, I think that is wonderful. On the other hand, we can sit down and eat caviar and soup beans together and we are both happy and what we are eating doesn't have anything to do with our relationship. What they can learn is up to them.

If all at once the world was covered and archaeologists came in millions of years from now and got the written material, the television programs, and the movies and [tried] to figure out what this culture was, I don't think there would be any question that there [was] definitely an attempt to annihilate the hillbilly culture. [Who] takes up the fight of the poor hillbilly nationally?

Burt Reynolds was nominated for an Academy Award for his role in *Deliverance*, which showed the Appalachians as retarded [and] so old they was disintegrating. That, and two homosexuals, are all the Appalachians you saw in the movie. The same night Marlon Brando received an award for his role in *The Godfather*, which if anything was an attack on Italian-Americans, and he refused it to call attention to the plight of the American Indians.

One of our congressmen was evaluated by Ralph Nader [as remaining] "typically hillbilly." What the hell does that mean? If you are reading that in Ohio it means a whole lot different thing than it does to me when I read it. Anybody that watches *Hee Haw*, *Green Acres*, [or] reads Al Capp [knows] the stereotype, [but] this broad generalization of, "This is what a hillbilly is," is wrong. I can't describe [one] any better than I can describe a black man, or a red man, or a New Yorker. They are just people and all of them have little unique characteristics.

America's composed of many different groups and many different cultures and that's what's making the country great. It's resembling a fruit cake where you have cherries, and dates, and nuts and they all retain their own identity, but then there's this batter stuff that puts it all together and makes it taste good. Why would you want to take that fruit cake, which is a pretty tasty item, put it into a big mixer and tear it all to hell, just so it'll all be alike?

What we have lacked in the mountains is people who can relate to the technically advanced aspects of society but still retain the personal characteristics that are necessary to relate to the people down here. You have got to separate people's minds from people's way of living. If the way of living means that they are not getting the right kind of food, they don't have a decent place to live, they don't have a chance to get an education, to get a job, then I think something has to be done about that. But loving your family, liking your country, [and liking] soup beans, corn-

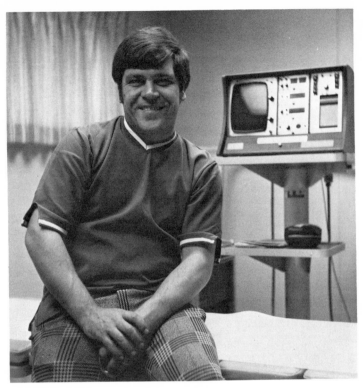

Benny Bailey

bread, and onions, I don't think people ought to be put down for having those kinds of ways.

People have been very accepting and very supportive of the clinic in a whole number of ways. [There are] about 15,000 people in Knott County and we have got about 21,000 active patient charts. The other thing they have done very well is pay. We use a modified sliding scale and we discount patients' bills about $4,000 a month, but after the discount 94 percent of the people pay their bill before they leave the building. Knowing a little about the people you are serving [has] contributed to the success of the clinic. Telling someone in these mountains who is sixty years old to quit eating salt is wasting your time. He is not going to quit eating salt—I'm not going to quit eating salt, I don't know what food tastes like without salt—but you can tell them to eliminate bologna, wieners, pickles, and decrease their salt [intake]. Another thing that is important [at the clinic] is the attention people get. When you come into [a] clinic, more than likely there is something wrong with you, or you think there is something wrong, and too many times you are rushed in and rushed out and nobody ever really asks what is wrong. The fact that we are able to take time with each patient [and] that we are able to treat the entire family from the kid's runny nose to grandpa's arthritis, helped.

What we are saying is by taking good management principles, which run all the way from the most technically advanced things that this country has to offer down to personnel, and applying them to the field of health you [can] make a viable corporation [that] certainly doesn't have a profit motive, but does have a motive to remain independent of outside funds. The success or failure of East Kentucky Health Services Center doesn't depend on anybody outside the area, it depends on people right here. If [people] come and use the facility and pay us for using it, we'll exist; if they don't we flunk. [The center's future] is not going to be decided in some board room in New Jersey or in some office building in Washington; it will be decided here. The thing to realize when you get old is that you have got to turn things over to some young people and that is hard. Hell, I'm thirty-one [and] there are some things I would rather be controlling right now that I just had to get out of because it is not my time anymore.

There's very few problems poor people have that couldn't be solved with money. As long as I've got the money, the problems I have as a poor person are solved. We always said if you want to be an alcoholic, it's better to be a rich alcoholic because you drink those drinks that have lemons and orange juice [and] it gives you a little nourishment. In the wine, you don't have anything. It's all right for John D. Rockefeller, IV, to come to West Virginia where he's a VISTA worker, do good things for people, and not take any money from VISTA. I could never do anything like that. If I don't bring my check home every month, goddamnit, I'd starve to death! It's all [right] for John Kennedy to donate his presidential salary to charity. If I were President today, I'd have to take what money I made to live.

What we are going to have to realize is that Appalachia is not an isolated part of Kentucky, or the United States, or the world. We all have to live somewhere, some of us choose to live in Appalachia, some of us choose to live in New York, and I don't think that ought to interfere with the quality of life that people have. They have things in Lexington, in Louisville, in California, that we need and I don't think we have to shut our minds to those types of things. The only time that we shut our minds is when they come in and say, "We'll run it for you." That is what has happened to us in the past. There used to be all kinds of charities in the mountains run by people from the East, people who like to come down and get rid of their pangs of conscience. Everybody has always wanted to take care of us. First the coal companies come in and said, "We'll build you a house, we'll put wall-to-wall floors in it. You can buy your food at the company store. We'll paint your house, take out your garbage. If you need a new car, we'll loan you the money. Everything is cut out of your check, you just keep on working." All at once, bingo! it is over.

Then the federal government came in and said, "Don't worry about it, boys. We are going to give you food stamps. We'll subsidize your housing. We'll create jobs for you. We'll take care of you." You are a kept people. Your livelihood is not controlled [by] how hard you work, how much you believe in God, how much you love America; it is controlled in the board rooms [of] Pittsburgh and New York, or on the floor of Congress. That has to do something to the psyche of a person. People are so damn dependent upon the people who own the coal, what are we going to do after coal is gone?

I agree coal is probably one of the answers to the energy problem and coal here in these mountains has to be mined to meet the needs of the nation, [just as] we had to take oil out of Oklahoma and Texas, and iron ore out of Minnesota. I don't think, though, that we ought to destroy Oklahoma and Texas and Minnesota to get the iron and the oil. I don't think we ought to destroy Appalachia to get the coal. I am very much opposed to strip mining. If there's going to be mining there has to be responsible mining. If we can't mine coal without killing people, or without tearing the land to hell, I don't think we ought to do it. With the technology that this nation has, surely they can find a way to get the coal and leave the land in as good shape as it was before they took it. Surely they can find a way to make it safe. There has been over 100,000 miners killed in this nation's coal mines. We wouldn't allow the assembly lines and automobile plants to run if they killed a hundred thousand men. Some way you have to figure in the social cost of production and we just refuse to deal with that issue. There must be a safe way to mine coal, and there must be a right way to mine it, and it can be done without tearing the nation all to pieces.

Like Benny Bailey, Simeon Fields is educated, successful, and has more than a passing interest in politics. Unlike Benny, he believes Appalachians have already made the prudent decision to meld with mainstream America. Simeon, the nephew of Ruby Watts who talked about politics in Chapter 1, is a native of Knott County's Nealy Creek and a graduate of three colleges. He began teaching in 1946 at age seventeen in a one-room school on Defeated Creek and later entered the navy, which provided him with the opportunity for travel and advancement. In 1973 Simeon retired as a lieutenant commander and attempted to follow his Uncle Ruby's political footsteps by campaigning for a seat in the Kentucky House of Representatives. He placed third in a field of nine candidates. After the election he was hired by Alice Lloyd College as a fund-raiser whose special duty was courting the coal industry's dollars. The assignment was a fitting one because Simeon views the coal industry as the Appalachian people's helping friend. To demonstrate the point, Simeon proudly points to the eighty-two acres of land that he owns on Troublesome Creek. He says the hillside where the stripping is being done was "good for absolutely nothing except squirrels and wild life," until the strip miners came along.

As you travel around the world letting people know that you are from the mountains of eastern Kentucky, sometimes you are treated like you are not quite as good as somebody else. The whole country has looked at us as being backward, having to have a hand-out to live. [Now] coal is changing that image; they know that this is a wealthy region. The mountains of eastern Kentucky have been the butt of many jokes about backward people. Years ago people stuck up their nose at Blue Grass music. [Today] Earl Scruggs, the five-string banjo king, is accepted in all parts of society. Look what is happening today in Nashville; [look at the popularity of] the *Hee Haw* show, Doc and Merle Watson. People are starting to see the value of the heritage that we have in the mountains. Our music, and our way of life, is not something to turn your nose up at, but something to respect.

I don't think you can put mountaineers into a straitjacket and say, "This is what they are," because here you find the lazy hillbilly waiting on the welfare check every month. Up the road you will find a guy who has worked sixteen hours a day all of his life and wouldn't take a welfare check if you offered it to him. On the hill is a coal operator who might have $20,000 in the bank and he may live in a mansion, or he may live in a log cabin. Another guy might have a million dollars and he might still drive his twenty-year-old Chevrolet. Another who makes $10,000 a year might be sporting a Cadillac De Ville. There is no way you can put mountaineers into a mold.

People who worry about getting into the mainstream of America are people who are overly concerned about trying to protect this image that doesn't exist. They are laboring under the false impression that we, as a people in eastern Kentucky, represent a certain breed and we don't. Everywhere you go you see a different way of life—you can say it is a different "heritage," a different "culture"—but throw them all together in a melting pot situation and see how quickly they adjust. I can't see why we would ever want to reject progress from [the] standpoint [of] bringing in industry and work and maybe higher taxes, better revenue for the schools, better health care, for the sake of trying to save a heritage. The heritage takes care of itself.

While most people pick Knott County as the most backward county in Kentucky, and Kentucky [as] the most backward state in the nation, I think there is a great potential here. We are sitting in the midst of some of the richest minerals in the world, and yet people have low incomes. It is almost a mystery the way the capital hasn't been returned to the mountains. Not only do we have an exodus of human resources, but our mineral wealth has eluded us completely. Now we are seeing it come back. Our population has been increasing for the last two or three years; these people who went to Detroit in 1957 are being laid off because the economy is bad. What do they do? They read about all this great coal-mining wealth that we have. They have seen coal operators flashing their diamond rings and driving their Cadillacs on television programs such as 60 *Minutes*. A lot of people have the impression that money is flowing freely down here in the mountains and that there is all kinds of work. They remember the days when they could live for $30-a-month rent, and they could buy groceries for $50. They come back home, settle down, [and] find out their rent is $125, their food costs more than it did in Detroit, and there are no jobs.

Even though we are affluent with our coal these days, we are so far behind that it is going to take twenty years to even start to catch up. Visit a county seat in the Blue Grass and compare: their courthouses, their nursing homes, their hospitals, their emergency ambulance services, their water and sewage disposal system, their surfacing of highways. We have got a long way to go in the mountains and our biggest problem is learning to put the resources we have to proper use.

The coal severance tax* money ought to be used to give us what we need in the way of ambulance services, nursing homes, a sewage disposal system, garbage dumps, better highways, and better bridges across our creeks. At the same time a portion of it ought to be used for planning for various factories twenty years from now. When they first passed the severance tax law they said you can only use this money for certain things, [such] as building an access road to some industrial activity like a shoe factory, which theoretically would be in competition with the coal company, but you cannot use this money to build an access road to a coal tipple. See what I'm getting at? They refused to recognize coal mining as an industry and yet they were collecting $100 million off the coal in severance taxes each year.

This year Knott County got about one million dollars. That is a million dollars more than [we] would have gotten had [it] not been for the coal severance tax, but let's say that we were getting 75 percent of the severance tax. Maybe we would [have] been getting three million instead of one. Our problem here in the mountains [is] with our political system and the leadership that we end up with in the courthouses, the legislature, and the Congress. We just haven't learned to use the revenues that we have gotten to the best advantage.

It is almost pathetic that our dollars are not doing us any more good than they are doing. Public officials need to be accountable to the people for how they use the money and that means local audits issued in the paper. How many times do you see this kind of thing in the mountains? Look at our last blacktopping job on

* The severance tax is a state tax on coal taken from the ground that is allocated on a per tonnage basis. In 1974 the state legislature agreed to return one half of the surplus (over budget) severance tax on coal money to the counties from which the coal was mined. The 1975 boom created a much greater surplus than anticipated and eastern Kentucky's counties enjoyed a windfall. The 1976 legislature altered the program, establishing greater controls and requiring the money to be spent in certain specified areas, such as for road-building and economic development.

the mountain. Instead of having the roadway prepared for that blacktop [by] putting in posts and shoring along the edge, they just paid the big bill to get it blacktopped [and] within a week the road was breaking off again. We spent almost $300,000 for a survey for a new Highway 80 from Hazard to Allen and according to *The Courier-Journal* the state has no plans for the financing of this new road. How can you spend $300,000 with no plan?

The biggest thing wrong with this region is politics and I don't believe I'm saying this from [the] standpoint of having lost a race. I am a man with three college degrees. I ran for the state legislature. My opponent has an eighth-grade education. My opponent won, I lost. The people did not elect me even though theoretically I am much, much better qualified to serve in the legislature. For the record, I want to say my opponent is a fine man and I like him, but I do think that I am more capable of serving in the legislature than he. My point is this: the mountain counties traditionally have sent men—I don't know of any woman that has ever been elected from the mountains—to Frankfort who are good politicians, who can shake hands well, but who are not necessarily qualified to serve. Our political structure in the mountains is such that it is awfully difficult to get elected to anything unless you are on the inside of that power structure. In other words, on election day those polls are controlled, maybe not illegally, but they are controlled by the power structure of the particular county. The guy that is in that power structure is usually the guy who has been around for forty or fifty years, who knows everybody, who has done some favors for this guy or that guy, who has maybe kept some guy from going to jail, gotten somebody out of jail, and therefore he has got people obligated to him. When these individuals go to Frankfort to serve, how much leadership do you get out of them? Traditionally the mountain counties send the farmer, the carpenter, the mailman, the bus drivers, and they have to match wits against the lawyers, the schoolteachers, the doctors from other parts of the state. This is what we are up against when it comes to not being able to get our coal severance tax passed.

Does the average Knott County voter want to be dominated by the power structure? You would think maybe there is something to this inasmuch as when they come to the polls to vote the average voter in Knott County wants somebody to be standing there at the door [who will] tell him: "I want you to vote for this guy for judge, this guy for circuit court clerk, this guy for tax commissioner, this guy for state legislature." That average voter is lost, he doesn't know who to vote for. Many, many of them will come early in the morning and wait until closing time in the evenings before they vote unless somebody comes along, takes them over to one side, [and] makes peace with them.* In some cases we still have a few illiterates who can't read and write who are led inside the polls and shown how to vote.

Right now we are seeing the greatest need in our history for energy [and] the good Lord gave us our oil, and our gas, and our coal [to be used]. [Through] deep mining we have left almost as much coal under the earth as we have taken out. That coal probably can never be reclaimed economically; therefore it will stay under the mountains from now on, never doing anybody any good. This is one of the beauties of strip mining. [When] you take the land off the coal, every usable block of coal in the area is taken to market where it will serve to solve the energy crisis. Safety is another thing. You don't have roof tops falling in on miners and methane gas explosives on a strip-mine site. When you plan from the beginning how that land is going to be restored to a higher use, then strip mining is the answer. By no means should [the earth] be put back to its original contour; that would be tragic to pile dirt back up to a peak again like it was before and let the elements wash it back down into the valleys. I'm an advocate of good strip mining, but only if it is good.

You might say I have an ulterior motive for feeling the way I do. I have got eighty-two acres on Troublesome Creek and I'm one of the lucky people, I own my coal. I have one side of the

* "Making peace" is a euphemism for vote buying.

mountain leased right now and the strip miners, in my estima-
tion, are doing a beautiful job of putting in silt dams and moving
the dirt in accordance with a plan. I am absolutely confident that
my land will be much more valuable [than] it was before. The top
of that mountain which before was nothing more than a jagged
peak, good for absolutely nothing except squirrels and wild life,
will now be flat and long enough to land a large aircraft.

I have the greatest admiration for people like Mr. Caudill who
wrote *Night Comes to the Cumberlands*, [but] when he said in effect the whole Appalachian region will someday be a waste land
[because of strip mining], I don't agree, not at all. To me, strip
mining, if planned properly from beginning to end, is probably as
fine a method as there is to get coal out of the ground.

I was glad to see Ollie Combs stand up for her property and
her home. All you have to do is drive up Clear Creek, and across
the mountain down into Lotts Creek, and you can see what great
destruction was done in those days. I don't believe that can happen anymore. Today we have laws that tell you, in a sort of way,
how to strip mine without destroying the land. The laws are getting better and reclamation is getting bigger. Under the current
law, good responsible operators are doing everything they can to
make a profit, to restore the land, to protect the environment,
and some of them are really eating into their profit in order to do
it right.

I think we probably have the brightest future of any area of the
United States of America. Appalachia can be a recreational playground for the entire Eastern seaboard. With our natural resources and our great natural contours of the earth where we can
build dams and have fishing, [we have the] ability to build a
tourist attraction [and] at the same time use the water for game
and wild life and [for] producing energy. The money, the human
resources, climate, weather [are] all here and going to stay regardless of how we push it around with a bulldozer.

*From Richard Jackson's point of view, transforming Central
Appalachia into a playground for Easterners is mountain people's*

*worst alternative. Richard has degrees from Western Carolina
College and the University of North Carolina and is active in several of the Episcopal Church's Appalachian projects. He lives in
Banner Elk, North Carolina, but grew up a hundred miles away
in Henderson County across the road from a summer camp that
exuded postcard-charm. There were rustic-looking cabins that
boasted amenities beyond the reach of most local folk, a swim-
ming pool, and a pavilion for dancing in the moonlight. Occasionally, a tourist or two would leave the comforts of camp to
mingle with the local people. Two such pleasure-seekers found
their way into an article, called "Come Frost," that Richard wrote
for the September 1974 issue of* Mountain Review *magazine. He
opened the article by writing:*

A friend of my uncle had gone into the county seat for more
apple-tree spray, having run out about halfway through the orchard. He had to wait, so he walked uptown in his smelly, yellow, spray-splattered overalls and sat down on one of the long,
green benches which lined the sidewalks of the summer resort
town. Two matron-type ladies from Florida occupied the other
end of the bench. After he had been there for a few minutes, one
of the ladies sniffed critically and remarked that mountain towns
certainly had some dirty, undesirable people in them. The orchard man turned, looked at them carefully, and agreed with the
lady's observation. He added, "One nice thing about it, tho'—
come frost and they all go back home."

That's the kind of story I grew up hearing, and I suspect similar ones circulated in many tourist towns then and still do today.
Those were days before I found out that I was a "mountain white,"
"ridge-runner," "hillbilly," resident of a place called Appalachia.
I thought a mine was either a big hole like a well or one of those
unimpressive, scratched-out places where people had dug out a
little mica. I was lucky, I guess, to be born and raised away from
coal mines, in an area of the mountains undisturbed by big machines—unless one counted the train loads of summer people
which came and went every spring and fall. Tourists were

regarded as something like an unseasonal snow—a nuisance, but an interesting topic of conversation nonetheless. Often enough, when a gathering of people fell to swapping stories about summer folks, someone would point out that they were a help with taxes and brought a lot of money into town. I wonder now if I remember accurately that the ones who made such comments

(Photograph by Lyn Adams)

Richard Jackson

always wore ties and starched shirts. In any case, once the economics were mentioned, some agreed and others simply regarded the pragmatist as a kill-joy, since the group nearly always broke up, or changed the subject to more serious, and less interesting, topics.

Experience and self-education have deepened Richard's reservations about the morality of tourism and second homes for the rich. In his oral history interview he posed some provocative alternatives for the future.

As the old saw goes, "travel is broadening," [but] I don't think it's worth a damn most of the time. It's an effort to escape from something; to get stimulated by seeing something that's either quaint, or new, or strange. I resented, and still do resent, being quaint, stimulating, and strange. It's like being background music for somebody's else's Technicolor daydreams.

If the early tourists who came into the area as summer-home people had learned, and been able to adopt, some of the values they encountered in the mountains we might not be in quite the mess we're in right now. Instead, they brought in values and viewpoints and imposed them so that Appalachia is not just an economic colony, it is a cultural colony as well. I've got a lot of trouble with that. I had it educated out of me at one point. My mother was very ambitious and she was the one that kept this relationship with the folks at the camp open. My father was a little grumpy about that. Mother was the one who insisted that I attend city schools, as opposed to country schools where I could have worn overalls and gone barefooted. I remember being laughed at for the first six years of public school. The first thing they'd do was modify my language. I found out early that's what made me different. When you dropped your writing stick and called it a "pancil," or when you said "cheer" instead of "chair," that wasn't going to get you a good reaction at all. On the basis of that experience I've decided that what makes a hillbilly is language, very much the way skin color makes a black a "Nigger."

What they did in the process of educating me was take some things from me that I have since regarded as valuable. I wish I could get them back. [For example], my dad had an infuriating economic habit; it used to drive me crazy, but I got educated out of it. His economic view was: "It's enough, ain't it?" That idea, I think, is one of the most radical concepts that can be applied in the United States at the present time: [if] people [would] decide what to them is enough and stop when they got there. If it's five million dollars, okay, but when you get to five million dollars, quit. That way we might stop this senseless, pointless thing called "development."

There's a real confusion between wealth and money; they aren't the same thing. Maybe the time's passed [since] people in the mountains, or people in the Ozarks, knew the difference, but they used to know the difference. Wealth was having enough land to feed you and tools to work it. Now we talk about [wealth] in terms of money. That's a lousy salad; coins are not chewable at all.

As long as we continue to measure the worth of a person by his economic status—and we do that—we're going to have that problem. In order for me to be all right somebody else has got to be in bad shape. Now this sets up what I call the professional do-gooder attitude. [For example] you've got an Appalachian sitting here and you've got a bunch of folks who say, "Look at all that timber and minerals, we can get it for a song." They come in and get it because they're one up. They leave. Then the missionaries, with precisely the same attitude, say, "Aha! There's some folks that need help. I can prove I'm a worthwhile human being by going over there and helping them. I ain't going to be affected by them, I'm just going to help them." In order for a guy to be a good missionary somebody else has got to be really down and out. The initial assumption is: I'm so much better off, and so much superior to these other folks, that I'm going to do some-thing—rip them off, help them, save them—instead of recogniz-

ing that [we're] all in the same leaky rowboat and if one end
sinks the other end ain't going to be far behind.

[In our culture] we have to eat by virtue of somebody else's
sweat and somebody else's guilt. Most of us would be horrified at
the thought of having to go out and slit a cow's throat and hang it
up and let the blood drain out [so] we can eat meat. But we're
very willing to have somebody else do that for us and then regard
them as crude. This stuff about getting back to "the simpler life,"
there's no such thing. Getting back to the "basic life" [is] totally
different because it's going to get your hands dirty and sweaty
and all kinds of grim terrible things. We aren't [going to do
that].

Granted, development and tourism contain some beneficial
side effects, [but] they are largely accidental [and] are allowed to
continue only because it doesn't cost anybody anything. As soon
as it costs anything they stop. You take a guy who doesn't have a
job and you give him a job making four bucks an hour, more
money [than] he's made in his life, and at the end of three
months you lay him off. It's going to take him x number of
months [before he can] get back [on] public assistance. If he's got
a family, it's not going to take him too long to figure out that the
next time they come along [offering] four bucks an hour he better
not touch it. Then he gets labeled as a deadbeat, [as] too lazy to
work. He's not too lazy to work, he's too smart to work because if
he takes that job for three months he's going to have to really
struggle for the other nine. If you wanted to design a system that
would keep people on welfare you couldn't do any better than
what we got. If a person is hungry you don't give him a program,
you give him food. If somebody's poor, you don't give him a program, you give him money. In terms of standard of living we
have to decide what "enough" is. We have to decide that for ourselves and make sure other people have the freedom to decide it
for themselves. There is nothing beautiful [or] romantic about an
enforced marginal existence. There *is* something beautiful about
people who have decided that in order to live in a pretty good

place they are willing to make some sacrifices in terms of convenience.

I am not opposed to anyone from Florida or anywhere else who wants to jump into a community at that community's level and find out what's going on, [but] I've got a lot of trouble with folks who want to come in and insulate themselves in a walled community, or a house that's eighty times above the lifestyle of others. The phenomenon we have in this country of walled communities [is] a very curious thing to me. [I wish] there were some way to get across to the group at Grandfather Company, or Hound Ears, or Sugar, or Beech,* "There's not a damn thing in there I want and [you] don't need to put that guard in the gate for me." Who is that guard [supposed] to keep out? What's it protecting? This is an indication of the escape kind of stuff that's going on. I think they're running from the anger of blacks, and Chicanos, and poor whites in the urban areas.

Last night I was talking to a group of folks [who said], "They have a right to escape the rat race," and my question is: Whose rat race is it? It's their rat race and if the guy doesn't like where he lives I wonder what would happen if he spent his eighty thousand there instead of bringing it up here. There isn't anything in their community that they couldn't have if they'd spend the money there instead of trying to drag the city here. I could have some patience with the attempts to escape if people would only pay something for that. I don't mean in terms of economics, but in terms of personal inconvenience. They aren't willing to do that. They move in here and then build all the crap that they said they were trying to escape from in the city. Pretty soon you got traffic problems, you got 7–11's stacked up on every corner, you got service stations, and all the attendant services they expect in the city. They forget the same mentality that built those treeless, monotonous suburbs around metropolitan areas are doing the development up here and the impetus is the same. The impetus is

* These are luxury resorts in the western North Carolina Blue Ridge. Grandfather Company is a firm that specialized in building hotels and high-priced homes.

not to help the economic base of the Appalachians. The impetus is not to find people an alternative to their rotten existence in the city. The impetus is to make a buck. And given that impetus they will make the buck however they can. If that means bulldozing the mountain, then by God it'll be bulldozed.

Essentially, I guess, tourism is one group of folks moving from one place to another to look at somebody else, and in a way I can see the guard at the gate to protect the privacy of the people on the other side of the gate. Now, if that's true then it means that privacy is an okay thing in our culture if you can afford it, and if you can't then you're exposed to [a] steady stream of traffic on Sunday afternoon. My fantasy is that of some guy saying, "God, Maw, look at them! Aren't they weird?" People in suburbs would get upset if you did that to them.

Privacy is part of the issue, but the saddest, the most discouraging thing about it is the people who are in those walled communities are lonely for a community and their impetus is to build a community. That makes them no different from the kids who are building communes in Spencer, West Virginia, or in Nevada. The sad thing is that there is no historical data to indicate that you can build a community. It is not a damned automobile. Communities are accidental. I've got to live with whoever falls in next door. "Love your neighbor as yourself," is not an empty commandment, but you can't love your neighbor without any concept of who he is. If he's there three months and then he's gone, where is neighbor? At the same time any time there's a community there's a certain amount of shit to be shoveled and, as Americans, every time it looks like the shovel is coming our way we move.

Loving one's neighbor means being responsible to him as well as for him, and willing to be affected by him, as opposed to just [being] willing to affect him, which is part of my objection to a great many of the church and federal programs. It's sort of a professional do-gooder viewpoint: "I'm here to help. I don't know what all you other slobs are here for, but I'm here to help." By and large the Appalachian Regional Commission, a lot of church programs, and a lot of the people who are in development, want to help because their perception is that the local folks are so sorry that there's no way they're going to make it if they don't get help. The local folks aren't sorry and they deserve better than just being waitresses and security patrols and dirt movers in order that others can act out some advertising concept of the "good" life.

So, there's a loss of dignity that is perpetuated upon a group of people. I agree with Gandhi's view of what violence is: it's any time you deprive another person of their dignity. What's going on in western North Carolina and a lot of other places is just plain violence.

The thing that has blown my mind is the number of people who wouldn't lift a finger to stop development, wouldn't lift a finger to bring it in, but grieve for the fact that it's here. If you announced in the paper tomorrow that the whole of Avery County has been taken over by the federal government to become a national park, people would gnash their teeth and say, "Oh, hell!" They wouldn't like it, it'd grieve them, but they probably wouldn't do much about it. That comes from a long and basic sense of "let things be." It seems to me that rural people—and by that I mean anybody who is grounded in [the] basics about what staying alive means—understand that a thing built on evil will collapse [under] its own weight, and their grief is [that] it happened in their lifetime.

The place where action needs to be taken is any time you can clearly identify that somebody has got their foot in the back of somebody else's neck. We can do that when it's one person on one person because most folks will listen to another person, [but] when it's a corporation it's a hard thing to do. If I could take dead aim at, say, Shell Oil Company or TVA and pull the trigger, I know very well that neither Shell nor TVA would even hiccup, [but] the guy who runs the station downtown might bleed to death. We have within corporations the ability to pass pain on to those who can least afford it. With the gas shortage it wasn't the folks who drive the Lincolns and Cadillacs who were hurt; it was the guy who had to commute from here to Hickory in the '59 Chevrolet that hurt. That's the nature of our system; it's demeaning, and we need to change it. At the same time we need to realize that we can rearrange systems till hell freezes over, [but] if we don't do something about our internal personal spirit we haven't done a thing.

We have tons of historical data that prove our systems don't work and now we're fixin' to do a bicentennial to celebrate American history. We should do a litany of repentance for American history. We have chewed up culture after culture and spit out the bones.

Appalachians have stood to the side of mainstream America because it's a colony. Its resources have historically been used to swell the wealth of people outside its boundaries [and] to me that makes it a colony. The sad thing is that strip mining is just as ugly as sin and I don't think anybody can look at that even through half-closed eyes from forty miles away and say it's a good thing. Some folks may look at it and say it's necessary—I think not—but [it is] ugly and we haven't been able to get it stopped. If we can't get strip mining stopped then I don't think we've got a prayer with development and so it's going to keep on until it destroys what attracted [people to] it to begin with.

What I would like to hear [is people] quit claiming goodness for it. If I hear one more person try to rationalize the Vietnamese War I think I'm going to go nuts, and I'm getting that way about development. If one more person tells me what great things it does for the tax base, and what wonderful jobs it provides for all these poor slobs that live in the mountains, it's just going to start pushing my tendency to nonviolence to its cracking point. I'd rather [developers would] just be accurate and say, "I'm up here to make a buck and here's how I'm going to do it."

I couldn't save North Carolina if they made me governor; hell, I can't even save Banner Elk, but there are a few things I'd love to see tried. I would like to see us try the Old Testament model of economics: the concept of Jubilee, restoration of property to original owners, and the forgiveness of whatever debts there may be against a man every fifty years. It'd be nice if somebody said, "No more will anybody be able to own land in the county in which they do not reside."

Wouldn't it be interesting if the date a corporation was incorporated it had to declare its death date and that it wouldn't survive more than seventy years—a man's life span? A corporation's a legal entity, it can hold property and be sued, but the damn thing never dies and you can't put it in jail. All of which serves to keep the rest of us in line. It would be nice to make them a little more human.

I would like to see the tax structure manipulated so that it reflects what the community wants to have happen to it. They are trying this in Vermont and several other northern states now and are taxing people who have summer homes, people who do not live in a community year round, on a higher base than they are the permanent residents. This works to discourage large-scale development and big resorts, and at the same time encourages and gives a tax break to the small farmer and small businessman. The way the tax structure is set up here now works against anything that is small. Likewise, in some places they are giving tax breaks to people who use solar energy and I think this should be tried here.

I am even crazy enough to want decentralization of the schools because when you consolidate schools you're taking away people's freedom and the impact that they can have on the local system. I would like to see schools, especially private schools, give something other than lip service to the quality of life in the mountains. We need educational programs that encourage people to stay in the mountains. We need to teach young people shrub farming, and truck farming and other skills that will really be of service to the community. The education system has blown it badly. Nowadays we are finding young people who do not know how to garden, who do not know how to can, and these are the same young people who are just a generation or two away from those who made their living by doing these things, and we've got a world on our hands that's got a lot of hungry people. I just don't know how we can keep on missing the point. Finally, I guess I have to admit that the "Appalachian problem" doesn't seem to me to be political, economic, or social. I believe it is a spiritual problem and its name is greed.

THE NARRATORS

LUTHER ADDINGTON has been busy since his birth in 1899 in Scott County, Virginia. He has hunted ginseng, managed a railroad store, written scrip for a coal company, sold Fuller brushes, written children's books, taught school, and served as Wise County school superintendent for thirty-five years. Retirement finds him studying local and church history and living in Wise, Virginia.

TALMADGE ALLEN began a career in the coal mines at fifteen in 1926, when his father became physically incapable of supporting the family. In 1967 he retired home to Hueysville, Kentucky, with only one kind thought about mining life: on the farm a man has no spare time; in the coal camps he calls his time his own after completing an eight- to fifteen-hour work shift.

BENNY BAILEY, who was born in Spewing Camp, Kentucky, in 1944, recognized eastern Kentucky's need for more and better health services in the late 1960's. By 1973 he and a young physician, Grady Stumbo, had raised more than a million dollars in private grants and donations and opened the non-profit, nationally acclaimed East Kentucky Health Services Center in Mallie, Kentucky. He lives near the clinic.

LAWRENCE BALDRIDGE, born in 1936, was reared in Hueysville, Kentucky, by strong believers in the Old Regular Baptist Church. Later he parted from that fold and became a Missionary Baptist. He is pastor of a church near his home in Pippa Passes, Kentucky, and plays an active role in community projects.

LEWIS BURKE realized an ambition to live at his Skull Hollow homeplace near Weeksbury, Kentucky, when he abandoned high-paying but perilous northern construction jobs in favor of risks in Kentucky's deep mines. Less hazardous work on strip-mine sites holds no appeal because he decries this mining method.

JIM BYRD was a jack-of-all-trades before retirement. He built houses, lakes, railroads, gun forts, office buildings, and banjos, which he still plays at home near Valle Crucis, North Carolina, where he was born in 1899.

BARBARA MOSLEY CAUDILL has spent much of her adult life battling the forces that prompted many of her kinfolk and neighbors to leave Appalachia's hills and migrate North. She was born in 1928, makes cornshuck dolls, and has no intention of leaving her Ulvah, Kentucky, home.

CHARLES CLARK, the son of a coal company law man, was born in 1913 near Van Lear, Kentucky. He gave up mining because of its hazardous working conditions and in 1938 he left the coal industry to become a school principal. From 1950 until his retirement he was superintendent of Floyd County, Kentucky, schools. He lives in Prestonsburg, Kentucky.

PEARL CORNETT planned on having a teaching career near Town Mountain, Kentucky, where he was born in 1915, but a school system that paid whites more than blacks foiled his intentions. In 1951 he left home and migrated to Cleveland, Ohio, where he became an arc welder until retirement in 1973. He died in 1976.

ELROY DOWDY, of Doran, Virginia, has twice been the victim of mechanization in the coal mines. First he was out of work for two years because employers preferred machines to men. Then in 1974, at age fifty-three, he became disabled in a man-trip car accident.

LEONARD EVERSOLE lives in Buckhorn, Kentucky, near his homeplace. A hunter and trapper by trade, he spent most of his life scouting the hills for ginseng, yellowroot, muskrat, and mink and sending his catch to dry-goods firms in exchange for boots, overalls, and cash.

SIMEON FIELDS, a retired navy lieutenant commander, thinks the coal industry is Appalachia's ally in progress. He believes responsible surface mining is possible in the mountains and has leased his land for a strip mine operation near his home in Knott County, Kentucky.

DOCK BURDINE FRANKLIN arrived home from World War I in 1920, at age twenty-three, observed working conditions in the mines, and decided to earn his living some other way. He opened the D. B. Franklin General Merchandise Store near his Sergent, Kentucky, home and has been there ever since. He sells everything from boots to potato chips.

CORA REYNOLDS FRAZIER bases her belief that reading certain Bible verses will tame any wild schoolboy upon teaching experiences that began in 1923. She was born in 1904 near Mayking, Kentucky. Retirement in Whitesburg, Kentucky, includes occasional substitute teaching.

BESSIE FIELDS SMITH GAYHEART confronted eastern Kentucky's bleak job market early in life and made a hard decision that her time would be better spent at home than commuting to some meager job. She lives near Cordia, Kentucky, where she was born in 1931, and uses volunteer activities to champion the rights of low-income persons and to oppose strip mining.

MARVIN GULLETT was born in 1918 in Kentucky's Blue Diamond mining camp in Perry County. Like his father, he mined coal, but his career was interrupted in the forties by health problems. Today he gardens and writes poetry at home in Busy, Kentucky.

DR. STANLEY GULLETT was born in 1912 near West Liberty, Kentucky. He was a dentist but trimmed his practice to a false-teeth-only trade several years before his death in 1975 to allow more time for hunting and fishing.

ELBERT (EBB) HERALD is a retired farmer, well-digger, store clerk, blacksmith, and logger. He was born in 1911 near Lost Creek, Kentucky, where he continues to live, and uses the free time retirement provides to preach in an Old Regular Baptist church and make hickory walking canes.

MILBURN (BIG BUD) JACKSON knows the terrors of underground mining accidents but believes he is no more endangered in the mines than his wife is when she sits on a porch. He was born in 1931 and lives in Cranes Nest, Virginia, near the mechanized mine where he works.

RICHARD JACKSON grew up across the road from a tourist camp in Henderson County, North Carolina. He decried what he perceived as the waste and vacuity of tourism then, and now. He lives in Banner Elk, North Carolina.

SAM JOHNSON preached the gospel from the time he became a steady churchgoer at age sixteen, in 1908, until his death in 1975 at home near Leburn, Kentucky. He also farmed, logged, and traded, but he seldom mentioned these things, as secular activities had little meaning for him.

OSCAR KILBURN, born in 1932, worked in the coal mines near Wooton, Kentucky, close to where he lives. In the mid-sixties he quit mining to make a career of trading mules, horses, and hound dogs, because "there's a little money made in it, then again you don't have to work hard."

ROBERT LAMPKINS reluctantly makes beer-can flip-tops for an aluminum company. He wanted to start a heavy equipment company near his Blacksburg, Virginia, home but those plans were balked by racial prejudice and an inability to borrow large sums of money.

HARRY LAVIERS, the son of a Welsh pioneer in eastern Kentucky's coal industry, was born in Wellston, Ohio, in 1900. LaViers followed in his father's footsteps and helped develop the bituminous coal industry. He is chairman of the board of Southeast Coal Company in Paintsville, Kentucky, where he lives.

JOHN CALDWELL CALHOUN MAYO, JR., the son of a schoolteacher who almost single-handedly developed eastern Kentucky's coalfields, was born in Paintsville, Kentucky, in 1900. He has moved from mining into banking and serves as chairman of the board of the Second National Bank in Ashland, Kentucky, near his home.

GABE NEWSOME, born in 1909, began mining before unionization became widespread. When bosses started driving him like a mule he joined the ranks of the union men and has encouraged other miners to do likewise ever since. He lives near Dorton, Kentucky, and runs a secondhand store.

MOSS NOBLE was born in Noble, Kentucky, in 1900. A lifelong interest in Republican politics netted him several appointed posts, such as assistant United States attorney for the eastern Kentucky district, but defeat at the polls. He practices law near his home in Jackson, Kentucky.

ORLA PACE migrated from Kentucky's Laurel County under sad circumstances in 1975, at age fourteen. Both her parents died that year and she had the choice of living at home or in Cincinnati, with married sisters. She chose Cincinnati but remains ambivalent about the decision.

WILLIE (WILL) PENNINGTON reluctantly followed his forebears' tracks in the mid-1950's by migrating from Hooker, Kentucky, where he was born in 1942, to Cincinnati. He eventually adjusted to city life and has remained to become a schoolteacher and administrator. He lives in Sharonville, Ohio.

MELVIN PROFITT recoiled from slave-like conditions on the Wolfe County, Kentucky, tenant farms of his youth and in 1921, at age seventeen, began a career in the coal mines. In the late 1960's black-lung disease ended his mining career and he retired near Hazel Green, Kentucky, to play banjos and write about the not so good days of his youth.

MONROE QUILLEN began his mining career in 1920, at age ten, by digging coal from a seam near home in Whitaker, Kentucky. In 1948 he left the mines to sell Chevrolet cars and trucks. He is retired and does carpentry work in the Whitaker area.

DELPHIA RAMEY spent her youth plowing, hoeing, and raising livestock. She was born in 1906 near a Marrowbone, Kentucky, coal town where she and her parents sold their produce. Warm days find her still tending a garden at home in Wheelwright, Kentucky.

BOYD FREDERICK REED left his Shamokin, Pennsylvania, home in 1927, at age thirty, and purchased a financially troubled Floyd County, Kentucky, coal-mining company. His Turner-Elkhorn Mining Company suffered more setbacks in the thirties that eventually led him to support miners' unionization efforts. He is retired in name only and still puts in a full day at Turner-Elkhorn near his Drift, Kentucky, home.

FLORA RIFE remembers life was tough on the southwestern Virginia farm where she was born in 1904, but it got tougher during the Depression. She and her husband met the challenge by moving from their coal camp home to a farm. Today she lives and gardens in Weeksbury, Kentucky.

HENRY P. (BUCK) SCALF has spent a lifetime studying the people of eastern Kentucky, their idiosyncrasies, genealogy, and social history. He has taught school, written thousands of newspaper articles, fought strip mining, and authored several books, including *Kentucky's Last Frontier*, a well-documented look at eastern Kentucky history. He lives near Stanville, Kentucky, where he was born in 1902.

FRED LORING SEELY, JR., the son and grandson of men who parlayed a few western North Carolina health spas into a spectacular inn and tourist industry, is a retired navy lieutenant. Born at Asheville's Grove Park inn in 1913, he now lives in Tryon, North Carolina, and designs commercial needlepoint patterns.

DR. MARY FRANCES SHUFORD, a family physician, was born in her family's rambling old tourist home on Orange Street in Asheville, North Carolina. She claims, "I've got twinges in my hinges and don't get around as much as I used to," but still practices medicine at home on Orange Street.

WILLIAM GOBEL SLOAN left his home near Pippa Passes, Kentucky, in 1920, at age sixteen, to mine coal because his father was "poor, dirt poor." Mining conditions were terrible; when they got worse he helped with local unionization efforts. He is retired but remains a card-carrying union member at home in Haysi, Virginia.

ALICE SLONE, founder of the Lotts Creek Settlement School near Cordia, Kentucky, where she lives, was born in 1904 near Pippa Passes, Kentucky. She is still doing what she has done for many years: running the school, fighting strip mining, and writing poetry.

VERNA MAE SLONE entered life on the banks of Caney Creek near Pippa Passes, Kentucky, in 1914, liked what she saw, and stayed put. She has made more than seven hundred quilts and written an autobiography, entitled *Kitteneye*, that reveals her real passion: correcting the misconceptions about mountaineers spread by non-Appalachian writers and television producers.

STEVE TOMKO, at age two, was brought from the tenant farms of Austria-Hungary to the coalfields of southwestern Virginia in 1902. Like his father, he mined coal until retirement. Today he tends garden and swaps stories at home near Wise, Virginia.

FRANCES ADDIS TURNER, born in 1911 near Van Lear, Kentucky, was reared in a variety of coal camps. Her father's executive position allowed her to reside above the camps' Silk Stocking Rows and observe coal-town life from a rare perspective. She teaches high school English at McDowell High School, near her Price, Kentucky, home.

SAMUEL VANDERMEER, a native of Paterson, New Jersey, was a missionary in the hills of eastern Kentucky until shortly before his death at Berea, Kentucky, in 1975. His ministry embraced both secular and spiritual concerns as he taught school, lobbied for mountain roads, fought disease, and built churches.

RUBY WATTS set out to serve his community by becoming a Democratic politician. Whether in elective or appointed offices, he maintains constituents' faith by remaining close to friends, family, and Knott County, Kentucky. He was born in 1905 and lives near Pine Top, Kentucky.

DR. CRATIS WILLIAMS, the scion of several legal distillers, was born in 1907 near Louisa, Kentucky. His distinguished career as a teacher and scholar ended only in the formal sense in 1976, when he retired as special assistant to the chancellor of Appalachian State University in Boone, North Carolina, where he continues studying and writing.

WARREN WRIGHT was born in 1920 near Burdine, Kentucky. As a youth he paid little heed to the land, people, and heritage that were his. All that changed in 1961, when coal company employees tried to strip mine his land at Burdine. Since then he has devoted his life to studying and writing, and working with grass-roots organizations in eastern Kentucky.

WILLIAM T. (CHID) WRIGHT, a member of the Town Council in Pound, Virginia, where he lives, is a retired coal miner and schoolteacher. He is also the author of *Devil John Wright of the Cumberlands*, a biography of his father, a mountain law man. He was born in McRoberts, Kentucky, in 1897.

INDEX

The names of the narrators appear in boldface